THE WORKS OF JOHN MILTON

Joannis Miltoni

ANGLI

PRO

POPULO ANGLICANO

DEFENSIO

SECUNDA.

Contra infamem libellum anonymum
cui titulus,

*Regii sanguinis clamor ad
cœlum adversus parri-
cidas Anglicanos.*

LONDINI,
Typis Neucomianis, 1654.

THE WORKS OF
JOHN MILTON

VOLUME VIII

NEW YORK
Columbia University Press
1 9 3 3

PRINTED IN THE UNITED STATES OF AMERICA
BY THE PRINTING HOUSE OF WILLIAM EDWIN RUDGE, INC.
MOUNT VERNON, NEW YORK

CONTENTS

JOANNIS MILTONI
ANGLI
PRO POPULO ANGLICANO
DEFENSIO SECUNDA

JOANNIS MILTONI

ANGLI

Pro Populo Anglicano Defensio II^{da}

CONTRA

INFAMEN LIBELLUM ANONYMUM, CUI TITULUS,

Regii sanguinis clamor ad cœlum,
adversus parricidas Anglicanos.

QUOD in omni vita hominum, omníque genere officii est primum, ut grati semper erga Deum, ejúsque memores beneficiorum simus, tum præsertim, siqua supra spem votúmque evenerint, utì, ob ea,
5 singulares atque solennes gratias quamprimùm referamus, id mihi nunc in ipso limine orationis tribus potissimùm de causis video esse faciendum. Primùm, iis me natum temporibus patriæ, quibus civium virtus eximia, & supergressa omnes majorum laudes magnitudo animi atque constantia, obtestata
10 priùs Deum, eundémque sequuta manifestissimum ducem, editis post orbem conditum exemplis factísque fortissimis, & gravi dominatione rempublicam, & indignissimâ servitute religionem liberavit. Deinde, cùm extitissent subitò multi, qui, ut est ferè ingenium vulgi, egregiè facta odiosè crimina-
15 rentur, unúsque, præ cæteris, literatorio fastu, & conccptâ de

JOHN MILTON
AN ENGLISHMAN HIS

Second Defence of the People of England

AGAINST

THE INFAMOUS ANONYMOUS LIBEL, ENTITLED,

The Cry of the Royal Blood to Heaven, Against the English Parricides.

A S IT is the first of duties, throughout the life of man, and in every condition, to be ever thankful to God, and mindful of his benefits; and as it should be our earliest and especial care, when events have been prosperous beyond our hopes and even our wishes, to return, on that ac-
5 count, our peculiar and solemn thanks—this I now feel in-cumbent on myself; and chiefly for three reasons. First, that I was born in those times of my country, when the effulgent virtue of its citizens—when their magnanimity and steadi-
10 ness, surpassing the highest praise of their ancestors, under the inspection of God first implored, and under his manifest guidance, setting examples and performing deeds of valour, the greatest since the foundation of the world—delivered the Commonwealth from a grievous domination, and religion
15 from a most debasing thraldom. And secondly, when there

se gregalium suorum opinione inflatus ac fidens, conscripto in nos libro admodum infami, tyrannorum omnium patrocinium nefariè suscepisset, me potiùs quàm alium quemvis, neque tanti nominis adversario, neque tantis rebus dicendis visum imparem, ab ipsis patriæ liberatoribus has partes accepisse communi omnium consensu ultrò delatas, ut causam & populi Anglicani, & ipsius adeò Libertatis, siquis unquam alius, publicè defenderem. Postremò, in re tam arduâ & expectationis plenâ, neque civium meorum de me sive spem, sive Judicium illud fefellisse, neque exterorum quamplurimis cùm doctis viris, tum rerum peritis non satisfecisse; adversarium verò, quamvis audacissimum, ità profligâsse, ut animo simul & existimatione fractâ cederet; triennióque toto, quo postea vixit, multa licèt minatus ac fremens, nullam tamen ampliùs molestiam nobis exhiberet, nisi quòd vilissimorum quorundam hominum obscuram operam subsidio sibi corrogaret, & laudatores nescio quos ineptos atque immodicos, ad inopinatam ac recentem infamiam, siquo modo posset, sarciendam subornaret; quod statim patebit. Hæc ego divinitus mihi accidisse bona, & magna quidem ratus, appositissima denique non modò ad persolvendas numini ex debito gratias,

suddenly appeared many, who, as is customary with the vulgar, hatefully calumniated deeds nobly done; and when one,
above the rest, inflated and confident with literary pride, and
with the opinion entertained of him by those of his own herd,
5 nefariously undertook the defence of all tyrants, in a book
beyond example scandalous, levelled against us — that I,
rather than another, deemed not unequal to an adversary of so
great a name, nor to speaking on so great a subject, accepted,
of those very deliverers of the country, and by general consent,
10 the part spontaneously assigned me; namely, to defend publicly (if any one ever did) the cause of the people of England,
and thus of liberty itself. Lastly, I return thanks to God, that,
in a task so arduous, so full of expectation, I neither disappointed the hopes nor the opinions of my fellow-citizens, nor
15 failed to satisfy no small number of foreigners, as well among
the learned, as among persons conversant with public affairs;
that I even so completely routed my adversary, though of the
most audacious order, that he retired with his spirit broken,
his reputation shattered; and for the three years which he
20 afterwards lived, much as in his rage he threatened, he gave
us no farther trouble, than to solicit, for his support, the secret
services of certain persons of the vilest character, and to suborn
I know not what senseless and unconscionable applauders, to
patch up, if possible, his unexpected and recent ignominy.
25 This will immediately appear. As I conceived these fortunate,
and even great events to have happened to me from above, and
indeed, that they were particularly suited not only to discharge
my debt of gratitude to the Deity, but to supply the most fa-

sed ad auspicium quoque optimum instituti operis capien-
dum, cum veneratione, ut facio, imprimis commemoranda
esse duxi. Nam quis est qui patriæ decora non arbitretur sua?
quid patriæ cujusquam esse magìs decori aut gloriæ potest,
5 quàm libertas, non civili tantùm vitæ, sed divino etiam cultui
restituta? quæ gens, quæ civitas aut feliciùs aut fortiùs hanc
sibi utrobique peperit? Etenim fortitudo, cùm non tota in
bello atque armis eniteat, sed contra omnes æquè formidines
diffundat vim suam atque intrepida sit, Græci quidem illi,
10 quos maximè admiramur, & Romani, ad tollendos ex civitatibus tyrannos nullam ferè virtutem, præter studium libertatis,
expedita arma, promptásque manus attulere; Cætera omnia
in proclivi, inter laudes omnium & plausus, & læta omina,
peragebant; nec tam ad discrimen & ambiguum facinus
15 quàm ad certamen virtutis gloriosissimum atque pulcherri-
mum, ad præmia denique & coronas spémque immortalitatis
certissimam properabant. Nondum enim Tyrannis res sacra
erat; nondum tyranni, Christi scilicet proreges atque vicarii
repentè facti, cùm benevolentiâ non possent, cæcâ vulgi super-
20 stitione sese munierant: nondum Clericorum malis artibus at-
tonita plebs, ad barbariem eâ fœdiorem, quæ stolidissimos
mortalium infamat Indos, degeneraverat. Illi enim noxios
sibi Dæmonas, quos abigere non possunt, pro Diis colunt; hæc
Tyrannos nè liceret tollere cùm posset, impotentissimos crea-

vourable omen for my proposed work, I thought it behoved
me to begin, as I do, with the reverend mention of them. And
who is there who considers not the honourable achievements
of his country as his own? And what can be more for the
5 honour or glory of any country, than liberty, restored alike
to civil life, and to divine worship? What nation, what city
has struggled for it, in both kinds, more successfully or more
courageously? Indeed as courage shines out not exclusively in
war and arms, but displays its intrepid power equally against
10 every species of fear, those Greeks and Romans, whom we
most admire, brought along with them, for the expulsion of
tyrants from their states, scarcely any other virtue but zeal for
liberty, accompanied with ready arms, and eager hands.
The rest they achieved from the impulse thence derived,
15 amid the general shout, applause, and joyous circumstance.
They were even less eager for dangerous and uncertain enter-
prise, than for the trial of virtue fair and glorious, and for
rewards and crowns, and the certain hope of immortal fame.
For, the sovereign authority was not yet consecrated to ty-
20 rants. Tyrants, suddenly transformed into viceroys, forsooth,
and vicars of Christ, could not yet exercise their power through
royal grace; had not yet fortified themselves by the blind superstition of the vulgar. The lower orders, stupefied by the
wicked arts of priests, had not yet degenerated into a barbarism
25 viler than what disgraces the Indians, dullest of mortals: for
these merely worship as gods those malignant demons they
are unable to put to flight; while those, that they might not
cashier tyrants when they had it in their power, exalted them

bat in se Deos; & humani generis pestes in suam perniciem
consecrabat. At contra has omnes traditarum diu opinionum,
religionum, calumniarum, atque terrorum densissimas acies,
hoste ipso vehementiùs ab aliis formidatas, decertandum An-
5 glis erat. Quæ omnia, edocti meliùs, proculdubio cœlitus
imbuti, tantâ causæ fiduciâ, tantâ animorum firmitate ac virtute superârunt, ut cùm numero populus sanè magnus essent,
animis tamen tam erectis támque excelsis, vulgus esse desie-
rint; Britanniáque ipsa posthac, quæ tyrannorum terra ferax
10 dicta olim est, nunc liberatorum longè feracior, perpetuâ se-
culorum omnium celebratione dici meruerit. Quos non legum
contemptus aut violatio in effrænatam licentiam effudit; non
virtutis & gloriæ falsa species, aut stulta veterum æmulatio
inani nomine libertatis incendit, sed innocentia vitæ, morúm-
15 que sanctitas rectum atque solum iter ad libertatem veram
docuit, legum & religionis Justissima defensio necessariò ar-
mavit. Atque illi quidem Deo perinde confisi, servitutem Ho-
nestissimis armis pepulere: cujus laudis etsi nullam partem
mihi vendico, à reprehensione tamen vel timiditatis vel igna-
20 viæ, siqua infertur, facilè me tueor. Neque enim militiæ
labores & pericula sic defugi, ut non aliâ ratione, & operam,
multò utiliorem, nec minore cum periculo meis civibus na-
vârim, & animum dubiis in rebus neque demissum unquam,

into gods most impotent to rule over them—deifying the pests of the human race for their own destruction. Now against all these close embattlements of long-received opinions, religions, slanders, and terrors, more dreaded far by others than the enemy himself, had Englishmen to contend; and being better taught, and without doubt inspired from heaven, such was their confidence in their cause, such their firmness and strength of mind, that all these they overcame. Hence, though, in number, they were indeed a great people, yet were they, in spirit, so erect and lofty, that they were no longer a mere populace; even Britain herself, which heretofore has been said to be a land fruitful in tyrants, shall henceforth deserve the perpetual celebration of succeeding ages, as a country far more fruitful in deliverers. These men were never let loose, by a contempt or violation of the laws, to an unreigned licence; they were inflamed by no delusive vision of virtue and of glory, or by any foolish emulation of the ancients for the empty name of liberty; they were taught the straight and only way to true liberty, by innocence of life and sanctity of manners; they were compelled by necessity to arm in the just defence of the laws and of religion. Thus, confident of the divine aid, they drove out slavery in their glorious warfare. Of this glory, though I claim no share for myself, it is easy for me to defend myself against the charge, if any such be brought against me, either of timidity or of cowardice. For, if I avoided the toils and the perils of war, it was only that I might earnestly toil for my fellow-citizens in another way, with much greater utility, and with no less peril. In doubtful postures of our affairs, my mind

neque ullius invidiæ, vel etiam mortis plus æquo metuentem
præstiterim. Nam cùm ab adolescentulo humanioribus essem
studiis, ut qui maximè deditus, & ingenio semper quàm corpore validior, posthabitâ castrensi operâ, quâ me gregarius
5 quilibet robustior facilè superâsset, ad ea me contuli, quibus
plus potui; ut parte meî meliore ac potiore, si saperem, non
deteriore, ad rationes patriæ, causámque hanc præstantissi-
mam, quantum maximè possem momentum accederem. Sic
itaque existimabam, si illos Deus res gerere tam præclaras
10 voluit, esse itidem alios à quibus gestas dici pro dignitate atque
ornari, & defensam armis veritatem, ratione etiam, (quod
unicum est præsidium verè ac propriè humanum) defendi
voluerit. Unde est, ut dum illos invictos acie viros admiror,
de mea interim provincia non querar; immo mihi gratuler, &
15 gratias insuper largitori munerum cœlesti iterum summas
agam obtigisse talem, ut aliis invidenda multò magìs, quàm
mihi ullo modo pœnitenda videatur. Et me quidem nemini
vel infimo libens confero; nec verbum de me ullum insolentius facio: ad causam verò omnium nobilissimam ac celeberri-

never betrayed any symptom of despondence, nor was I more afraid than became me of malice, or even of death. Devoted even from a child to the more humanizing studies, and always stronger in mind than in body, I set an inferior value
5 upon the service of the camp, in which I might have been easily surpassed by any ordinary man of a more robust make, and betook myself to those occupations, where my services could be of more avail; that, if I were wise, I might contribute my utmost power, from the higher and more excellent, not
10 from the lower parts of my nature, to the designs of my country, and to this transcendent cause. I thought, therefore, that if it were the will of God those men should perform such gallant exploits, it must be likewise his will, that when performed, there should be others to set them forth with becoming
15 dignity and ornament; and that the truth, after being defended by arms, should be alike defended by reason—the only defence which is truly and properly human. Hence it is, that while I admire those men, unconquered in the field, I complain not of the part allotted to myself; nay, I may rather con-
20 gratulate myself, and once again return my highest thanks to the heavenly bestower of gifts, that such a lot has fallen to me, as may be viewed, with much greater reason, as a subject of envy to others, than in any way as a cause of repentance to myself. It is not my wish, however, to make a comparison of
25 myself with any one, not even with the humblest; nor is it from any arrogant feeling that I have spoken a single word in my own behalf. But when I turn my mind to that cause, of all others the most noble and most renowned, and to this

mam, & hoc simul defensores ipsos defendendi munus orna-
tissimum, ipsorum mihi suffragiis attributum atque judiciis,
quoties animum refero, fateor me mihi vix temperare, quin
altiùs atque audentiùs quàm pro exordii ratione insurgam; &
5 grandius quiddam, quod eloqui possim, quæram: quandoquidem oratores illos antiquos & insignes, quantum ego ab
illis non dicendi solum, sed & loquendi facultate, (in extranea
præsertim, quâ utor necessariò, linguâ, & persæpe mihi nequaquam satisfacio) haud dubiè vincor, tantùm omnes om-
10 nium ætatum, materiæ nobilitate & argumento vincam. Quod
& rei tantam expectationem ac celebritatem adjecit, ut jam
ipse me sentiam non in foro aut rostris, uno duntaxat populo,
vel Romano, vel Atheniensi circumfusum; sed attentâ, &
considente quasi totâ penè Europâ, & judicium ferente, ad
15 universos quacunque gravissimorum hominum, urbium, gentium, consessus atque conventus, & priore defensione, dixisse,
& hac rursus dicturum. Jam videor mihi, ingressus iter, trans-
marinos tractus & porrectas latè regiones, sublimis perlustrare;
vultus innumeros atque ignotos, animi sensus mecum con-
20 junctissimos. Hinc Germanorum virile & infestum servituti
robur, indè Francorum vividi digníque nomine liberales impetus, hinc Hispanorum consulta virtus, Italorum inde sedata

splendid office of defending even the defenders—an office
assigned me by their own suffrages and judgments, I confess
it is with difficulty I restrain myself from soaring to a more
daring height than is suitable to the purpose of an exordium,
5 and from casting about for something of more grandeur, to
which I may give utterance: for, to whatever degree I am surpassed (of which there can be little doubt) by the ancient,
illustrious orators, not only as an orator, but also as a linguist
(and particularly in a foreign tongue, which I employ of
10 necessity, and in which I am often very far from satisfying
myself) I shall surpass no less the orators of all ages in the
nobleness and in the instructiveness of my subject. This it is,
which has imparted such expectation, such celebrity to this
theme, that I now feel myself not in the forum or on the ros-
15 trum, surrounded by a single people only, whether Roman or
Athenian, but, as it were, by listening Europe, attending, and
passing judgment. I feel that I addressed myself in my former
defence, and that I shall again address myself in this, to all
sittings and assemblies, wherever are to be found men of the
20 highest authority; wherever there are cities and nations. I
imagine myself to have set out upon my travels, and that
I behold from on high, tracts beyond the seas, and wide-
extended regions; that I behold countenances strange and
numberless, and all, in feelings of mind, my closest friends
25 and neighbours. Here is presented to my eyes the manly
strength of the Germans, disdainful of slavery; there the lively
and generous impetuosity of the Franks, worthily so called;
on this side, the considerate virtue of the Spaniards; on that,

suíque compos magnanimitas ob oculos versatur. Quicquid uspiam liberorum pectorum, quicquid ingenui, quicquid magnanimi aut prudens latet, aut se palàm profitetur, alii tacitè favere, alii apertè suffragari, accurrere alii & plausu 5 accipere, alii tandem vero victi, dedititios se tradere. Videor jam mihi, tantis circumseptus copiis, ab Herculeis usque columnis, ad extremos Liberi Patris terminos, libertatem diu pulsam atque exulem, longo intervallo domum ubique gentium reducere: Et, quod Triptolemus olim fertur, sed longè 10 nobiliorem Cereali illâ frugem, ex civitate mea gentibus importare; restitutum nempe civilem liberúmque vitæ cultum, per urbes, per regna, pérque nationes disseminare. Sed nec ignotus planè, nec fortasse non gratus rursum advenero; si sum idem, qui pugnacissimum tyrannorum satellitem, & 15 opinione plerorumque, & suî fiduciâ insuperabilem antea creditum, cùm nos nostrásque acies contumeliosè lacesseret, & Optimates nostri me primùm intuerentur, singulari certamine congressus, adacto convitiantis in jugulum hoc stylo, immò suismet ipsius telis, collocavi; & nisi velim tot undique 20 lectorum intelligentium calculis atque sententiis, neutiquam addictis mihi aut obnoxiis diffidere prorsus & derogare, opima spolia retuli. Hæc sine ulla vaniloquentia ità esse re verâ, vel illud maximè argumento esse potest, quod ego nec sine Dei

the sedate and composed magnanimity of the Italians. Wherever there are natures free, ingenuous, magnanimous, either they are prudently concealed or openly professed. Some favour in silence, others give their suffrages in public; some hasten
5 to receive me with shouts of applause, others, in fine, vanquished by truth, surrender themselves captive. Encompassed by such countless multitudes, it seems to me, that, from the columns of Hercules to the farthest borders of India, that throughout this vast expanse, I am bringing back, bringing home to
10 every nation, liberty, so long driven out, so long an exile; and as is recorded of Triptolemus of old, that I am importing fruits for the nations, from my own city, but of a far nobler kind than those fruits of Ceres; that I am spreading abroad among the cities, the kingdoms, and nations, the restored culture of
15 citizenship and freedom of life. But if I am he, who laid low that redoubted satellite of tyrants, hitherto deemed invincible in the general opinion, and in his own conceit; if I am he, who, when he disdainfully defied us and our embattled might, (and our chief men turning their eyes first upon me) engaged
20 him in single combat, and with this stylus, the weapon of his choice, stabbed the reviler to the heart, and bore off abundant spoils;—unless I should choose to discredit, and wholly to disparage the estimates and opinions of hosts of intelligent readers on all sides, far from being devoted or under
25 obligations to me; if I am he, I say, I shall return as one not utterly unknown, perhaps even not unwelcome. That all this is true, without any extravagant talking, is most clearly proved even from the following circumstances: when Salmasius, or

nutu reor accidisse, quòd, cùm à Regina Suecorum Serenissima, quâ vivit opinor nemo, aut olim vixit, vel optimarum
artium, vel doctorum hominum studiosior, honorificè sanè
esset invitatus, venissétque & Salmasius & Salmasia, (uter enim
5 horum is erat, uxoris palàm dominatus cum fama tum domi
incertum admodum reddiderat) quo in loco peregrinus magno in honore degebat, ibi eum nostra Defensio nihil tale metuentem occupavit. Quâ statim à pluribus perlectâ, Regina
quidem, quæ & ipsa cum primis perlegerat, de suâ pristinâ
10 benignitate ac munificentiâ, id solum spectans quod se dignum erat, in hospitem nihil remisit: de cætero, si audita sæpius & quæ arcana non sunt, licet referre, tanta animorum
facta subitò mutatio est, ut qui nudiustertius summâ gratiâ
floruerat, nunc penè obsolesceret; nec ità multò post discedens
15 cum bona venia hoc unum in dubio permultis relinqueret,
honoratiórne advenerit, an contemptior abierit. Sed neque
aliis in locis detrimentum levius fecisse famæ satìs constat. Verùm hæc omnia non eò attuli, quò me cuiquam venditarem,
neque enim est opus; sed quò id duntaxat latiùs ostenderem,

Salmasia (for of what sex he was, was rendered extremely doubtful, from his being plainly ruled by his wife, alike in matters regarding his reputation, and in his domestic concerns) when Salmasius, or Salmasia, then, had indeed the
5 honour of being invited by the most serene, the queen of Sweden (than whom there lives not, I think, nor has ever lived one, who has more studiously cultivated the liberal arts, or who is a more generous patroness of men of letters) and when arrived in that country, of being treated, though a
10 foreigner, with great distinction—he was there surprised, while dreaming of no such thing, by our Defence— an event which I must think could not have happened but by the will of God. Here it was immediately perused by no small number; and the queen, who was among its first readers, attentive
15 only to what became her own dignity, remitted nothing, indeed, of her former grace and munificence towards her guest. For the rest, if it be allowable to disclose what I have often heard, and which is no secret, so remarkable a change was suddenly wrought in the sentiments of people, that the man,
20 who, of yesterday, blossomed in the meridian beams of favour, is to-day almost withered; and on his leaving Sweden, which he did, with good leave, not long after, it became a matter of doubt with many persons, whether his arrival was attended with more honour, or his departure with more contempt. It
25 sufficiently appears also, that his reputation sustained no less injury in other places. But as to all these matters, I am not so situated as to be forced to trumpet my own praises. This is not at all necessary. I would only show more clearly that I had no

quod initio institui, quas ob causas, & quàm non leves, ab
agendis Deo Optimo Maximo gratiis potissimùm sim exorsus;
mihíque procemium hoc fore honestissimum atque pulcher-
rimum, in quo præcipuè, tot argumentis enumeratis, demon-
5 strare liceat, me, haud expertem licèt calamitatum humanarum, me tamen, résque meas Deo curæ esse; me maximis
prope de rebus, & ad patriæ necessaria tempora accommodatis,
& civilis vitæ religionísque ex usu maximè futuris, non uno
pro populo, nedum uno pro reo, sed pro universo potiùs ho-
10 minum genere, contra humanæ libertatis hostes, quasi in
communi omnium gentium & frequentissimo concursu dis-
serentem, divino favore & auxilio adjutum atque auctum:
quo ego majus aut gloriosius quicquam mihi tribuere, neque
possim ullo tempore neque cupiam. Eundem proinde immor-
15 talem Deum oro, ut consuetâ ejus ope ac benignitate solâ
fretus, quâ integritate, diligentiâ, fide, felicitate etiam, fortissimè justissiméque simul facta haud ità pridem defendi,
eâdem, vel eâ amplius, Authores ipsos, méque tantis viris
ignominiæ causâ, non honoris additum ab immeritis oppro-
20 briis, atque calumniis vindicare sufficiam. Quòd si est, qui
contemni hæc satiùs arbitretur potuisse, fateor equidem, si
apud eos qui nos rectè nôssent hæc spargerentur: cæteris quâ
tandem ratione constabit non esse verum quicquid adversarius

light reasons for beginning, as I did, with giving my especial
thanks to God most high and most excellent; I would show
that this proem, in which I am able to evince by so many
proofs, that I and my concerns (though in no wise free from
5 the ills of humanity) are under the care of the Deity—must
redound to my honour and fair fame; I would show that I
am aided by the divine favour and help, in undertakings of
the greatest magnitude, planned for the needed service of my
country, and tending to be of the highest use to society and to
10 religion, not in respect of one people only, much less of one
unprincipled man, but rather of the universal race of man,
against the enemies of man's freedom—addressing myself, as
it were, to the multitudes of all nations gathered together and
crowded into one vast congregation. It is not possible for me,
15 nor can it ever be my desire, to ascribe to myself any thing
greater or more glorious. Wherefore I implore the same immortal God, that as, upheld solely by his wonted aid and goodness, I have both justly and intrepidly defended deeds hitherto
unparalleled, I may not be deficient in vindicating with the
20 same or even greater, integrity, diligence, fidelity, and even
success the authors, and myself also, conjoined as I am with
so many others, in unmerited reproach and calumny, for
purposes of ignominy instead of honour. And if there be any
one who thinks that these things would have been better
25 passed over in contempt, I do not dispute it, admitting these
things to have been scattered among those who have understood us rightly; but how shall it be made appear at last to the
rest of mankind, that the lies which our adversary has told are

noster est mentitus? cùm autem, data, quæ par est, opera, à
nobis erit, ut quo præcessit calumnia, eodem vindex quoque
veritas sequatur, & illos de nobis perperam sentire opinor desi-
turos, & istum fortasse mendaciorum pudebit: si non pudu-
5 erit, tum demùm, satiùs contempserimus. Huic interea responsum pro meritis celeriùs expedivissem, nisi se falsis rumo-
ribus hactenus muniisset; dum sæpius denuntiaret, ad incudem
sudare Salmasium, nova volumina in nos fabricare, jam jámque editurum: ex quo hoc solum est consequutus, ut male-
10 dicentiæ pœnas aliquanto seriùs daret: expectandum enim
duxi potiùs, ut potiori viribus adversario, integrum me ser-
varem. Sed cum Salmasio debellatum jam puto mihi esse,
utpote mortuo; & quemadmodum mortuo, non dicam: non
enim ut ille mihi cæcitatem, sic ego illi mortem vitio vertam.
15 Quanquam sunt, qui nos etiam necis ejus reos faciunt, illósque
nostros nimis acriter strictos aculeos; quos dum repugnando
altiùs sibi infixit, dum quod præ manibus habebat opus, vidit
spissiùs procedere, tempus responsionis abiisse, operis gratiam periisse, recordatione amissæ famæ, existimationis, Prin-
20 cipum denique favoris, ob rem regiam malè defensam, erga

not truths? Yet, as we shall do our endeavour, which is no
more than just, that however far slander has gone before, so
far the avenger truth shall follow after, it is my belief that
those who have been deceived will cease to think wrongfully
5 of us, and that the adversary will peradventure be ashamed of
his lies; and if he is not ashamed, that then it would at last be
better to treat him with contempt. Meanwhile, I should have
prepared a suitable reply to him with more despatch, if he had
not all along entrenched himself in delusive rumours; giving
10 out every now and then his menacing warnings, that Salmasius was sweating at the anvil, and fabricating new volumes against us, which he was even on the point of publishing.
By all this he merely effected that the punishment he would
suffer for his slanderous tongue should be deferred: for I
15 thought it behoved me to wait, that I might reserve my strength
entire against the more potent adversary. But with Salmasius
I imagine my battling is now at an end, for he is among the
dead. And how he died I shall not undertake to say: for I will
not impute to him his death as a crime, as he did to me my
20 blindness. There are not wanting, however, those who lay the
guilt of his death upon me, and upon those stings of mine
which were but too sharp; and which, by resisting, he caused
to sink the deeper. And while he saw the work he had in hand
advance slower and slower; saw that the time for reply was
25 gone by; saw that the grace of his work was no more: stung,
moreover, by the recollection, that his fame, his estimation
had perished; in fine, that the favour shown him by princes
had abated, by reason of his poor defence of the royal cause—

se imminuti, triennali tandem mœstitiâ, & animi magis ægri-
tudine, quàm morbo confectum obiisse. Utcunque sit, si
iterum cum hoste satìs mihi cognito, si bella etiam posthuma
gerenda sunt, cujus feroces ac strenuos impetus facilè sustinui,
5 ejus languentes & moribundos conatus non est ut reformidem.

   Nunc verò ad hoc quicquid est hominis, qui nos inclamat,
aliquando veniamus: clamorem quidem audio, non Regii
sanguinis, ut præ se fert titulus, sed obscuri cujuspiam nebu-
lonis; clamantem enim nusquam reperio. Eho! quis es? ho-
10 móne an nemo? hominum certè infimi, nè mancipia quidem,
sine nomine sunt. Sempérne ergò mihi cum anonymis res
erit? at verò hi regios haberi se vel maximè volunt: miror si
regibus sic persuaserint. Regum sequaces atque amicos regum
non pudet; quo pacto igitur sunt isti regibus amici? non dant
15 munera; immo verò libentiùs multò accipiunt: res suas non
impendunt, qui ne nomina quidem causæ regiæ dare audent:
quid ergó? verba dant, sed nec verba gratìs dare suis regibus,
vel satìs benevoli in animum inducunt, vel satìs constantes nomine adscripto audent. Me quidem ὦ ἄνδρες ἀνώνυμοι, fas
20 enim sit Græcè quos Latinè quid nominem non reperio, me inquam, cum vester ille Claudius de Jure Regio, materiâ sanè gra-

he is said, after three years of chagrin, to have died, worn away by sickness of mind, more than from any bodily disease. But however this may be, if I must engage him a second time— if I must wage even a posthumous war with an enemy, who is

5 now sufficiently well known to me, as I have found no difficulty in sustaining the ferocity of his most vigorous charge, I can have no reason to dread his feeble and dying efforts.

But, at length, let us now proceed to the personage, such as he is, who raises this cry against us. I hear the cry indeed, not

10 of the royal blood, as the title would make us believe, but of some skulking scoundrel: for the crier himself I no where find. Ho there! who are you? A man, or nobody? Certainly of the most beggarly order of men; for slaves even are not without a name. Shall I for ever be concerned with the name-

15 less? Such, however, would be accounted king's men in a degree above their fellows. I should wonder if they persuaded kings of this. The followers and the friends of kings are not ashamed of kings. How then are these men friends to kings? They make no presents; on the contrary, they are far more

20 ready to receive them. Those are not the men to expend their fortunes upon the royal cause, who venture not to bestow even their names. What then? They bestow words; but they have not enough good-will to persuade themselves, they have not enough constancy to have the courage to subscribe their

25 names, and thus to bestow even words upon their kings for nothing. But ὦ ἄνδρες ἀνώνυμοι, anonymous Sirs! (for I may be allowed to address you in Greek, as I find no name for you in Latin) since your Claudius had undertaken to write, with-

tiosissimâ, sine nomine tamen orsus esset scribere, & exemplo
possem uti, usque adeò neque mei, neque causæ puditum est,
ut ad rem tantam accedere, nisi nomen palàm professus, turpe
ducerem. Quod ego in Republica palàm videor contra Reges,
5 cur vos in Regno, vel Regum sub patrocinio, non nisi furtim
& clanculum, contra Rempublicam audetis? cur in tuto pa-
vidi, cur in luce nocturni, summam potentiam, summam
gratiam, timiditate invidiosâ planè, atque suspectâ obscuratis?
satísne vobis ut præsidii sit in Regibus veremini? sic tecti, sic
10 obvoluti non vos mehercule ad asserendum jus Regium defensores, sed ad ærarium compilandum fures potiùs videmini
venisse. Equidem quod sum, profiteor; quod Regibus nego
jus esse, vel in regno quovis legitimo pernegare ausim: nemo
me læserit Monarcha, quin se priùs damnet, tyrannum fassus.
15 Si tyrannos insector, quid hoc ad Reges? quos ego à tyrannis
longissimè sejungo. Quantum à viro malo distat vir bonus,
tantundem à tyranno discrepare Regem contendo: Unde effi-
citur, tyrannum non modò non esse Regem, sed Regi quidem
adversissimum semper imminere. Et sanè qui monumenta
20 rerum percurrit, plures à tyrannis quàm à populo oppressos
Reges, atque sublatos inveniet. Qui igitur tollendos affirmat
tyrannos, non Reges, sed inimicissimos Regibus, immo in-

out a name, on the right of kings, a subject truly gracious, I
might have followed his example, but that I was not so much
ashamed either of myself or of my cause: besides, I thought
it dishonorable to go to a subject of such grandeur, without
5 openly declaring my name. How is it, that what I am seen to
do openly against kings, in a commonwealth, you have not the
spirit to attempt, unless secretly and by stealth, against a commonwealth in a kingdom, and under the patronage of kings?
Why cast a cloud over the supreme power, the sovereign grace,
10 by this invidious and suspicious timidity?—timorous when in
safety, dark in the midst of light. Are you afraid lest kings
should be too weak to protect you? Thus cloaked, thus
muffled up, by Jove, one would think you come not as defenders to assert the right of kings, but as thieves to rob the
15 treasury. Now what I am, I openly profess to be. The right
which I deny to kings, I would boldly persist in denying, in
any legitimate kingdom. No monarch could injure me, without first condemning himself, by the confession that he was a
tyrant. If I inveigh against tyrants, what is that to kings? be-
20 tween whom and tyrants I make the widest difference. As
much as a good man differs from a bad, so much, do I maintain, that a king differs from a tyrant. Whence it follows, that
a tyrant is not only no king, but is ever the most irreconcilable
enemy to a king. And in fact, he who runs over the records of
25 history will find that more kings have been overpowered and
displaced by tyrants, than by the people. He who affirms,
therefore, that tyrants ought to be displaced, affirms not that
kings are to be displaced, but the bitterest foes to kings—foes,

festissimos regum hostes tollendos affirmat. Vos contrà, quod
regibus jus datis, ut quicquid libeat jus sit, non est jus, sed injuria, sed scelus, sed ipsa pernicies: venenato isto munere, non
salutari, quos supra omnem vim atque periculum fore prædi-
5 catis, eos ipsi occiditis; regem & tyrannum idem esse, siquidem idem utrobique Jus est, statuitis. Nam si isto suo Jure,
Rex non utitur, (utetur autem nunquam quamdiu Rex, non
tyrannus, erit,) non hoc Regi, sed viro assignandum est. Quid
autem absurdius illo jure Regio fingi queat, quo si quis utatur,
10 quoties Rex vult esse, toties esse vir bonus desinat: quoties vir
esse bonus maluerit, toties se arguerit non esse Regem? quo
quid in Reges dici contumeliosius potest? Hoc jus qui docet,
ipse sit oportet injustissimus, atque omnium pessimus: pejor
autem quo pacto fiat, quàm si quales format ac fingit alios,
15 talis ipse imprimis fuerit? Quòd si omnis vir bonus, ut antiquorum secta quædam magnificè sanè philosophatur, est Rex,
pari ratione sequitur, omnem virum malum pro suo quemque
modulo tyrannum esse: neque enim magnum, nè hoc nomine
intumescat, sed infimum quiddam est tyrannus; & quantò
20 omnium maximus, tantò omnium vilissimus, & maximè ser-
vilis. Alii enim suis tantùm vitiis volentes serviunt; Hic non

which, above all others are most hostile to kings. On the other hand, the right which you give to kings, that whatever they may choose to will, *that* shall be right, is not right, but wrong, but iniquity, but perdition itself. By a gift thus 5 poisonous, instead of salutary, you become yourselves the murderers of those, who as you affirm, should be above all violence and all danger: you make a king and a tyrant identical, inasmuch as you ascribe the same right to both. And admitting that a king makes no use of this right of his (which he 10 never will, as long as he shall be simply a king, and no tyrant) this is to be attributed not to the king, but to the man. Now what can be imagined more absurd than this kingly right, which if any king uses, that is, whenever he would be a king, he would cease to be a good man; whenever he should choose 15 rather to be a good man, he would prove himself to be no king? What greater contumely can be cast upon kings? He who teaches this right must himself be most unjust—yea, the worst of his kind: for how can he be worse, than by first becoming himself such a one, as he thus moulds and fashions 20 others. But if every good man is a king, as a certain sect of the ancients magnificently philosophized, it follows, by parity of reason, that every bad man, according to his proportion, is a tyrant: and that he may not be puffed up with this name let it be observed, that a tyrant, so far from being anything great, 25 is the meanest of earthly things; that as far as he surpasses all in the elevation of his rank, so far is he the vilest of all, and the most a slave. For others are the willing slaves, only of their own vices; he is obliged to be the slave, even against his will,

modò suis, sed ministrorum etiam atque satellitum importunis-
simis flagitiis etiam nolens cogitur servire; & suas quasdam
tyrannides abjectissimo cuique suorum concedere: Tyranni
igitur servorum infimi, suis serviunt etiam servitiis. Quamob-
5 rem rectè hoc nomen vel in minimum quemque tyrannorum
pugilem, vel in hunc etiam clamatorem poterit convenire; qui
in hac causa tyrannica cur tam strenuè vociferetur, ex his quæ
dicta sunt, quæque mox dicentur, satìs liquebit: utì etiam cur
anonymus: aut enim turpiter conductus, clamorem hunc
10 suum, regio sanguini, Salmasium sequutus, vendidit aut infamis doctrinæ conscientiâ pallens, aut vitâ flagitiosus ac turpis,
latere si cupit, mirum non est: aut fortassis ità se parat, ut
sicubi spem quæstûs uberiorem odoretur, desertis quandoque
regibus integrum sibi sit, ad quamlibet etiam futuram rem-
15 publicam transfugere; nè tunc quidem sine exemplo magni
sui Salmasii, qui affulgente lucro captus, ab orthodoxis ad
Episcopos, à popularibus ad regios, etiam senex defecit. Tu
igitur iste è gurgustio clamator, qui sis non fallis; frustrà tibi
ista latibula quæsisti: extrahêre, mihi crede, neque Plutonis
20 ista galea diutiùs te teget: dejerabis, quoad vixeris, me aut
cæcum non esse, aut tibi saltem non connivere. Quis igitur
sit, quod genus hominis, quâ spe adductus, quibus illecebris,

not of his own vices only, but of the most importunate profligacies of his ministers and satellites; he is obliged to yield the
subordinate branches of his tyranny to the most worthless of
his creatures. Tyrants, therefore, are the most abject of slaves;
5 they are slaves even to their own slaves. Hence, this name may
be correctly applied even to the most insignificant pugilist of
tyrants—nay to this crier; the reason of whose vociferating so
furiously, in this tyrannous cause, will sufficiently appear
from what has been already said, and from what shall be said
10 presently; as likewise, the reason of his being anonymous.
For either he is basely hired, like Salmasius, and has sold this
cry of his to the royal blood; or it were nothing strange, if,
smitten with a fearful consciousness of the infamy of its doctrine, or if, from his flagitious and scandalous life, he is de-
15 sirous of concealment; perhaps even he places himself in such
a position, as to snuff a more promising hope of gain from
another quarter, that he may be free, in his own conscience, to
desert kings at a future time, for some commonwealth, though
yet to be established: and even in this case, he would not be
20 without an example in his great Salmasius, who, captivated by
the glittering reward, revolted in his old age, from the orthodox to the bishops, from the popular party to the royalists. We
are at no loss then to discover, who you are—crier as you are,
from some paltry hovel; it is in vain you try to lurk unknown;
25 be assured you shall be dragged to light, nor shall that Pluto's
helmet any longer protect you: I will make you swear to the
latest day of your life, either that I am not blind, or at least that
I am not purblind in respect of you. Listen now, if you have

quibus lenociniis delinitus, ad hanc causam regiam accesserit, (Milesia propemodum, aut Baiana fabula est) si vacat, nunc audite.

Est *Morus* quidam, partim Scotus, partim Gallus; nè tota
5 hominis infamia, gens una, aut regio nimiùm laboraret; homo improbus, & cùm aliorum, tum, quod gravissimum est, amicorum, quos ex intimis inimicissimos sibi fecit, testimoniis quam plurimis infidus, mendax, ingratus, maledicus, & virorum perpetuus obtrectator & fœminarum, quarum nec pudi-
10 citiæ plus unquam parcere, quàm famæ consuevit. Is, ut primæ ætatis obscuriora præteream, primùm Genevæ Græcas literas docuit; verùm, sæpius licet nomen suum Græcè Morum discipulis interpretatus, stultum & nequam ipse dediscere nequivit, Quin eo potiùs furore est agitatus cùm tot scelerum esset
15 sibi conscius, quamvìs fortasse nondum compertus, ut pastoris in Ecclesia munus ambire, atque istis moribus inquinare non horresceret. Verùm haud diu Presbyterorum censuram effugere potuit, mulierarius ac vanus, multisque aliis criminibus notatus, multis ab orthodoxâ fide erroribus damnatus,
20 quos & turpiter ejuravit, & ejuratos impiè retinuit; tandem adulterii manifestus. Hospitis ancillam quandam fortè ada-

time (and it is a sort of Milesian, or Baian tale) while I relate
who he is, whence sprung, influenced by what expectation, by
what allurements, coaxed by what panderly offices, he came
to this cause of kings.

5   He is one "More," part Scot, part Frenchman, (that one
nation or country may not lie under the whole infamy of his
character) an unprincipled fellow, who, according to general
report, and what is of most weight, according to the testimony
of his friends (whom from fast friends he has made his great-
10 est enemies) is without fidelity, without veracity, without
gratitude; an evil-speaker, an unceasing slanderer of men, as
likewise of women, whose modesty he is as little accustomed
to spare, as their good name. This personage, to pass over the
obscurity of his early life, first made his appearance as teacher
15 of Greek at Geneva; and though he often explained to his
scholars the meaning of his own name, Morus, in Greek, he
could not himself unlearn to be a fool and a profligate; besides,
his being conscious of so many crimes, though perhaps not yet
detected, served the more to work him up to such a pitch of
20 madness, that he felt no horror at becoming a candidate for,
and at defiling with his scandalous manners, the office of
pastor in the church. But he could not long escape the censure
of the presbyters. A trifler, and given to women, marked also
for various other offences, convicted of numerous aberrations
25 from the orthodox faith, which he was so base as to recant on
oath, and so impious as to retain, he last of all turns out a no-
torious adulterer. He happened to be seized with a lawless
passion for a servant girl of his host; and though the girl was

maverat; eam paulò pòst etiam alteri nuptam sectari non de-
stitit; tuguriolum quoddam intrare hortuli, solum cum sola,
vicini sæpe animadverterant. Citra adulterium, inquis; poterat enim quidvis aliud: sanè quidem; poterat confabulari,
nimirum de re hortensi, prælectiones quasdam suas sciolæ fortasse fœminæ & audiendi cupidæ expromere de hortis, Alcinoï
putà vel Adonidis; poterat nunc areolas laudare, umbram
tantummodo desiderare, liceret modò ficui morum inserere,
complures indè sycomoros quàm citissimè enasci, ambula-
tionem amœnissimam; modum deinde insitionis mulieri poterat monstrare: hæc & plura poterat, quis negat? veruntamen
presbyteris satisfacere non poterat, quin illum tanquam adulterum, censurâ ferirent, & pastoris munere indignum prorsus
judicarent: harum & hujusmodi accusationum capita in Bib-
liotheca illius urbis publica etiamnum asservantur. Interea,
dum hæc palàm nota non essent, ab ecclesia, quæ Middelbur-
gi erat Gallica, procurante Salmasio, in Hollandiam vocatus,
magnâ cum offensione Spanhemii, viri sanè docti, & pastoris
integerrimi, qui eum Genevæ antea probè noverat, literas
testimoniales, quas vocant, dum alii non ferendum existima-

married not long after to another, he still followed her; the neighbours had frequently observed them enter together a small lodge in the little garden. This amounts not, it may be said, to adultery; he might have been employed about some-
5 thing else. True, he might have been talking with her, for example, on the subject of gardening; he might have taken occasion from gardens, from those of Alcinous, suppose, or of Adonis, to introduce certain lecturings of his to the woman, who might have been a prodigy of understanding, and eager
10 to listen. He might now have praised the parterres; might even have wished for nothing more than shade; might have been allowed no other liberty than to engraft a mulberry in a fig, thence to raise, with the utmost dispatch, a line of syca-mores—a most delectable walk. Then he might have shown
15 the woman the manner of engrafting. All these things and many more he might have done; who denies it? But all these things would not satisfy the presbyters, but they must smite him with their censure as an adulterer, and sentence him as totally unworthy of the pastoral office. The heads of these and
20 of similar charges are still preserved in the public library of that city. In the meantime, while these proceedings were not publicly known, he receives by the influence of Salmasius, from the Gallican church at Middelburg, an invitation to Hol-land; and to the great offence of Spanheim (a man truly
25 learned, and a pastor of the first character, who had known him well before at Geneva,) contrived to obtain of the Gene-vese, but on condition only of his quitting Geneva, letters tes-timonial, as they are called, (and these, to tell the truth, were

rent, ut homo istiusmodi ecclesiæ testimonio ornaretur, alii quidvis potiùs ferendum, quàm ipsum hominem, ægrè à Genevensibus, & non aliâ quàm sui discessûs conditione, atque illas quidem frigidulas, tandem impetravit. In Hollan-
5 diam ut venit, ad salutandum Salmasium profectus, domi ejus in Uxoris ancillam, cui Pontiæ nomen erat, oculos nequiter conjecit: semper enim in ancillis prolabitur libido hominis; hinc summâ assiduitate Salmasium cœpit colere, &, quoties licuit, Pontiam. Nescio an ille commoditate hominis
10 & assentatione captus, an hic optabilem excogitâsse se conveniendæ eo sæpius Pontiæ occasionem ratus, prior sermones injecerit de responso Miltonii ad Salmasium. Ut ut fuit, Morus propugnandum suscipit Salmasium: Et Salmasius quidem Theologicam in ea urbe cathedram suâ operâ pollicetur Moro;
15 Morus & hanc & aliud insuper suaviculum, furtivos Pontiæ concubitus pollicetur sibi. Per causam consulendi de hoc opere Salmasium, dies ac noctes eam domum frequentat. Jámque ut olim Pyramus in morum, ità nunc repente morus in Pyramum transmutatus sibi videtur, Genevensis in Babylonium;
20 verùm illo juvene quantò improbior, tantò fortunatior, nunc suam Thisben, factâ sub eodem tecto copiâ, ut libitum est, Pontiam alloquitur; rimam in pariete conquirere opus non erat; Spondet matrimonium; eâ spe pellectam vitiat; eodém-

rather cold); though, at the same time, there were some who thought it not to be borne, that a man of his description should be graced with the testimony of the church; while others again were of opinion, that anything was to be borne, rather
5 than the man himself. On his arrival in Holland, and going to pay his respects to Salmasius, he cast his wanton eyes on the servant-girl of Salmasius's wife, whose name was Pontia: for the fellow's lust always lights upon waiting-maids. From this, he began to pay court to Salmasius with his utmost assiduity,
10 and, as often as he could, to Pontia. I know not, whether Salmasius, pleased with his adulation and struck with the thought of using him for his convenience, or whether More, thinking to contrive a desirable opportunity of meeting Pontia the more frequently, was the first to begin the conversation on
15 the subject of Milton's Answer to Salmasius. However this may be, More undertakes to defend Salmasius, and Salmasius on his part promises to procure for More the divinity-chair in that city: and More promises himself both this, and the additional douceur of Pontia's stolen embraces. On pretence of
20 consulting Salmasius about that work, he frequents his house day and night; and as Pyramus of old was transformed into a mulberry tree, so the mulberry now fancies itself suddenly changed into Pyramus—the Genevan into the Babylonian. But exceeding that youth in good fortune as much as he ex-
25 ceeds him in wickedness, he has now the liberty of speaking with his Thisbe, his Pontia, whenever he pleases, under the same roof; there is no need of searching for a chink in the wall. He promises her marriage: and with this delusive hope de-

que scelere, horreo dicere, sed dicendum est, Sacrosancti
Evangelii minister, hospitalem etiam domum constuprat. Ex
hoc demum congressu, mirum quiddam, & præter solitum
naturæ prodigiosum accidit, ut & fœmina & mas etiam conci-
5 peret, Pontia quidem Morillum, quod & Plinianum exerci-
tatorem diu postea exercuit Salmasium; Morus ovum hoc
irritum & ventosum, ex quo tympanites iste clamor regii sanguinis prorupit. Quod quidem primò regiis nostris in Belgio
esurientibus pergrata admodum sorbitio fuit; nunc rupto pu-
10 tamine, vitiosum ac putridum repertum aversantur. Nam
Morus hoc suo fœtu haud mediocriter inflatus, & Arausiacam
factionem totam demeruisse se sentiens, jam integras profes-
sionum cathedras spe improbâ devoraverat, & suam Pontiam
utpote ancillam & pauperculam, jam gravidam sceleratus
15 deseruerat. Illa despectam se atque delusam querens, &
synodi fidem & magistratûs imploravit. Sic tandem evulgata
hæc res, & conviviis penè omnibus, ac circulis diu risum &
cachinnos præbuit. Unde aliquis, & lepidi sanè, quisquis erat,
ingenii, hoc distichon,

20   *Galli ex concubitu gravidam te, Pontia, Mori,*
        Quis bene moratam, morigerámque neget?

bauches her; in committing which crime (I shudder with horror while I relate it, but it must be related) a minister of the holy gospel defiles even the house of his host. From this connection, there followed, in due time, something strange and
5 monstrous—out of the common course of nature. Not the female only, but the male conceived; Pontia a Moreling which, for a long time after, served to exercise the Plinian exercitator, Salmasius; More this addle and windy egg, from which burst forth that tympany—the *Cry of the Royal Blood*.
10 This was thought at first a most delicious sup for our hungry royalists in Belgium; but now the shell is broken, they turn with loathing from the rotten and offensive contents. As for More, inflated in no small degree with this birth of his, and thinking he had deserved well of the whole Orange faction,
15 he was already seizing, in his presumptuous expectations, new professorial chairs; and like a scoundrel as he is, had already deserted his poor, humble Pontia, she being only a waiting maid, and now great with child. Thus despised and deluded, she complained to the synod and magistrates, imploring their
20 protection. Hence the affair at length became public, and long furnished a subject for mirth and derision at almost all convivial meetings and parties. This gave occasion to somebody (and whoever he was, he had no contemptible genius for wit) to write the following distich:

25 As your belly, Pontia, 'gins to swell,
From tread of the Gallican;
That under More, you've been Mored, well,
Deny it not a man.

Sola Pontia non risit; sed nec querendo quicquam profecit;
Clamor enim regii sanguinis clamorem stupri, & stupratæ
mulierculæ ploratum facilè obruerat; Salmasius quoque illa-
tam sibi hanc totíque familiæ & injuriam & labem ægrè ferens,
5 séque ab amico & laudatore suo sic ludos factum, sic adversario
rursus obnoxium, accedente ad priores ejus in causa regia in-
felicitates forsitan hoc etiam infortunio, haud ità multò pòst
supremum diem obiit. Verùm aliquantò hæc posteriùs. Interim Salmasius, Salmacidis quodam fato, ut enim nomen, ità
10 & fabula non abludit, nescius Hermaphroditum se adjunxisse
sibi Morum tam gignendi, quàm pariendi compotem, quid is
domi genuisset ignarus, quod peperit exosculatur; librum
nempe istum in quo sentit se Magnum toties dici, & suo fortè
judicio dignè, aliorum certè stultè atque ridiculè laudatum.
15 Itaque typographum festinanter quærit; & fugientem ab se
jam diu famam, retinere frustrà conatus, quas laudes, quas potiùs fœdas suî adulationes per hunc atque alios miserè concu-
piverat, iis etiam divulgandis obstetricatur ipse atque subser-
vit. Ad hanc operam Vlaccus quidam est visus omnium maxi-
20 mè idoneus; huic facilè persuadet, non modò ut librum illum
excudendum curaret, quod nemo reprehendisset; sed etiam ut
Epistolæ ad Carolum videlicet missæ, multis in me, qui hominem nunquam nôram, probris & contumeliis refertæ, sub-

Pontia alone is not seen to smile; but she gained nothing from complaint: for the cry of the royal blood easily drowned the cry of her violated chastity, and the lamentation of a poor defiled girl. Salmasius too, full of vexation at the injury and
5 dishonour brought upon himself and household, and that he had been thus made the sport of his friend and panegyrist; that he was thus again at the mercy of his adversary—this new misfortune, added to his former ill-success in the royal cause, was perhaps the circumstance which not long after brought him
10 to his end. But of this by and by. In the meantime, Salmasius, not unlike in fate to Salmasis, (for as the name, so the tale is not inapt) unconscious that More, whom he had associated to himself, was an hermaphrodite, alike capable of procreation and of parturition, not aware of what More had begotten
15 at home, he fondles in ecstasy what he had brought forth— namely the book in which he found himself so often styled great; being, no doubt in his own estimation, worthily praised, though certainly, in the estimation of others, most absurdly and ridiculously. However, he goes with all haste
20 in search of a printer; and struggling in vain to keep hold of the fame which had been so long deserting him, those praises, or rather those gross flatteries, which he had pitifully coveted, through this man and others, he lends his obstetric services for bringing into the world. For this business one Vlaccus is
25 found to be the fittest of all others. Him he easily persuades not only to print the said book, which nobody could have blamed; but also to profess himself, by subscribing his name, the author of a letter addressed to Charles, full of reproaches

scripto nomine se profiteretur authorem. Nequis igitur mire-
tur cur se exorari tam facilè sit passus, ut me tam impudenter
nullâ de causâ lacesseret, & alienas etiam intemperies in se
transferre atque præstare tam pro nihilo duceret, erga omnes
5 etiam alios quemadmodum se gesserit, sicuti ego compertum
habeo, ostendam. Est Vlaccus unde gentium nescio, vagus
quidam librariolus, veterator atque decoctor notissimus; is
Londini aliquandiu bibliopola fuit clancularius; quâ ex urbe,
post innumeras fraudes, obæratus aufugit. Eundem Parisiis
10 fide cassum & malè agendo insignem, via tota Jacobæa cogno-
vit: unde olim quoque profugus nè multis quidem parasan-
gis audet appropinquare; nunc si cui opus est balatrone perdi-
tissimo atque venali, prostat Hagæcomitis Typographus re-
coctus. Hunc ut intelligatis, quid dicat, quídve agat, quàm
15 nihil pensi habeat, nihil esse tam sanctum, quod non lucro
vel exiguo posterius putet, séque non causâ publicâ, quod quis
putâsset, sic in me esse debacchatum, fatentem ipsum in se
testem producam. Is cum vidisset quod in Salmasium scripseram, nonnullis librariis æra meruisse, scribit ad amicos
20 quosdam meos mecum agerent, ut siquid haberem excudendum, sibi committeretur; se typis longè melioribus, quàm qui

and contumelies upon me, who had never any knowledge of
the man. That no one, however, may feel surprise, that he suffered himself so easily to be prevailed upon to set upon me
with such insolence without cause, and to think it, as he does,
5 so trifling a matter thus to become a proxy for venting other
people's fury, I shall show (for I have made the discovery)
how he has conducted himself towards the rest of mankind.

This Vlaccus, whose country I know not, is a sort of vaga-
bond bookseller, a spendthrift, and a practised impostor. For
10 some time, he carried on a clandestine trade, as a bookseller,
in London; from which city, after innumerable frauds, he
fled for debt. At Paris, the whole of the Rue St. Jacques
knew him for his total want of credit, and for his dishonest
practices; and having been formerly a fugitive from this city
15 also, he dares not approach it within many parasangs. At this
time, if any one has need of a venal and most incorrigible
rogue, he shows himself newly furbished up as a printer at the
Hague. Now, that you may know what he is saying, or what
he is doing; how totally without business he is; that there is
20 nothing so sacred which he would not regard as of less value
than even the most trifling gains; and that it was from no
public consideration, as any one would have thought, that he
raged so furiously against me—I shall produce himself as an
evidence witnessing against himself. He no sooner observed
25 that some booksellers had got money by what I had written
against Salmasius, than he writes to certain friends of mine to
use their interest with me, that, if I had any thing to print, it
might be thrown into his hands; assuring them it should be

priùs excudisset, mandaturum: respondi per eosdem, non
habere me in præsentia, quod excuso esset opus. Ecce autem!
cui suam operam tam officiosè modò detulerat, in eum haud
ità multò post, scripti contumeliosissimi non excusor solùm
5 sed & author, subdititius licèt, prodit. Indignantur amici;
rescribit impudentissimus, mirari se simplicitatem eorum, &
rerum imperitiam, qui officii rationem aut honesti ab se exi-
gant aut desiderent, cùm videant quibus rebus quæstum faciat:
se ab ipso Salmasio illam epistolam cum libro accepisse; qui
10 rogabat id utì suâ gratiâ vellet facere quod fecit; si Miltonio,
vel cuivis alteri visum esset respondere, nullum sibi esse scru-
pulum; siquidem eâdem suâ operâ uti voluerint: id est, vel
in Salmasium vel in Carolum; namque id erat solum quod in
responso ejusmodi futurum expectare poterat. Quid plura?
15 hominem videtis; ad reliquos nunc pergo, non enim unus est
duntaxat, qui hanc in nos regii Clamoris quasi tragœdiam
adornavit: en igitur initio, ut solet, dramatis personæ: Clamor
prologus, Vlaccus Balatro, aut, si mavultis, Salmasius Vlacci
Balatronis persona & lacernis involutus, Duo Poetastri Cere-
20 visiali vappâ temulenti, Morus adulter & stuprator. Mirificos
sanè tragœdos! bellum certamen mihi paratum! verùm quales-
cunque sortiti, quoniam alios atque hujusmodi adversarios

printed in far better type than what had been used by my former printer. I replied, through the medium of those friends, that at present I had nothing to print. But behold! not long after, he comes forth as the author (the suppositious
5 one indeed) of a production full of the grossest abuse against the very man to whom lately he had so officiously offered his services. My friends express their indignation. The fellow, unrivalled in impudence, writes in answer, that he is astonished at their simplicity and ignorance of the world, in expect-
10 ing or even in desiring any regard to duty or honesty from him, seeing by what business he got his livelihood; that he had received the said letter, together with the book, from Salmasius himself, who asked him, as a favour, whether he would do what he has actually done; that if Milton, or any one else,
15 should think proper to reply, and chose to make use of his labour, he had no scruple: that is, either against Salmasius, or against Charles: for in such reply, this was the only thing which he could expect to happen. I need say no more; you see the man.
20　I now proceed to the rest: for there were more than one concerned in getting up this tragedy, as they would make it, of the royal cry. Here then in the beginning, according to custom, you have the *dramatis personæ*: The cry, by way of prologue; Vlaccus, a paltry rogue; or if you will, Salmasius,
25 disguised as the rogue Vlaccus; two poetasters, drunk with stale beer; More, adulterer and whore-master. Admirable set of tragedians, truly! the battle in array with which I have to encounter! But as our cause could hardly be expected to have

vix est ut causa nostra habere possit, nunc singulos aggrediamur; hoc tantùm præfati, si cui minus gravitatis nostra alicubi refutatio habere videbitur, cogitare eum debere, non cum gravi adversario, sed cum grege histrionico, nobis rem esse;
5 ad quem dum refutationis genus accommodandum erat, non semper quid magis decuisset, sed quid illis dignum esset, spectandum duximus.

Regii sanguinis clamor ad cœlum adversùs parricidas
   Anglicanos.

10 Siquidem non Jure fusum ostendisses, More, istum sanguinem, haud incredibile narrares: nunc, quemadmodum primis restituti Evangelii temporibus, Monachi, cùm argumentis minùs valerent, ad spectra nescio quæ, & ficta monstra decurrere solebant; sic vos, postquam omnia defecere, ad clamores
15 nusquam auditos, & obsoletas fraterculorum artes revertimini. Voces è cœlo audire quemquam nostrorum, longè abest ut credas; ego te clamores ab Inferis audîsse, quod postulas, facilè crediderim. Verùm hunc regii sanguinis clamorem dic sodes quis audivit? Te ais: nugæ: Primùm enim malè audis:
20 Ad cœlum autem qui clamor perveniat, si quis præter Deum, justi puto soli & integerrimi quique audiunt, ut qui possint,

different adversaries, let us now attack them, such as they are, one after another; only premising, that if any one should think our refutation deficient in gravity, he should consider that we have not to do with a grave adversary, but with a herd of play-
5 ers; to which, while it was necessary to accommodate the nature of the refutation, we thought it proper to have in view not always what would be most suitable to decorum, but what would most suit them.

The Cry of the Royal Blood to Heaven against the English Parricides.

If, More, you had shown that blood to have been unjustly
10 shed, your account might have worn an appearance of plausibility. But, as in the early periods of the reformation, the monks, from their weakness in argument, were used to have recourse to all manner of spectres and imaginary monsters; so you, after all other things have failed, resort to cries which
15 were never heard and to arts of despicable friars, which are grown out of date. You would be far enough from giving credit to any one of our party, who should affirm that he had heard voices from heaven; though I should have little difficulty in believing (with which you charge me) that you had
20 heard cries from hell. But tell us, I beseech you, who heard this cry of the royal blood? You say that you heard it: trash! for in the first place, you are never favoured in what you hear; and the cry which ascends to heaven, if heard by any but God, is heard, as I must think, by the just and the upright alone;
25 inasmuch as they being themselves void of offence, are author-

immunes ipsi, iram Dei consciis denuntiare. Tu verò quorsum audires, an ut satyram cynædus scriberes? videris enim eodem tempore, & ementitus hunc clamorem ad cœlum, & cum Pontia furtim libidinatus esse. Multa te impediunt, More, 5 multa intus forísque circumsonant, quæ te res istiusmodi ad cœlum perlatas audire non sinunt; & si nihil aliud, certè qui contra ipsum te ad cœlum quamplurimus fit clamor. Clamat contra te, si nescis, Mœcha illa tua hortensis, tuo maximè Pastoris sui exemplo, deceptam se esse questa; clamat contra 10 te maritus, cujus torum violâsti; clamat Pontia, cui pactum nuptiale temerâsti; clamat, siquis est, quem probro genitum, infantulum abdicâsti; horum omnium clamores ad cœlum contra te, si non audis, neque illum regii sanguinis audiveris: interea libellus iste, non regii sanguinis clamor ad cœlum, sed 15 lascivientis Mori hinnitus ad Pontiam, rectiùs inscribetur. Quæ sequitur Epistola prolixa quidem, & bene putida, partim Carolo, partim Miltonio, alteri amplificandò, alteri infamando, dedicatur. Ab ipso statim initio Authorem discite: *Caroli Regna*, inquit, *in Sacrilegam parricidarum, &* (*quia verba* 20 *desunt idonea, Tertullianeâ voce abutimur*) *Deicidarum potestatem venerunt.* Hæc sive Salmasiæa, sive Moræa, sive

ized to denounce the wrath of God on the guilty. But to what
end should you hear it?—That, lecher as you are, you might
write a satire? For it appears, that at the very time you were
forging this cry to heaven, you were slyly playing the wanton
5 with Pontia. You have many impediments, More, you have
many things ringing within and without, which will not
suffer you to hear things of that nature which have reached to
heaven; and if you had nothing else to prevent you, the loud
cry which is raised to heaven against yourself, would certainly
10 be sufficient. That strumpet of yours of the garden, who has
complained, that what most of all led to her seduction was the
example of yourself her own pastor, is crying, whether you
know it or not, against you; the husband whose bed you violated is crying against you; Pontia is crying, with whom you
15 broke your nuptial compact; and if any one is crying, that little
infant is crying, whom you begot in shame, and abandoned a
helpless babe. If you hear not all these cries to heaven against
yourself, you never could have heard the cry of the royal blood.
At the same time, this libel, instead of being called the cry of
20 the royal blood to heaven, may be more properly inscribed—
More's lascivious neighing for his Pontia.

The prolix and stale epistle which follows is devoted in part
to Charles, in part to Milton, to extol the one, and to vilify the
other. From the very beginning, you may form your judg-
25 ment of the author. "The dominions of Charles (says he)
have fallen into the sacrilegious hands of parricides, and (because proper words could not be found, we are abused in a
word from Tertullian) of deicides." Whether his rant is to be

Vlaccæa sartago sit, prætereamus. Hoc verò aliis ridendum,
Carolo indignandum profectò est, quod paulò pòst, *neminem,*
ait, *vivere felicitatis Caroli studiosiorem.* Quíne eandem &
epistolandi, & excudendi operam Caroli hostibus detulisti, te
5 vivit nemo felicitatis ejus studiosior? Miserum profectò dicis
regem sic ab amicis omnibus derelictum, ut qui intimi re-
stant, iis Vappa typographus comparare se audeat. Miserri-
mum, cujus fidelissimis, Vlaccus perfidus fide ac studio non
cedat: quo quid insolentius de se, contemptius de rege ami-
10 císque regiis pronunciare potuit? neque hoc minùs ridicu-
lum, induci Idiotam & operarium de rebus gravissimis ac regiis
virtutibus philosophantem, eáque dicentem, qualiacunque
sunt, quibus nec Salmasius ipse, nec Morus meliora dixisset.
Equidem Salmasium, ut sæpe aliàs, ità hoc loco haud obscurè,
15 si multâ lectione, judicio tamen puerili & nullius usûs hominem deprehendi; qui cùm legere potuisset summos in Spar-
tanâ civitate optimè institutâ magistratus, si quid fortè viro
malo excidisset sapienter dictum, id ei adimi jussisse, & in
virum aliquem bonum ac frugi sortitione conferri, adeò id
20 omne quod decorum dicitur ignorârit, ut è contra, quas pro-

referred to Salmasius, to More, or to Vlaccus, let us pass it by.
But what he says a little after—"That there lives not the man
who is more studious to promote the happiness of Charles,"
though only ridiculous to others, must rouse the indignation
5 of Charles. And is there no one alive more studious of his happiness than you, who have offered to the enemies of Charles,
your services in the very same way—that is, to write a letter,
and afterwards to print it? Well might you call the king
miserable, in being thus deserted by his friends, when a ras-
10 cally printer can presume to rank himself among the few more
intimate friends which remain: miserable indeed, when his
most faithful friends do not surpass in faith and studious regard the perfidious Vlaccus. What could he say more arrogant, as it respects himself, or more contemptuous, as it re-
15 gards the king and his friends the royalists? Nor is it less
ridiculous to introduce an illiterate mechanic philosophizing
on the weightiest subjects, and on the virtues of kings; utter-
ing sentiments, such as they are, which could not have been
bettered either by Salmasius or More. To tell the truth, I have
20 discovered Salmasius, here, as often elsewhere, and by no
obscure signs, to be a man, though of great reading, of an
unexercised and puerile judgment. Though he must have read
—that the chief magistrates in the excellently modelled commonwealth of Sparta, if any wise saying happened to fall from
25 a worthless character, ordered it to be taken from him, and
conferred by lot upon some man of virtue and prudence—he
was yet so ignorant of every thing that is called decorum, as
to do quite the reverse—as to suffer opinions, which he

bum atque prudentem decere sententias arbitraretur, eas homini nequissimo attribui sustineret. Bono es animo, Carole:
veterator Vlaccus, *quæ sua est in Deum fiducia,* bono animo
te esse jubet. *Noli tot mala perdere:* Vlaccus decoctor per-
5 ditissimus, qui bona omnia, siqua habuit, perdidit, author
tibi est, perdere ut nolis mala: *Fruere novercante fortunâ:*
Potin'es ut nè fruare, hortatore præsertim tali, qui alienis
etiam fortunis frui per fas & nefas tot annis consuevit? *In
sapientiam penitùs ingurgitâsti, & ingurgita:* sic monet, sic
10 præcipit regum Institutor sanè optimus Vlaccus gurges, qui
arreptâ atramentosis manibus, coriaceâ lagenâ, inter combi-
bones operas, ingenti haustu, sapientiam tibi propinat. Hæc
audet tuus Vlaccus, tam præclara monita, nomine etiam conscripto, quæ Salmasius, quæ Morus, cæteríque pugiles tui aut
15 timidi non audent, aut superbi non dignantur; nimirum quoties te monito est opus aut defenso, alieno semper nomine,
atque periculo, non suo, sapientes aut fortes sunt. Desinat
ergò, quisquis hic est, *strenuam & animosam facundiam*
ipse suam inaniter jactare; dum *vir,* si diis placet, *insignis,*
20 *decoro ingenio nomen suum celeberrimum* edere metuit;
librum, quo regium sanguinem ulcisci se ait, ne dicare quidem Carolo nisi per Vlaccum interpretem & vicarium ausus,

thought becoming in an honest and prudent person, to be put into the mouth of a man who is an arrant scoundrel. Be of good cheer, Charles: the scoundrel Vlaccus, "from his trust in God," bids you be of good cheer. "Don't throw so many 5 sufferings away": Vlaccus, the most prodigal of spendthrifts, who has thrown away his whole substance, if he ever had any, counsels you not to throw away your sufferings. "Make use of fortune, who is thus acting towards you as a stepmother." And can you avoid making use of her, especially when you 10 have such an adviser, who, for so many years, has been in the habit, right or wrong, of using other people's fortunes? "You have drunk deep of wisdom; drink on": so counsels, so directs the drunken Vlaccus, the unrivalled preceptor of kings, who, amidst his fellow-workmen and pot-companions, seizing 15 the leathern flaggon with his inky hands, drinks a mighty draught to your wisdom. Such are the goodly counsels, to which your Vlaccus ventures to put his name, and which Salmasius and More, with the rest of your champions, are either too timid, or too proud to acknowledge: that is, when- 20 ever you require to be advised or defended, they are always wise or brave, not in their own name, but in the name of another, and at another's hazard. Whoever this personage may be, therefore, let him cease idly to vaunt his "bold and manly eloquence," when the man, who is eminent (please 25 the gods) for the elegance of his genius, was afraid to give up "his very celebrated name." The book, in which he has avenged, as he says, the royal blood, he dared not even dedicate to Charles, but through his confident and deputy Vlaccus;

verbis typographi miserè contentus significare, *librum* se, sine nomine, *si pateris, O Rex, tuo nomini dicatum ire.* Sic functus Carolo in me impetum parat minitabundus: *Post hæc procemia, tubam terribilem inflabit* ὁ θαυμάσιος *ille Sal-*
5 *masius.* Salubritatem prædicis & concentûs musici novum genus futurum; isti enim tubæ terribili, cùm inflabitur, nulla aptior excogitari symphonia poterit, quàm si affatim oppedetur. Buccam verò Salmasius nimis inflatam ne afferat moneo; quo enim attulerit inflatiorem, eò mihi crede, opportu-
10 niorem ad Colaphos præbebit; qui thaumasii Salmasii rhythmicum hunc sonum, quo delectaris, buccis ambabus resonantibus, numerose reddent. Pergis cornicari. *Qui nec parem nec secundum habet, in universo literarum & scientiarum orbe.* Vestram fidem! Eruditi, quotquot estis, vestram fidem!
15 Siccine vobis omnibus anteferri Cimicem Grammaticum, cujus res atque spes omnis in glossario vertebatur? quem vel extremum meritò occupet scabies, si cum viris verè doctis comparetur. Hæc autem, nisi ab infimo quopiam & infra Vlaccum ipsum væcorde affirmari tam fatuè nequiverunt.
20 *Quique jam stupendam & infinitam eruditionem cœlesti junctam ingenio ad causam tuæ majestatis contulit.* Si meministis quod suprà narravi, ipsum Salmasium, attulisse hanc

meanly content to signify, in the words of his printer, "that, with your permission, O king, he was going," without a name, "to dedicate the book to your name."

Having thus dispatched Charles, he is now preparing, with no little blustering, his attack upon me: "After these preludes, the wonderful Salmasius will blow the terrible trumpet." You prognosticate health, and give us notice of a new kind of musical harmony: for when that terrible trumpet shall be blown, we can think of no fitter accompaniment for it than a reiterated crepitation. But I would advise Salmasius not to inflate his cheek overmuch: for you may take my word for it, that the more it is swollen out, the fairer will he present it for slaps, in musical response, while both his cheeks ring again, to this modulated tone of the wonderful Salmasius, with which you are so delighted.—You continue to croak. "Who has neither an equal nor a second in the whole circle of literature and of science." Can you believe it, ye learned, whoever you are, can you believe it, that this book-worm of a grammarian, whose whole ability and hope turned upon a glossary, does thus indeed rank above you all? A man whom the devil might well take as the hindermost, if compared with men truly learned.—But the assertions which follow are so foolish, that they could never have been made, but by some low fellow, and infatuated to a degree even below Vlaccus: "And who has now brought to your majesty's cause an erudition stupendous, infinite, conjoined with a celestial genius." If you recollect what I have told you above, that it was Salmasius himself who brought this epistle, together with the book, to be printed;

epistolam cum libro excudendam, vel ab ipso scriptam, vel ab anonymo quovis, vernámque typographum exorâsse, ut quod author nollet, ipse suum nomen adscriberet, cognoscetis profectò pusilli omnino, & abjectissimi hominem ingenii suis
5 laudibus tam miserè velificantem, & immensa encomia tam stolidi laudatoris aucupantem. *Opus æternum frustrà sugillantibus nonnullis, jurisconsulti mirari satìs nequeunt quòd homo Gallus ità subitò res Anglicas, leges, decreta, instrumenta, ità teneat, enodet, &c.* Immo quàm ineptierit in
10 nostris legibus & psittacus fuerit, nostris etiam jurisconsultis testibus abunde ostendimus. *Sed ipse mox alterâ, quam in Rebelles molitur, impressione, simul Theonum ora comprimet, simul Miltonum nobis pro eo ac meretur concastigatum dabit.* Tu igitur ut pisciculus ille anteambulo, præcurris Balæ-
15 nam Salmasium, impressiones in hæc littora minitantem; nos ferramenta acuimus, expressuri si quid habent impressiones & concastigationes illæ sive olei sive gari. Bonitatem interea magni viri mirabimur plusquam Pythagoricam, qui animalia quoque miseratus, & præsertim pisces, quorum carnibus ne
20 quadragesima quidem parcit, iis tam decenter involvendis tot volumina destinârit, tot pauperum millibus, Thunnorum, credo, aut Scombrorum, chartaceas in singulos tunicas testamento legârit.

that it was written either by himself, or by some person who
was nameless; that he entreated the obsequious typographer
to put his name to it, as the author himself would not —you
will judge him to be a man of a mind most weak and abject;
5 thus pitifully spreading his sails to catch the breeze of his own
panegyric, thus artfully endeavouring to entrap the immoderate praises of so senseless an encomiast!—"In vain do a few
buffet the immortal work; the lawyers cannot sufficiently
admire, that a Frenchman should so soon make himself mas-
10 ter of English affairs, laws, acts of parliament, instruments,
and disentangle them," &c. Nay, what nonsense he has talked,
what a mere parrot he has been, on the subject of our laws, we
have abundantly shown, and in the opinion too of our lawyers.—"But soon, he himself, in another impression which he
15 is meditating upon the rebels, will at once stop the mouths of
the Theons, and chastise Milton for us according to his de-
serts." You yourself, then, like the little fish which goes before
the whale as a client his patron, are merely the harbinger of
the whale Salmasius, who is threatening an invasion of our
20 shores! We sharpen our harpoons and instruments of iron,
that we may secure whatever oil or pickle may be obtained
from that invasion and meditated castigation of us. Meanwhile, we admire the more than Pythagorean benevolence of
the great man, who, compassionating even animals, and above
25 all fish, to whose flesh even Lent shows no indulgence, could
have destined so many volumes to enwrap them decently, and
out of so many thousands of poor tunnies, may be, or herrings,
could have bequeathed a papercoat for each!

Gaudete Scombri, & quicquid est piscium salo,
Qui frigidâ hyeme incolitis algentes freta,
Vestrûm misertus ille Salmasius eques
Bonus amicire nuditatem cogitat;
5 *Chartæque largus apparat papyrinos*
Vobis cucullos præferentes Claudii
Insignia nomenque & decus Salmasii,
Gestetis ut per omne cetarium forum
Equitis clientes, scriniis mungentium
10 *Cubito virorum, & capsulis gratissimos.*

Hæc habui in Editionem diu exspectatam tam nobilis libri; cujus impressionem, dum, ut ais, molitur Salmasius, tu ejus domum, More, fædissimâ compressione Pontiæ contaminâsti. Et videtur sanè ad hoc opus absolvendum, Salmasius diu mul-
15 túmque incubuisse; paucis enim ante mortem diebus, cùm vir quidam doctus, à quo hoc ipsum accepi, misisset qui ex eo quæreret, ecquando apparatûs partem secundam in Prima- tum Papæ editurus esset, respondit, ad illud opus non ante reversurum se, quàm absolvisset quod adhuc commentaretur
20 adversùs Miltonium. Ità ego etiam Papæ refutandus præfe- ror; & quem illi primatum in Ecclesia negavit, eum mihi ultro in inimicitia sua concedit; sic ego primatui Papæ jam jam evertendo salutem attuli; ego redivivum hunc Catilinam,

Rejoice ye herrings, and ye fish beside,
That, the winter chill, in cold friths abide;
For the good Salmasius, that piteous knight,
Of paper liberal, saddens at your plight;
5   Your nakedness to clothe, he'll frocks prepare,
The insignia, name, and honours that shall bear
Of Claude Saumaize; that through the fishy mart,
You all may wear your paper liveries smart,
As clients of the knight; a prize to those,
10   Who on their tunic's sleeve do wipe their nose.

I wrote these lines on the long-expected edition of this far-famed work; and while, as you tell us, Salmasius was meditating this impression, you, More, were contaminating his house, by a most shameless commerce with Pontia. It appears indeed, that Salmasius long applied himself, and with great earnestness, to finish the work: for, a few days before his death, when a certain literary man, from whom I had the account, sent to inquire of him, when he intended to publish the second part of what he had prepared against the pope's supremacy, he replied, that he should not return to that work, till he had completed what he had still in hand against Milton. And so, I am even preferred to the pope for refutation. That pre-eminence which he denies him in the church, he spontaneously concedes to me in his enmity. It seems then I have made a timely diversion for the supremacy of his holiness, since it was to have been overturned without delay. I have diverted from the walls of Rome this new Catiline, though not

non in toga, ut consul olim Tullius, nè per somnum quidem, sed aliud omnino agens, Romanis mœnibus averti; non unus profectò cardinalatus mihi hoc nomine debebitur; vereor, nè translato in me regum nuper nostrorum titulo, Defensor fidei

5 ab Romano Pontifice appellandus sim. Videtis quantus invidiæ artifex in me concitandæ, Salmasius fuerit; verùm ipse viderit, qui tam honestâ provinciâ turpiter relictâ, alienis se controversiis immiscuerit, ab Ecclesiæ causa, ad civiles & externas, quarum suâ nihil intererat, se traduxerit; cum Papa

10 inducias fecerit; & quod fœdissimum fuit, cum Episcopis, post bellum apertissimum, in gratiam redierit. Veniamus nunc ad mea crimina; éstne quod in vita aut moribus reprehendat? Certè nihil: quid ergo? quod nemo nisi immanis, ac barbarus fecisset, formam mihi ac cæcitatem objectat.

15   *Monstrum, horrendum, informe, ingens, cui lumen*
       ademptum.

Nunquam existimabam equidem fore, ut de forma, cum Cyclope certamen mihi esset; verùm statim se revocat. *Quanquam nec ingens, quo nihil est exilius, exsanguius, con-*

20 *tractius.* Tametsi virum nihil attinet de forma dicere, tamen quando hìc quoque est, unde gratias Deo agam, & mendaces

invested in the consular robe, as of old the consul Tullius, nor was it done in a dream, but in a very different manner; and shall merit for this service something beyond a mere cardinal-ship; I even suspect that the Roman pontiff, transferring to

5 me the title of our kings, will hail me as defender of the faith. You see what an artificer of envy Salmasius has been to me; yet, it is his place to see to it, who, basely deserting so hon-orable an office to mix in strangers' controversies, withdrew himself from the cause of the church, to political and foreign

10 concerns, with which his own had nothing to do; who made a truce with the pope; and what was baser than all, became reconciled to the bishops, after declaring open war against them.

Let us come now to the charges against me. Can he find

15 any thing to blame in my life or manners? Clearly nothing. What does he do then? He does what none but a brute and barbarian would have done; he upbraids me with my person, and with my blindness.

A monster horrid, ugly, huge, and blind.

20 I certainly never thought I should have to contend with the cyclops for the point of beauty! But he immediately corrects himself. "He is not huge, it is true: for nothing can be more lean, bloodless, and shrivelled." Though it is to little purpose for a man to speak of his beauty; yet at last, as I have reason, in

25 this particular also, for giving thanks to God, and am able to confound liars, lest any one should haply think me some monster with a dog's head, or a rhinoceros (as the Spanish

redarguam, nè quis, (quod Hispanorum vulgus de hæreticis,
quos vocant, plus nimio Sacerdotibus suis credulum opinatur)
me fortè Cynocephalum quempiam, aut Rhinocerota esse
putet, dicam. Deformis quidem à nemine, quod sciam, qui
5   modò me vidit, sum unquam habitus; formosus nécne, minùs
laboro; staturâ fateor non sum procerâ: sed quæ mediocri
tamen quàm parvæ propior sit: sed quid si parvâ, quâ &
summi sæpe tum pace tum bello viri fuere? quanquam parva
cur dicitur, quæ ad virtutem satìs magna est? sed neque exilis
10   admodum, eo sanè animo iisque viribus ut cùm ætas vitæque
ratio sic ferebat, nec ferrum tractare, nec stringere quotidiano
usu exercitatus nescirem; eo accinctus, ut plerumque eram,
cuivis vel multò robustiori exæquatum me putabam, securus
quid mihi quis injuriæ vir viro inferre posset. Idem hodie
15   animus, eædem vires, oculi non iidem; ità tamen extrinsecus
illæsi, ità sine nube clari ac lucidi, ut eorum qui acutissimùm
cernunt: in hac solùm parte, memet invito, simulator sum: in
vultu, quo *nihil exsanguius* esse dixit, is manet etiamnum
color exsangui & pallenti planè contrarius, ut quadragenario
20   major vix sit cui non denis prope annis, videar natu minor;
neque corpore contracto neque cute. In his ego si ulla ex parte

vulgar, trusting but too much to their priests, imagine of heretics) I will say a few words.

No one, who has only seen me, has ever to my knowledge, thought me ugly: whether handsome or not, is a point I shall
5 not determine. My stature, I own, is not tall; but may approach nearer to the middle than to the small size. And what if small, as many men have been, who were of the very first rank, both in peace and war; and why should that stature be called small, which is large enough for every virtuous pur-
10 pose? But it is not true, that I am thus lean beyond example; on the contrary, I possess that spirit and strength, that, when my age and manner of life so inclined me, I was neither unskilled in handling my sword, nor unpractised in its daily use. Armed with this weapon, as I commonly was, I thought my-
15 self a match for any man, though far my superior in strength, and secure from any insult which one man could offer to another. At this day, I have the same spirit, the same strength, my eyes only are not the same; yet, to external appearance, they are as completely without injury, as clear and bright,
20 without the semblance of a cloud, as the eyes of those whose sight is the most perfect. In this respect only am I a dissembler; and here, it is against my will. In my countenance, than which, as he has said, there is "nothing more bloodless," there still remains a colour so very opposite to the bloodless and pale,
25 that, though turned of forty, there is scarcely any one who would not think me younger by nearly ten years. It is equally untrue, that either my body or my skin is shrivelled. In these particulars, were I guilty of any falsehood, I should deservedly

mentior, multis millibus popularium meorum, qui de facie
me nôrunt, exteris etiam non paucis, ridiculus meritò sim:
Sin iste in re minimè necessariâ, tam impudenter & gratuitò
mendax comperietur, poteritis de reliquo eandem conjectu-
5 ram facere. Atque hæc de forma mea vel coactus: de tua
quanquam & contemptissimam accepi, & habitantis in te
improbitatis atque malitiæ vivam imaginem, neque ego dicere, neque ullus audire curat. Utinam de cæcitate pariter
liceret inhumanum hunc refellere adversarium; sed non
10 licet; feramus igitur: non est miserum esse cæcum; miserum est cæcitatem non posse ferre: quidni autem feram,
quod unumquemque ità parare se oportet, ut si acciderit, non
ægrè ferat, quod & humanitus accidere cuivis mortalium, &
præstantissimis quibusdam, atque optimis omni memoriâ
15 viris accidisse sciam: sive illos memorem vetustatis ultimæ
priscos vates, ac sapientissimos; quorum calamitatem, & Dii,
ut fertur, multò potioribus donis compensârunt, & homines
eo honore affecerunt, ut ipsos inculpare maluerint deos, quàm
cæcitatem illis crimini dare. De augure Tiresia quod traditur,
20 vulgò notum. De Phineo sic cecinit Apollonius in Argo-
nauticis:

expose myself to the ridicule of many thousands of my countrymen, who know me personally, and even of foreigners not
a few. Now if this man be detected of telling such impudent
and unfounded falsehoods, on a subject it was not at all neces-
5 sary for him to meddle with, you may form a correspondent
conjecture as to the rest.

    Thus much have I been even constrained to say of my per-
son. Of your person, though I have understood it to be most
contemptible, and the living image of the wickedness and
10 malice which dwell within you, I neither care to speak, nor
do others care to hear. Would it were equally in my power to
confute this inhuman adversary on the subject of my blindness! but, it is not. Then, let us bear it. To be blind is not miserable; not to be able to bear blindness, that is miserable. But
15 why should I be unable to bear that which it behoves every one
to be prepared to bear, should the accident happen to himself,
without repining? Why should I be unable to bear what I
know may happen to any mortal being,—what I know has
actually happened to some of the most eminent and the best of
20 men, on the records of memory? Or shall I mention those old
poets, ancientest and wisest, whose calamity the gods are said
to have recompensed with far more excelling gifts, and men
to have honoured with that high honour, as to choose rather to
blame the gods themselves, than to impute their blindness to
25 them as a crime. What is handed down of the augur Tire-
sias is well known. Of Phineus thus sang Apollonius in his
Argonautics:

Οὐδ᾽ ὅσσον ὀπίζετο καὶ Διὸς αὐτοῦ
Χρείων ἀτρεκέως ἱερὸν νόον ἀνθρώποισι.
Τῷ καί οἱ γῆρας μὲν ἐπὶ δηναιὸν ἴαλλεν
᾽Εκ δ᾽ἔλετ᾽ ὀφθαλμῶν γλυκερὸν φάος.

5   *— neque est veritus Iovem ipsum*
Edens veraciter mentem divinam hominibus:
Quare & senectam ei diuturnam dedit,
Eripuit autem oculorum dulce lumen.

Cæterum deus & ipse veritas est: in qua homines edocenda
10 quò quis veracior eò similior deo acceptiórque sit, oportet.
Non est pium veritatis invidentem deum credere; aut nolle
hominibus quàm liberrimè impertitam: Ob nullam igitur
noxam, divinus vir, & humani generis erudiendi studiosissi-
mus, ut philosophorum etiam complures, caruisse luminibus
15 videtur. Sive illos commemorem civili prudentiâ, gestísque
rebus admirabiles olim viros; primùm Timoleontem Corin-
thium, & civitatis suæ, & Siciliæ totius liberatorem; quo virum
meliorem, aut in republica sanctiorem nulla ætas tulit; tum
Appium Claudium, cujus in Senatu pulcrè dicta sententia,
20 Italiam Pyrrho, gravi hoste, seipsum cæcitate non liberavit;
tum Cæcilium Metellum Pontificem, qui non urbem solùm,
sed & fatum urbis Palladium, & penitissima sacra dum ab
incendio servavit, suos oculos perdidit; quanquam aliàs certè
Deus pietati tam egregiæ favere se, etiam inter gentes, testatus
25 est: quod tali igitur viro usu venit, ponendum in malis esse

Not Jove himself he feared; his daring ken
With truth disclosed the will of fate to men;
With length of years did Jove him hence requite,
But his eyes bereft of the day's sweet light.

5   But God himself is truth; and the more closely any one ad-
heres to truth, in teaching it to mankind, the more nearly
must he resemble God, the more acceptable must he be to him.
It is impious to believe God to be jealous of truth, or to be an
enemy to the utmost freedom of its communication to men. It
10 does not appear, therefore, that it was for any crime, that this
ancient sage, who was so zealous to enlighten human kind,
and that many among the philosophers, were deprived of
light. Or, should I mention those men of old, so deserving
of admiration for their civil wisdom, as also for their great
15 actions? And first, Timoleon of Corinth—the deliverer of his
own city, and of all Sicily—than whom, a better man or more
revered in the commonwealth no age has produced. Next,
Appius Claudius, who, by nobly declaring his sentiments in
the senate, delivered Italy from Pyrrhus, a formidable enemy;
20 but himself delivered not from blindness. Then Cæcilius Me-
tellus the high-priest, who lost his eyes, in saving from the
flames not the city only, but the Palladium, on which hung
the destiny of the city, as also the most sacred of the religious
mysteries; though on other occasions it is certain that God has
25 declared that his favour attends a devotedness so extraordinary, even among the Gentiles. What therefore has happened
to such a man, I can hardly think should be considered as an

vix putem. Quid alios recentiorum temporum adjungam,
vel illum Venetiarum Principem Dandulum longè omnium
præstantissimum; vel Boëmorum Ziscam ducem fortissimum,
orthodoxæ fidei propugnatorem? Quid summi nominis theo-
5 logos Hieronymum Zanchium, nonnullósque alios? cùm &
ipsum Isaacum Patriarcham, quo nemo unquam mortalium
Deo charior fuit, annos haud paucos, cæcum vixisse constet;
aliquot fortasse, Jacobum etiam ejus filium, & ipsum Deo
haud minùs dilectum: cùm denique Christi servatoris nostri
10 divino testimonio compertissimum sit, illum hominem ab
se sanatum, neque ob suum, neque ob parentum suorum aliquod peccatum, etiam ab utero cæcum fuisse. Ad me quod
attinet, te testor, Deus, mentis intimæ, cogitationúmque omnium indagator, me nullius rei, (quanquam hoc apud me
15 sæpius, & quàm maximè potui, seriò quæsivi, & recessus vitæ
omnes excussi) nullius vel recèns vel olim commissi, mihi-
met conscium esse, cujus atrocitas hanc mihi præ cæteris calamitatem creare, aut accersisse meritò potuerit. Quod etiam
ullo tempore scripsi (quoniam hoc nunc me luere quasi pia-
20 culum regii existimant, atque adeò triumphant) testor itidem
Deum, me nihil istiusmodi scripsisse, quod non rectum &
verum, Deóque gratum esse, & persuaserim tum mihi, &
etiamnum persuasus sim; ídque nullâ ambitione, lucro, aut
gloriâ ductus; sed officii, sed honesti, sed pietatis in patriam
25 ratione solâ; nec reipublicæ tantùm, sed Ecclesiæ quoque
liberandæ causâ potissimùm fecisse: adeò ut cùm datum

evil. Why should I add others of later times—as Dandolo prince of Venice, the first man by far of all his compatriots; or Ziska the gallant duke of Bohemia, champion of the orthodox faith? Why divines of highest name, Hieronymus Zanchius, with some others? When it is well known, that the patriarch Isaac himself, than whom no mortal was ever more dear to God, lived blind no small number of years; and for some time, perhaps Jacob also his son, of God no less beloved; when, in fine, it is beyond all doubt, from the divine testimony of Christ our Saviour, that the man whom he healed had been blind even from the womb, for no sin either of himself or of his parents. As for myself, I call thee, O God, to witness, the searcher of the inmost spirit, and of every thought, that I am not conscious of any offense (though, to the utmost of my power, I have often seriously examined myself on this point, though I have visited all the recesses of my heart) recently committed or long ago, the heinousness of which could have justly caused, could have called down this calamity upon me above others. Whatever I have written, yea, at any time (since the royalists in their exultation imagine I am now suffering for it, by way of atonement, as they will have it) I call the same God to witness, that I have written nothing, which I was not persuaded at the time, and am still persuaded, was right, and true, and pleasing to God; and this without being moved by ambition, by lucre, or by glory; but solely by a sense of duty, of grace, and of devotion to my country; that, above all, I have done this, with a view not only to the deliverance of the commonwealth, but likewise of the church. Hence, when

mihi publicè esset illud in defensionem regiam negotium,
eodémque tempore & adversâ simul valetudine, & oculo jam
penè altero amisso conflictarer, prædiceréntque disertè medici,
si hunc laborem suscepissem, fore, ut utrumque brevi amit-
5 terem, nihil istâ præmonitione deterritus, non medici nè
Æsculapii quidem Epidaurii ex adyto vocem, sed divinioris
cujusdam intus monitoris viderer mihi audire; duásque sortes,
fatali quodam nutu, jam mihi propositas, hinc cæcitatem,
indè officium; aut oculorum jacturam necessariò faciendam,
10 aut summum officium deserendum: occurrebántque animo
bina illa fata, quæ retulisse Delphis consulentem de se matrem,
narrat Thetidis filius.

Διχθαδίας κῆρας φερέμεν θανάτοιο τέλοσδε.

Εἰ μέν κ'αὖθι μένων Τρώων πόλιν ἀμφιμάχωμαι

15 Ὤλετο μέν μοι νόστος, ἀτὰρ κλέος ἄφθιτον ἔσται.

Εἰ δέ κεν οἴκαδ' ἵκωμι φίλην ἐς πατρίδα γαῖαν.

Ὤλετό μοι κλέος ἐσθλὸν, ἐπὶ δηρὸν δέ μοι αἰὼν

Ἔσσεται.

Iliad. 9.

20 *Duplicia fata ducere ad mortis finem:*
Si hic manens circa Troum urbem pugnavero,
Amittitur mihi reditus; sed Gloria immortalis erit,
Si domum revertor dulce ad Patrium solum,
Amittitur mihi Gloria pulcra, sed diuturna vita
25 *Erit.*

Unde sic mecum reputabam, multos graviore malo minus
bonum, morte gloriam, redemisse; mihi contrà majus bo-

that office against the royal defence was publicly assigned me,
and at a time when not only my health was unfavorable, but
when I had nearly lost the sight of my other eye; and my
physicians expressly foretold, that if I undertook the task, I
5 should in a short time lose both—in no wise dismayed at this
warning, methought it was no physician's voice I heard—not
the voice even of Æsculapius from the shrine of Epidaurus—
but of some diviner monitor within; methought, that, by a
certain fatality in my birth, two destinies were set before me,
10 on the one hand, blindness, on the other, duty—that I must
necessarily incur the loss of my eyes, or desert a sovereign duty.
Nor did I fail to recollect the two-fold destiny, which the son
of Thetis reports that his mother brought back concerning
himself, when she went to consult the oracle at Delphi:

15   Two fates conduct me to the realms of night:
    If staying here around Troy-town I fight,
    I return no more; but my glory fair
    Shall shine immortal, and my deeds declare:
    If to my dear and native land I'm led,
20   Long is my life; but my glory is fled.
                       Iliad 9.

Hence I thought with myself, that there were many who
purchased a less good with a greater evil; for example—glory,
with death. On the contrary, I proposed to purchase a greater
good with a less evil; namely, at the price of blindness only,
25 to perform one of the noblest acts of duty; and duty, being a

num minore cum malo proponi: ut possem cùm cæcitate sola
vel honestissimum officii munus implere; quod ut ipsâ gloriâ
per se est solidius, ità cuique optatius atque antiquius debet
esse. Hac igitur tam brevi luminum usurâ, quantâ maxima
5 quivi cum utilitate publica, quoad liceret, fruendum esse
statui. Videtis quid prætulerim, quid amiserim, quâ inductus
ratione: desinant ergò judiciorum Dei calumniatores maledicere, déque me somnia sibi fingere; sic denique habento;
me sortis meæ neque pigere neque pœnitere; immotum atque
10 fixum in sententia perstare; Deum iratum neque sentire,
neque habere, immò maximis in rebus clementiam ejus
& benignitatem erga me paternam experiri atque agnoscere;
in hoc præsertim, quòd solante ipso atque animum confir-
mante in ejus divina voluntate acquiescam; quid is largitus
15 mihi sit, quàm quid negaverit sæpius cogitans: postremò nolle
me cum suo quovis rectissimè facto, facti mei conscientiam
permutare, aut recordationem ejus gratam mihi semper atque
tranquillam deponere. Ad cæcitatem denique quod attinet,
malle me, si necesse est, meam, quàm vel suam, More, vel
20 tuam. Vestra imis sensibus immersa, nequid sani videatis aut
solidi, mentem obcæcat: mea, quam objicitis, colorem tantummodo rebus & superficiem demit; quod verum ac stabile
in iis est, contemplationi mentis non adimit. Quàm multa

thing in its own nature more substantial even than glory, ought on that account to be more desired and venerated. I decided, therefore, that, as the use of light would be allowed me for so short a time, it ought to be enjoyed with the greatest

5 possible utility to the public. These are the reasons of my choice; these the causes of my loss. Let the slanderers, then, of the judgments of God cease their revilings; let them desist from their dreamy forgeries concerning me; in fine, let them know, that I neither repine at, nor repent me of my lot; that

10 I remain fixed, immovable in my opinion; that I neither believe, nor have found that God is angry; nay, that in things of the greatest moment I have experienced, and that I acknowledge his mercy, and his paternal goodness towards me; that above all, in regard of this calamity, I acquiesce in his divine

15 will, for it is he himself who comforts and upholds my spirit —being ever more mindful of what he shall bestow upon me than of what he shall deny me; last of all, that I would not exchange my own consciousness of what I have done, for any act of theirs however well performed, or lose the recollection

20 of it, which is always so calm and delightful to me. As to blindness, I would rather at last have mine, if it must be so, than either theirs, More, or yours. Yours, immersed in the lowest sense, so blinds your minds, that you can see nothing sound or solid; mine, with which you reproach me, deprives

25 things merely of their colour and surface; but takes not from the mind's contemplation whatever is real and permanent in them. Besides, how many things are there, which I should choose not to see; how many which I might be unwilling to

deinde sunt quæ videre nollem, quàm multa quæ possem libens non videre, quàm pauca reliqua sunt quæ videre cupiam. Sed neque ego cæcis, afflictis, mœrentibus, imbecillis, tametsi vos id miserum ducitis, aggregari me discrucior; quandoquidem spes est, eo me propiùs ad misericordiam summi patris atque tutelam pertinere. Est quoddam per imbecillitatem, præeunte Apostolo, ad maximas vires iter: sim ego debilissimus, dummodo in mea debilitate immortalis ille & melior vigor eo se efficaciùs exerat; dummodo in meis tenebris divini vultûs lumen eo clariùs eluceat; tum enim infirmissimus ero simul & validissimus, cæcus eodem tempore & perspicacissimus; hac possim ego infirmitate consummari, hac perfici, possim in hac obscuritate sic ego irradiari. Et sanè haud ultima Dei cura cæci sumus; qui nos, quò minus quicquam aliud præter ipsum cernere valemus, eò clementiùs atque benigniùs respicere dignatur. Væ qui illudit nos, væ qui lædit, execratione publicâ devovendo; nos ab injuriis hominum non modò incolumes, sed penè sacros, divina lex reddidit, divinus favor; nec tam oculorum hebetudine, quàm cœlestium alarum umbrâ has nobis fecisse tenebras videtur; factas illustrare rursus interiore ac longè præstabiliore lumine haud rarò solet. Huc refero, quòd & amici officiosiùs nunc etiam quàm solebant, colunt, observant, adsunt; quòd &

see; and how few remaining things are there which I could
desire to see! Neither am I concerned at being classed, though
you think this a miserable thing, with the blind, with the afflicted, with the sorrowful, with the weak; since there is a
5 hope, that, on this account, I have a nearer claim to the mercy
and protection of the sovereign father. There is a way, and the
Apostle is my authority, through weakness to the greatest
strength. May I be one of the weakest, provided only in my
weakness that immortal and better vigour be put forth with
10 greater effect; provided only in my darkness the light of the
divine countenance does but the more brightly shine: for then
I shall at once be the weakest and the most mighty; shall be at
once blind, and of the most piercing sight. Thus, through this
infirmity should I be consummated, perfected; thus, through
15 this darkness should I be enrobed in light. And, in truth, we
who are blind, are not the last regarded by the providence of
God; who, as we are the less able to discern any thing but himself, beholds us with the greater clemency and benignity. Woe
be to him who makes a mock of us; woe be to him who in-
20 jures us; he deserves to be devoted to the public curse. The
divine law, the divine favour, has made us not merely secure,
but, as it were, sacred, from the injuries of men; nor would
seem to have brought this darkness upon us so much by in-
ducing a dimness of the eyes, as by the overshadowing of
25 heavenly wings; and not unfrequently is wont to illumine it
again, when produced, by an inward and far surpassing light.
To this I attribute the more than ordinary civilities, atten-
tions, and visits of friends; of whom there are some, with

nonnulli sunt, quibuscum Pyladéas atque Theséas alternare voces verorum amicorum liceat.

’Ορέστ. ῞Ερπε νῦν οἴαξ ποδός μοι. Πυ. φίλα γ᾽ ἔχων κηδεύματα,
   Vade gubernaculum mei pedis. Py. per gratam mihi
5   *habens curam.* Eurip. in Orest.

Et alibi,
   Δίδου χεῖρ᾽ ὑπηρέτῃ φίλῳ,
Da manum ministro amico.
   Δίδου δέρῃ σὴν χεῖρ᾽, ὁδηγήσω δ᾽ ἐγώ,
10   *Da collo manum tuam, ductor autem viæ ero tibi ego.* Id in Her. furent.

Non enim hoc casu factum me omnino nullum; non quicquid est probi aut cordati hominis, positum in oculis putant esse. Quin & summi quoque in republica viri, quandoquidem
15 non otio torpentem me, sed impigrum & summa discrimina pro libertate inter primos adeuntem oculi deseruerunt, ipsi non deserunt; verùm humana qualia sint, secum reputantes, tanquam emerito favent, indulgent, vacationem atque otium faciles concedunt; si quid est ornamenti, non detrahunt; si
20 quid publici muneris, non adimunt; si quid ex ea re commodi, non minuunt; & quamvis non æquè nunc utili, præbendum nihilo minùs benignè censent; eodem planè honore, ac si, ut olim Atheniensibus mos erat, in Prytanéo alendum de-

whom, as with true friends, I may hold the dialogue of Pylades and Orestes:

Orest. Go slowly on, and be the rudder of my feet.
Py. Precious is my charge.

5   *Eurip. in Orest.*
And in another place:
Give your hand to your friend and helper.
Throw your arm about my neck, and I will be your guide.
                                         Id. in Her. furent.

10   For they do not suppose that by this misfortune I am rendered altogether a nullity; they do not suppose that all which belongs to a man of sense and integrity is situated in his eyes. Besides, as I am not grown torpid by indolence, since my eyes have deserted me, but am still active, still ready to advance
15 among the foremost to the most arduous struggles for liberty; I am not therefore deserted even by men of the first rank in the state. On the contrary, such men, considering the condition of humanity, show me favour and indulgence, as to one who has completed his services; and readily grant me exemption
20 and retirement. They despoil me of no dignity, they deprive me not of any public office I before held; they disparage not the benefit which may have accrued from that particular service; and though they are aware that they are now to confer their favours upon one who is become less useful, they think it
25 ought to be done with no less benignity; indeed, with the same honour, as if, like the Athenians in ancient times, they had decreed a maintenance for me in the Prytaneum. Thus, while

crevissent. Sic mihi & apud Deum & apud homines cæcitatem solari meam quandiu licuerit, amissos honesti causâ oculos nemo meos lugeat; absit quoque ut ipse lugeam, aut vel animi satìs ut nè habeam quo cæcitatis convitiatores facilè

5 possim contemnere, vel veniæ ut nè possim faciliùs condonare. Ad te, quisquis es, redeo, qui parùm tibi constans, nunc pumilionem me, nunc Antæum vis esse: *Non aliud* postremò optas *libentiùs fœderatis Belgii Provinciis, quàm ut tam facilè, támque feliciter defungantur hoc Bello, quàm defungetur*

10 *Salmasius Miltonio.* Cui ego voto si facilè assensero, arbitror me nostris successibus Reíque Anglicanæ nec ominari malè, nec malè precari.

En verò iterum clamorem, alienum quendam & stridulum! anseres puto alicunde advolare: Jam sentio quid sit; memini

15 clamoris hanc esse tragœdiam; prodit Chorus: en duo Poëtastri; vel duo vel unus, biformi sanè specie & bicolore; Sphingémne dicam an Horatianum illud monstrum Poëticum, capite muliebri, cervice asininâ, variis indutum plumis, undique collatis membris: id profectò ipsissimum est. Rhap-

20 sodus videlicet quispiam, centonibus & pannis obsitus; unúsne an duo incertum, nam & Anonymus quoque est. Poëtas equidem verè dictos & diligo & colo, & audiendo sæpissimè

I can derive consolation in my blindness both from God and man, let no one be troubled that I have lost my eyes in an honorable cause; and far be it from me to be troubled at it; far be it from me to possess so little spirit as not to be able without difficulty to despise the revilers of my blindness, or so little placability, as not to be able, with still less difficulty, to forgive them.

I return to you, whoever you are, who, with no little inconsistency, will one while have me to be a dwarf, another while, an Antæus. But, at last, you express a wish: "Nothing better could befall the united provinces of Holland, than that they may make an end of this war as easily and as successfully, as Salmasius will make an end of Milton." In which wish I shall readily acquiesce, and am of opinion, that I am neither presaging ill nor praying ill for our success, and for the cause of England.

But hark! again some strange and cackling cry! I suppose a flight of geese is on the wing, coming from some quarter or other! Oh, I now perceive what it is. I remember that it is the clamour of a tragedy. The chorus makes its appearance. See, two poetasters; either two or one; but there are two different shapes and colours. Shall I call it a sphinx, or that poetical monster of Horace, with a woman's head, an ass's neck, arrayed in motley plumes, and with limbs borrowed from different animals? Aye, that is the very thing: that is, some rhapsodist, covered from head to foot with centos and patches; whether he is one or two is doubtful, as he also is without a name. Now poets who are truly so called, I love and

delector; illorum etiam plerósque tyrannis esse scio inimicissimos, si vel à primis exorsus ad Buchananum usque nostrum
recenserem: istos verò versiculorum nugivendos, quis non
oderit? quo genere hominum nihil stultius, aut vanius, aut
5 corruptius, aut mendacius. Laudant, vituperant, sine delectu,
sine discrimine, judicio, aut modo, nunc Principes, nunc ple-
beios, doctos juxtà atque indoctos, probos an improbos, perinde habent; prout Cantharus, aut spes nummuli, aut fatuus
ille furor inflat ac rapit; congestis undique & verborum &
10 rerum tot discoloribus ineptiis, támque putidis, ut laudatum
longè præstet sileri, & pravo, quod aïunt, vivere naso, quàm
sic laudari: vituperatus verò qui sit, haud mediocri sanè
honori sibi ducat, se tam absurdis, tam stolidis nebulonibus
displicere. Primus qui est, si modò bini sunt, dubito Poëta sit
15 an Cæmentarius; ità Salmasio os oblinit, immo totum quasi
parietem dealbat atque incrustat. Curru nempe *triumphan-*
tem inducit, Heroëm Gigantomachum, *hastilia* & *cæstus,* &
nescio quæ nugamenta armorum vibrantem, doctos omnes
pedibus quadrigam sequentes, sed post terga ejus innumeris
20 spatiis relictos, utpote *quem numen rebus trepidis salutem*
orbis admoverit; tandem ergo tali tempus erat tegi umbone

reverence; and it is one of the most frequent and delightful of my pleasures to listen to their song. Besides, I know that most of them, if I pass them in review from the very first down to our Buchanan, are the sworn foes of tyrants. But who can

5 endure these pedlers of verse?—a race of mortals than which nothing can be more foolish, more vain, corrupt, or lying. They praise or blame, without choice, without discrimination, without judgment or measure, now princes, now plebeians, alike the learned and unlearned, honest men and knaves,

10 as prompted by caprice,—as inspirited and transported by the bottle, by the hope of getting a little money, or by their own senseless fury; heaping together from all sides inconsistencies, both in words and things, so threadbare and of colours so incompatible, that it would be better far for the

15 person praised to be passed by in silence, and to live, as the saying is, on the sneers of contempt than to be thus praised: nay, he who has incurred their blame, may take it to himself as no ordinary honour, that he is not a favorite with these dull and paltry scoundrels. The foremost of them, if there are

20 really two, I am in doubt whether to call a poet or a mason, so unconscionably does he bedaub the person of Salmasius,—so like a perfect wall does he plaster and whitewash it. He introduces the giant-warring hero in a sort of "triumphal" car, brandishing his "spears and clubs," and I know not what

25 trumpery armour, with the whole host of the learned following on foot in the rear, but at an awful distance; like "the coming," forsooth, "of any God, in seasons of danger, for the salvation of the world: for at length the time was come, for kings to be

reges, parente nimirum *Juris & imperii.* Delirus necesse est fuerit & bis puer Salmasius, qui his laudibus non solùm tantopere sibi placuerit, sed excudendas etiam quàm primùm de se tam sedulò curaverit: Misellus etiam poëta atque inde-
5 corus, qui Grammaticum, quod genus hominum poëtis ministrum semper atque subserviens fuit, tam immodicis laudibus dignetur. Alter verò non versus facit, sed planè insanit, enthusiastarum omnium, quos tam rabidè insectatur, ipse amentissimus: hic Salmasii carnifex quasi sit, Syri Damæ filius, Lora-
10 rios invocat & Cadmum; veratro deinde ebrius, totam, quicquid ubique est, Servulorum & Ballionum sentinam, ex Indice Plautino evomit; credas linguâ Oscum non latinè loquentem, aut inferarum, quas natat, paludum coaxare ranam. Tum ut intelligatis, quantus sit Iamborum artifex, duabus syllabis
15 unâ in voce peccat, alterâ productâ, alterâ perperam correptâ. *Hi trucidato rege per horrendum nefas.*

Aufer istas, asine, *vacivitatum* tuarum clitellas; & tria verba, si potes, sani ac sobrii hominis tandem affer; si tua ista cucur-
20 bita & *blennum caput* vel ad punctum temporis potest sapere: interea te ego puerorum *virgidemiis* tuis cædendum trado

covered with such a shield by the parent," God wot, "of right and dominion." Surely, Salmasius must have been mad and twice a child, when he could not only be flattered with bepraisings so fulsome, but when he could use his utmost dili-
5 gence to get them printed with all possible dispatch! The poet too must have been a sorry poet, and unobservant of decorum, who could dignify with such immoderate eulogiums a grammarian,—a description of person, who has ever been a menial —merely subservient to poets. The other, so far from making
10 verses indeed, is absolutely beside himself—the maddest of all the enthusiasts, whom he persecutes with so much fury. As if he were executioner to Salmasius, a son of Syrus or Dama, he invokes the slave-whippers, and Cadmus; then, drunk with hellebore, he vomits out a whole sink of foul abuse collected,
15 with the help of an index to Plautus, from the mouths of slaves and mountebanks. You would think he was speaking Oscan instead of Latin, or croaking like one of the frogs of the marshy plains in which he swims. Then, to show you what an adept at iambics he is, he makes two false quantities in one
20 word, making the one long where it ought to be short, and the other short where it ought to be long.

Hi trucidato rege per horrendum nefas.

Away with your panniers "of emptiness," you ass! and at last utter three words, if you can, like a man in his sound and
25 sober senses, if that pumpkin head, if that "thick head" of yours be capable of common sense even for a moment. In the meantime I hand you over, you Orbilius you, to be flogged by

Orbilium. Tu mihi sic perge maledicere, ut *Cromuello* pejor tibi sim, quâ nullâ majore me laude afficere potuisti. Te verò benevolúmne dicam, an stolidum, an hostem insidiosum? benevolus certè non es, verba enim hostem indicant; cur ergò
5 tam stolidus fuisti vituperator, ut anteferre me tanto viro in buccam tibi venerit? ecquid tu non intelligis, an me putas non intelligere, quò graviora vestra in me esse odia ostenditis, eò vos ampliora mea in rempublicam merita prædicare, vestra tot opprobria, tot mea esse apud meos præconia? Nam si vos
10 me omnium maximè odistis, sanè ego vos omnium maximè exulceravi, vos ego maximè afflixi, causæque vestræ nocui: id si ità est, idem ego de meis civibus optimè quoque merui; hostis enim vel testimonium vel judicium, etsi aliàs leve admodùm, de suo tamen dolore longè est gravissimum. An Poëta
15 non meministi, cùm de Achillis mortui armis, Ajax & Ulysses contenderent, non Græcos populares set Trojanos hostes ex sententia Nestoris Judices datos?

Τοὔνεκα Τρωσὶν ἐφῶμεν ἐΰφροσι τήνδε δικάσσαι.

Quapropter Trojanis permittamus prudentibus hanc litem
20 *judicandam.*

Et paulò pòst,

your own scholars. Go on, and revile me in this way, as being,
in your eyes, "worse than Cromwell": for it is impossible for
you to bestow upon me higher praise. But am I to consider
you as a friend, or as a blockhead, or as an insidious enemy?
5 That you are not a friend is certain: for your words betray you
for an enemy. How then came you to be so great a blockhead,
as to take it into your head to prefer me for your accusation to
so great a personage? Do you imagine, that what you do not
comprehend, I also do not comprehend?—namely, that the
10 more inveterate you discover your hatred to be against me,
the greater do you proclaim my merits to be towards the commonwealth?—That with my own party your manifold reproaches do but declare my praise? For if you hate me to a
degree beyond all others, it is plain that I, of all others, have
15 galled you the most severely; that it is I, who have the most
humbled you; that it is I, who have done the most mischief to
your cause. If this be the fact, then it is I also, who have deserved the most highly of my fellow citizens: for the testimony or judgment of an enemy, though in other respects
20 abundantly trivial, is the weightiest of all on the subject of his
own pain. Do you not remember, when Ajax and Ulysses contended for the arms of the dead Achilles, that the poet, by the
counsel of Nestor, chose the judges not from among the
Greeks who were their countrymen, but from the Trojans,
25 who were their enemies?

Hence let the impartial Trojans judge the strife.

And a little after:

Οἵ ῥα δίχην ἰθεῖαν ἐπί σφισι ποιήσονται.
Οὔ τινι ἦρα φέροντες ἐπεὶ μάλα πάντας Ἀχαιοὺς
᾿Ισον ἐπεχθαίρουσι κακῆς μεμνημένοι ἄτης.

Qui justum judicium de iis fecerint,
5 *Nemini gratificantes, cùm vehementer omnes Achivos*
Æquè oderint, mali memores damni.

Hæc Smyrnæus ille, sive Calaber. Insidiosus itaque sis oportet, méque in invidiam conjicere labores, qui quod judicium
in hoste rectum atque sincerum esse solet, id dolo malo &
10 graviùs lædendi animo corrumpis atque depravas, ita non vir
modò sed & hostis depravatissimus es. Verùm ego, nullo negotio frustrabor te, vir bone; quanquam enim Ulyssem, id est,
quàm optimè de patria meritum me esse sanè perquàm vellem, tamen Achilleïa arma non ambio; cœlum in clypeo pic-
15 tum, quod alii, non ego, in certamine aspiciant, præferre,
onus non pictum sed verum, humeris portare, quod ego, non
alii sentiant, non quæro: Equidem cùm nullas omnino simul-
tates aut inimicitias ullo cum homine privatas geram, neque
ullus, quod sciam, mecum gerat, tot in me maledicta jactari,
20 tot probra torqueri, reipublicæ duntaxat causâ, non meâ, eo
æquiore animo fero: nec præmii & commodorum inde pro-
venientium, partem longè minimam, ignominiæ longè maximam pervenisse ad me queror; contentus quæ honesta factu

Now they a righteous judgment will declare,
As nor to one nor t'other love they bear;
For all the Greeks they hold in equal hate;
Darkly remembering their ruined state.

5   Thus far the Symrnæan, or Calaber. It follows, then, that you must be insidious, and labour to cast an odium upon me, since, by wicked arts, and with the purpose of inflicting a deeper injury, you pervert and deprave that kind of judgment which is usually unbiassed and sincere in an enemy: hence, you are not merely the most depraved of men, but the most depraved of enemies. But, my good man! I will render frustrate none of your endeavours: for though I could most ardently wish that I were Ulysses, that is, that I had deserved the most highly of all of my country; yet, I covet not the arms of Achilles; I seek not to carry before me the heavens painted on my shield, which others may look to in a contest, though I do not; it is my endeavour to bear on my shoulders, a real not a painted burden, to be felt by myself, rather than by others. Indeed, as I have no private malice or enmity against any man, nor, as far as I know, has any man against me, I am the less concerned at the torrent of abuse which is cast upon me, at the numberless reproaches which are hurled against me, as I bear all this not for myself, but for the sake of the commonwealth. Nor do I complain, that by far the least share of the reward and of the advantages thence proceeding and that by far the greatest share of the reproach, have attached to me; content to have had in view and to have prosecuted without reward,

sunt, ea propter se solùm appetisse, & gratìs persequi: Id alii viderint, túque scito, me illas *opimitates* atque *opes,* quas mihi exprobras, non attigisse, neque eo nomine quo maximè accusas, obolo factum ditiorem. Hic rursus infit Morus, & se-
5 cunda epistola causas scribendi refert; cuinam? *Lectori Christiano* nempe Mœchus & stuprator Morus salutem: piam sanè epistolam promittis; jam causas incipe. *Excitati sunt Europæarum gentium animi, maxime omnium Galli nostri reformati, ut parricidium & parricidas, &c. cognoscerent.*
10 Galli & ipsi reformati contra reges bella gesserunt; quid ulteriùs fuissent facturi, paribus usi rerum successibus, affirmari non potest: certè reges ipsorum, si qua earum rerum monumentis fides, ab illis haud minùs metuebant sibi, quàm à nobis noster: neque injuriâ, quoties meminissent quæ etiam illi
15 scriptitarunt, & minati sæpe sunt: Nolint igitur, quicquid tu causare, splendidè nimis de se polliceri, iniquiùs de nobis sentire. Pergit in causis. *Equidem ea Anglorum melioris notæ consuetudine sum usus.* Qui tibi sunt melioris notæ, viris bonis sunt pessimæ. *Ut ausim dicere me ista homi-*

those things which were honorable to be done, for their own sakes alone. This is what others should look to, and as for yourself, know that I have not so much as touched those "good things," "that wealth" with which you reproach me, nor am
5 made one half-penny the richer by that name, on account of which you bring your chief accusations against me.

Here More begins again, and in the second epistle gives his reasons for writing: and for writing to whom?—To "the Christian reader," forsooth, the adulterer and fornicator More
10 writes, greeting. You lead us to expect a truly pious epistle: come let us hear your reasons. "The minds of the nations of Europe and most of all our French protestants, were roused to become acquainted with the parricide and with the parricides," &c. The French, even the Protestants themselves, have
15 engaged in wars against the laws; what farther they would have done, if they had had the like success with ourselves, cannot now be known. It is certain, that their own kings, if any credit is to be given to the records of those transactions, stood in no less apprehension from them, than our king from
20 us: nor was this without reason, when they considered the spirit and multitude of the writings even of those reformers, and how often they had gone so far as to threaten. They were unwilling, therefore, whatever you pretend, to promise too splendidly of themselves, or to think unjustly of us.—He goes
25 on with his reasons. "Indeed, such have been my habits of intimacy with Englishmen of the better note";—Those who in your eyes are of the better note, are, in the eyes of men of virtue, of the worst note;—"That I might undertake to say I

num monstra nosse intus & in cute. Putabam te mœchas
tantummodo tuas & scorta; tu etiam monstra intus & in
cute. *Ut nomen meum premerem, facile impetrarunt Angli
quibuscum consuevi.* Et astutè quidem illi: siç enim spe-
5 rabant & se impudentiâ tuâ eò largiore fruituros, & te tuâ
famâ, etiam tum malâ, eo minus causæ nociturum. Noverant
enim te, & quàm esses olim bonus hortorum custos, & nunc
rasus licèt & pumicatus sacerdos, ut à Pontia ne Pilata quidem
abstinere manus potueris; nec de nihilo sanè, si enim à confi-
10 cienda carne carnifex dictus putatur, cur minùs tu conficiendo
Pontiam Pontifex factus ex sacerdote tibi videare? Hæc cùm
de te non nescirent alii, cùm non posses ipse quin tibimet con-
scires, tamen incredibili, & execrandâ quadam impietate palàm audes profiteri, te *Dei gloriam unice quærere, & vindi-*
15 *care:* & dum ipse turpissima quæris, simul accusare alios, quod
pietatis larvam criminibus imponant: cùm id nemo manifes-
tiùs ac sceleratiùs quàm tu ipse facis, unquam fecerit. *Ad re-*
rum ais *gestarum seriem magno* tibi *fuisse adjumento cum alios*
scriptores tum maxime elenchum motuum nuperorum in An-

know those monsters of men in heart and in grain." I thought you knew nobody but your adulteresses, and strumpets; and you also know monsters in heart and in grain.—"The Englishmen with whom I had intercourse easily prevailed upon me to suppress my name." And, in truth, not without a crafty policy: for in this way, they had the hope of being indulged with a larger measure of your impudence, and that you would do less mischief to the cause by your character, which was bad even at that time. For they had known you of old; had known what an excellent keeper of gardens you had formerly been; and though now a priest all shaven and spruce, that you could not keep your hands off not even from Pontia Pilate; nor without reason indeed: for if *carnifex* (an executioner) be supposed to be derived a *conficienda carne* (from dispatching flesh) why should you think it less likely, that from a priest you should be made *pontifex* (a high-priest) *conficiendo Pontiam,* (from dispatching Pontia)? though these stories about you were no secrets to other people; though it is impossible but that yourself must have been conscious of them; yet with an impiety which is scarcely credible, and which deserves execration, you dare openly to profess that "you are seeking only and vindicating only the glory of God"; and at the very time you yourself are pursuing the most scandalous courses, accuse others "of covering their crimes under the mask of piety"; though no man was ever more manifestly and more wickedly guilty of this than yourself.—"For the order of transactions (you say) you derived great assistance from other writers, and especially from *A View of the late*

glia. Næ tu ineptus homo es, qui tanto clamore facto, quod
tuum sit nihil afferas; sed scriptores tantùm, regiis partibus
addictos eóque meritò suspectos authores contra nos adducere
potuisti, quorum fides si elevabitur, progredi nequeas. Nos igi-
5 tur scriptores illos, si opus erit & elenchum elencho refutabi-
mus, non illis per te, sed tibi per illos, cum visum erit responde-
bimus; tibi quæ de tuo protuleris, videndum interea, ut tueri
queas; quæ cujusmodi sint, ab impio & planè Atheo homine
profecta, audiant nunc omnes pii & horrescant. *Jubet amor*
10 *dei & injuriæ sancto ejus nomini factæ sensus acerrimus cogit*
supplices manus ad deum attollere. Abde, abde obscœnas illas
manus, quas libidine & ambitione supinatus attollere non
vereris, nè cœlum ipsum quoque audeas iis manibus incestare,
quibus sacra religionis mysteria contrectando polluisti. Quam
15 enim divinam ultionem aliis temerarius & væcors imprecaris,
eam in ipsius tuum impurissimum caput devocasse te olim
intelliges.

Hactenus clamoris quasi præludia fuere; nunc, (summas
enim, & propè solas in hoc dramate partes clamor obtinet,)
20 quàm potest maximo hiatu, rictum diducit: in cœlum scilicet
iturus; quo si ascenderit, in neminem profectò acriùs clama-
bit quam in ipsum clamatorem Morum. *Cum omnibus secu-*

Troubles in England.'' You are indeed a trifling fellow: for
though you raise so great a clamour, you can bring nothing
that is your own; you could produce against us the writers only
who are devoted to the royalist faction—authors, for that very
reason justly suspected—and whose credit once invalidated,
you would be unable to proceed. We shall therefore refute
those writers, and if necessary, one view by another: as we see
occasion, we shall reply not to them through you, but to you
through them. In the meantime, it behoves you to be prepared to defend what you have brought forward of your own;
the nature of which, as it proceeds from a name evidently impious and atheistic, let all religious persons now hear, and
tremble with horror. "The love of God commands,—the
keenest sense of the injury done to his sacred name compels
us, to lift up our suppliant hands to God." Hide, O hide those
polluted hands, which, grovelling as you are in ambition and
lust, you have the presumption to lift up, lest you dare also to
pollute heaven itself with the touch that has already contami-
nated the sacred mysteries of religion. But that divine vengeance, which you rashly and absurdly imprecate upon others,
you will find hereafter you have called down upon your own
guilty head.

Thus far we have been listening merely to the preludes of
the cry; now (for the cry gets the principal, and almost the
only part, in this drama) the mouth is opened to its utmost
yawn, as the cry is to reach to heaven; and if it arrive thither,
it will, in truth, cry out against no one more sharply than
against the crier, More himself. "Since the majesty of kings

lis, sacra fuerit regum majestas, &c. Multa tu quidem More
vulgariter, multa malitiose in nos declamas, quæ nihil attinet: regis enim cædes, & tyranni supplicium non sunt idem,
More, non sunt; inter se distant longissimè, atque distabunt,
5 dum sensus & ratio, jus atque fas, rectíque & obliqui judicium
hominibus concedetur. Verùm de his satìs jam sæpiùs dictum,
satìs defensum est: non patiar qui tot diris inanibus lædere
non potes, ut repetitâ crambe nos demum occídas. De patientiâ, deinde & pietate bellè disputas: Sed

10   *de virtute loquutus*
   Clunem agitas: ego te ceventem, More, verebor?

Omnes aïs *reformatos, presertim Belgas & Gallos, factum
nostrum horruisse:* & statim, *bonis ubique non licuisse, idem
sentire & loqui.* Sed te tibi repugnare leviculum est; hoc
15 multò indignius atque atrocius; *præ nostro* inquis, *scelere,
nihil fuit Judæorum scelus, Christum crucifigentium, sive
hominum mentem, sive sceleris effectus compares.* Furiose!
túne Christi minister perpetratum facinus in Christum tam
leviter fers, quacunque demum *mente* vel *effectu* ut pari sce-

has, in all ages, been held sacred," &c. Indeed, More, you clamour many things against us, in your vulgarity, many in your malice, which are nothing to the purpose: for the murder of a king, and the punishment of a tyrant, are not the same,
5 More, they are not the same; they differ most widely, and will differ, as long as sense and reason, right and wrong, the power of distinguishing straight from crooked, shall be allowed to men. But as to these things enough has been often said already, enough defended. You who can do us no injury with
10 all your mighty blustering, shall not put an end to us at last by serving up your hash again. You have some fine things about patience; then about piety. But,

> You preach of virtue, while of flesh you're frail;
> What fear, though now as erst you wag your tail?

15 "All protestants, you say, especially the Dutch and the French, were struck with horror at what we have done"; and immediately after—"good men were no where at liberty to speak what they thought." But for you to contradict yourself is a trifling matter; what follows is of a far more disgraceful
20 and atrocious character: "In comparison of our wickedness (say you) the wickedness of the Jews in the crucifixion of Christ was nothing, whether we consider the intention of the men, or the effects of the crime." Maniac! and do you, a minister of Christ, make so light of the horrible crime committed
25 against Christ, as, whatever might have been "the intention" or "the effect," to dare to pronounce, that to kill any king is

lere interfectum quemlibet regem audeas dicere? Judæi certè
clarissimis indiciis dei filium agnovisse poterant; nos Carolum non esse tyrannum, nulla ratione potuimus intelligere.
Eventûs autem, ad minuendum scelus, ineptissimè facis men-
5 tionem: verùm semper animadverto regios, quò quisque acrior
est, eò leviùs ferre quicquid committitur in Christum, quàm
si quid in regem: cui tamen cùm Christi præcipuè causâ
obediendum doceant, facilè ostendunt se neque Christum
verè colere, neque regem: sed aliud quiddam sibi quærentes,
10 incredibilem hanc erga reges fidem ac religionem suam, vel
ambitioni, vel occultis quibusdam aliis cupiditatibus obten-
dere. *Prodiit ergo magnus literarum princeps Salmasius.*
Desine toties magnum illud, More; quod millies licèt inges-
seris, haud cuiquam profectò intelligenti persuaseris mag-
15 num esse Salmasium, sed minimum esse Morum, & nullius
pretii homulum, qui, quid deceat ignarus, magni cognomine
tam imperitè abutatur. Nos grammaticis atque criticis, quorum summa laus aut in alienis lucubrationibus edendis, aut
librariorum mendulis corrigendis versatur, industriam qui-
20 dem ac literarum scientiam, doctrinæ etiam haud contem-
nendæ laudem, ac præmia libenter concedimus, magni cog-
nomen haud largimur. Is solus magnus est appellandus, qui
res magnas aut gerit, aut docet, aut dignè scribit: res autem

equally sinful? The Jews, from the clearest signs, might certainly have recognized the Son of God; but it was impossible
that we, in any way, should have been made to comprehend
that Charles was not a tyrant. To mention the accidental con-
5 sequences with a view to diminish a crime, is most absurd. But
I always remark this in a royalist; according as he is the more
acrimonious, does he make less account of any offence committed against Christ, than against the king; and though he
teaches that the king ought to be obeyed chiefly for the sake
10 of Christ, he plainly makes it appear, that himself is no true
follower either of Christ, or of the king; but that, having
other selfish objects in view, he makes a display of this his in-
credible fidelity and devotion to his king, from ambition, or
from other passions which he conceals.—"Salmasius, there-
15 fore, the great prince of letters, came forward." Don't persist, More, in this manner in calling such a man great.
Though you should repeat it a thousand times, you would
never persuade any man of sense that Salmasius was a great
man; but rather that More is a most little one, a worthless
20 manikin, who, from his ignorance of propriety, abuses thus
absurdly the epithet of great. To grammarians and critics,
whose highest praise consists either in editing the works of
others, or in correcting the blunders of transcribers, we readily allow industry indeed and the knowledge of languages,
25 with the credit and rewards of a learning by no means to be
despised; but we do not bestow upon them the title of great.
He alone deserves the appellation of great, who either achieves
great things himself, or teaches how they may be achieved; or

magnæ sunt solæ, quæ vel vitam hanc nostram efficiunt bea-
tam, aut saltem cum honestate commodam atque jucundam,
vel ad alteram ducunt beatiorem. Horum verò Salmasius quid
egit? egit verò nihil; quid autem docuit aut scripsit magnum?
5 nisi fortè contra Episcopos, & primatum Papæ, quod ipse
postea & suis moribus, & aliis in nos pro episcopatu scriptis,
recantatum penitus evertit. Magnus ergo scriptor dici non
debet, qui aut nihil magnum, aut quod optimum in vita scrip-
serat, ei fædissimè renunciavit. *Literarum princeps* ut sit, &
10 Alphabeti per me licet; at verò tibi non *princeps* modò *litera-*
rum est, sed *patronus regum,* & *patronus quidem dignus*
tantis clientibus. Pulchrè tu quidem regibus consuluisti, ut
post alios insignes titulos, Claudii Salmasii clientes appellen-
tur. Eâ nimirum lege solvimini cunctis aliis legibus, Reges,
15 ut in clientelam Grammatico tradatis vos Salmasio, sceptra
ferulæ submittatis: *Debebunt ei Reges, dum stabit orbis, dig-*
nitatis & salutis suæ vindicias. Audite, Principes; qui pessimè
vos defendit, immo ne defendit quidem, nemo enim oppug-
navit, dignitatem & salutem vestram sibi imputat. Hoc nempe
20 solum consequuti sunt, qui superbissimum Grammaticum

who describes with suitable dignity the great achievements of
others. But those things only are great, which either make
this life of ours happy, or at least comfortable and agreeable as
far as is consistent with honesty, or which lead to another and
5 a happier life. Now what has Salmasius done of such things as
these? Clearly nothing. And what has he taught or written
that is great? Unless perhaps what he wrote, against the bishops and the pope's supremacy, which, being recanted by his
subsequent conduct, and by other writings in opposition to us
10 and in favour of episcopacy, he has rendered null. He, therefore, who had either never written any thing great, or who
basely disclaimed the best thing he ever wrote, is not entitled
to be called a great writer. He has my permission to be "the
prince of letters," and of the alphabet too; but in your appre-
15 hension he is not merely the "prince of letters," but "the patron of kings," and "a patron truly worthy of clients so
illustrious." Indeed, you have consulted admirably for kings,
when, in addition to their other notable titles, you would
have them to be styled the clients of Claudius Salmasius.
20 By the law, surely, that if you deliver yourselves up, ye kings,
to the patronage of Salmasius the grammarian, if you humble your sceptres to the rod, you are absolved from all other
laws.—"As long as the world shall stand, kings will owe
to him the vindication of their dignity and safety." Hear,
25 O ye princes! the man who has defended you so scurvily,
nay, who has defended you not at all, for he had nobody
to oppose him, affirms, that for your dignity and safety you
are indebted to him! Now this is all they have gained, who

sustinendis regum rationibus ex tinearum & blattarum foro
advocârunt. *Cui quantum res regia, tantundem etiam ecclesia
debebit;* non laudem sanè, sed meritissimam desertæ suæ
causæ notam. Nunc in laudes effunderis Defensionis regiæ;
5 *ingenium, doctrinam, infinitum prope rerum usum, & inti-
mam sacri & profani juris penum, concitatæ orationis vigorem, eloquentiam, facundiam aurei illius operis* admiraris,
quorum cum nihil affuisse homini contendo, (quid enim
Salmasio cum eloquentia?) tum aureum fuisse illud opus vel
10 centies fateor; tot enim Carolus aureos numeravit, ne dicam
quid Arausiacus etiam princeps in idem opus profuderit. *Nunquam major surrexit vir magnus, nunquam magis Salmasius:*
Et tantò quidem major ut se ruperit, quàm magnus enim
fuerit in illo opere jam vidimus; & siquid ejusdem argumenti,
15 ut fertur, posthumum reliquit, fortasse videbimus. Non equidem inficior, edito illo libro, Salmasium in ore omnium fuisse,
regiis mirè placuisse; *ab augustissima Sueciæ regina, amplis-
simis præmiis invitatum;* quinimò totâ illâ contentione Salmasio secunda omnia, adversa mihi penè omnia fuere. Pri-
20 mùm de illius eruditione, erat hominum summa opinio,
quam multis ab annis jam diu collegerat, libros conscribendo

have assisted the haughty grammarian, while, in a court of
moths and book-worms, he sustained the cause of kings.—
"Nor will the church owe him less than the cause of roy-
alty." It is not praise, then, that the church will owe him,
5 but a richly deserved mark of infamy, for deserting her cause.
—Now you would lavish your encomiums upon the royal defence; you admire "the genius, the learning, the acquaintance
with things little short of infinite, the profound knowledge
of the canon and civil law, the vigour of elevated language,
10 the eloquence, the grace of that golden work"—of all
which qualities I maintain that the man was wholly destitute (for what had Salmasius to do with eloquence?) But,
that the work was a golden work, this I acknowledge a hundred times over: for so many pieces of gold did Charles count
15 out; not to mention what the prince of Orange also bestowed
upon the same work.—"Never did a great man appear
greater; never did Salmasius": yes indeed, he was so much
greater that he burst: for how great he was in that work we
have already seen; and if he has left any posthumous work, as
20 is reported, on the same subject, we shall perhaps see again.
Now I do not deny, that, after the publication of that book,
Salmasius was in everybody's mouth, and that he pleased the
royalists to a miracle; that "he was invited, and amply re-
warded, by the most august the queen of Sweden"; nay, that,
25 in the whole of that contest, Salmasius had every thing in his
favour, and I almost every thing against me. In the first place,
of his erudition, the opinion of mankind could go no higher,
which opinion he had been collecting for many previous years,

multos, & bene magnos, non eos quidem plerúmque utiles,
sed abstrusissimis de rebus, & summorum authorum citatiun-
culis differtos; quo nihil citiùs literatorum vulgus in admi-
rationem rapit; me verò quis essem, nemo in iis ferè regioni-
5 bus nôrat; magnam ille suî expectationem concitârat, atten-
tior operi quàm solebat aliàs, ut in re tanta; ego mei nullam
potui movere: immò verò multi me ab illo dehortabantur,
tyronem cum veterano congressurum, partim invidentes, nè
utcunque mihi gloriæ foret cum tanto hoste decertâsse; par-
10 tim & mihi, & causæ metuentes, nè utriusque gravi cum ignominia victus discederem; causa denique speciosa atque plausi-
bilis, inveterata vulgi opinio, sive superstitio dicenda potiùs
est, & propensus in regium nomen favor Salmasio vires &
spiritus addiderat; eadem omnia contra me fecêre, quo magìs
15 est mirandum, quamprimum responsio nostra prodiit, non si
à plerísque avidè arriperetur videre gestientibus ecquis tam
præceps animi esset ut auderet cum Salmasio confligere, sed
tam esse placitam multis atque gratam, ut, non authoris, sed
ipsius veritatis ratione habitâ, qui modò summo in honore
20 fuerat Salmasius, nunc quasi detractâ, sub qua latuerat, per-
sonâ, & existimatione, & animo repentè caderet; séque asse-

by writing a multitude of books, and of no small bulk; not
books of general utility, but on the abstrusest subjects, and
stuffed with scraps of citation from eminent authors; than
which nothing sooner excites the wonderment of the literary
5 vulgar. On the contrary, who I was, scarcely any one in those
parts had ever heard. He, by applying a more than ordinary
diligence to the work, the subject being of such magnitude,
had awakened in respect of himself great expectation; while
it was not in my power to awaken any. Nay, as I should be a
10 raw recruit engaging with a veteran, there were many who
dissuaded me from the undertaking, partly out of envy, lest,
whatever the issue, I should gain glory from a contest with an
enemy so illustrious; partly, from apprehension for me and
for the cause, lest I should retire vanquished, to the heavy dis-
15 grace of both. Lastly the specious and plausible nature of his
cause, the rooted opinion of the vulgar, or which is more
properly called superstition, and the prepossession in favour of
the royal name, had given additional vigour and spirit to Salmasius — circumstances which all made against me. Hence
20 when our defence soon after made its appearance, it is less to
be wondered at, that it was seized with avidity by most persons, as they had an eager curiosity to see who could be so rash
as to presume to enter the lists with Salmasius, than that it
should give such pleasure and satisfaction to many; insomuch
25 that as respect was no longer had to the author, but to truth
itself, Salmasius, who was lately seated on the summit of
honour, now, as if the mask which disguised him had been
taken off, suddenly fell from his renown and from his confi-

rere, tametsi omnibus nervis id agens, quoad vixit postea non
valuerit. Te verò, serenissima Suecorum regina, tuúmque
illud acre judicium fallere haud diu potuit; tu veritatis partium studiis anteferendæ, Princeps atque Author propè dicam
5 cœlestis extitisti. Quamvis enim illum hominem eximiæ doctrinæ famâ, causæque regiæ patrocinio tunc temporis longè
omnium celeberrimum, à te invitatum, multis honoribus affe-
cisses, tamen prodeunte illo responso, & singulari æquanimi-
tate abs te perlecto, postquam vanitatis & apertissimæ cor-
10 ruptelæ redargutum Salmasium, multa leviter, multa immo-
deratè, falsa quædam, adversùs seipsum alia, & prioribus sententiis contraria disseruisse animadverteras, ad quæ, coram
accitus, ut ferunt, quod satìs responderet nihil habuit, ita
palàm animo affecta es, ut ab illo tempore neque hominem,
15 ut antea, colere, neque ejus ingenium aut doctrinam magni
facere, &, quod erat planè inopinatum, ejus adversario pro-
pensiùs favere, omnes te intelligerent. Quod enim erat in
tyrannos dictum, negabas id ad te ullo modo pertinere: unde
& apud te fructum, & apud alios famam rectissimæ conscien-
20 tiæ adepta es. Cùm enim tua facta satis declarent, tyrannum
te non esse, hæc tua tam aperta animi significatio adhuc clariùs demonstrabat, te ejus rei ne omnino quidem tibi esse con-

dence; and though he strained every nerve to recover himself, he was unable to accomplish it as long as he lived.

But you, most serene queen of the Swedes! and that nice discernment of yours, he could not long deceive. You have 5 stood forth the princess and the authoress little less (shall I say?) than heavenly, of preferring truth to the partialities of faction. For although you invited and loaded with honours the man, who, at that time, was celebrated above his fellows for pre-eminent learning, and for his defence of the royal 10 cause, yet, after that answer had appeared, which was perused by you with singular equanimity, and you had discovered that Salmasius was convicted of talking to no purpose, and of palpable misrepresentation; that he had said many things which are frivolous, many which are extravagant, some which are 15 false, others which go against himself, and are contrary to his former sentiments, and that when called into your presence, as the report goes, he could give no satisfactory reasons for all this—your mind underwent so visible a change, that, from that time, it was plain to everybody, that you neither paid the 20 same attention to the man as before, nor made much account of his genius and learning; and what was altogether unexpected, showed an evident inclination to favour his adversary. For you denied that what was spoken against tyrants could have any reference whatever to you; and by this you gained, 25 with yourself the fruit, with others the reputation, of a most upright conscience. As it is sufficiently plain from your actions, that you are no tyrant, this open declaration of your sentiments shows, in a still clearer light, that you are utterly

sciam. O me spe meâ omni feliciorem! (Eloquentiam enim,
nisi quæ in ipsa veritate Suada est, nullam mihi sumo) qui,
cùm in ea patriæ tempora incidissem, ut necesse esset in causâ
tam arduâ tâmque invidiosâ versari, ut jus omne regium im-
5 pugnare viderer, tam illustrem, tam verè regiam nactus sim
integritatis meæ testem atque interpretem, nullum me verbum fecisse contra reges, sed contra regum labes ac pestes
duntaxat tyrannos. Te verò magnanimam, Augusta, te tutam
undique divinâ planè virtute ac sapientiâ munitam! quæ quod
10 in jus tuum ac dignitatem poterat videri scriptum, non solùm
tam æquo animo atque sedato, tam incredibili mentis candore,
vultúsque verâ serenitate perlegere sustinuisti; sed contra
ipsum Patronum tuum ejusmodi sententiam ferre, ut ejus adversario palmam etiam adjudicare à plerisque existimeris.
15 Quo te honore, quâ te veneratione, Regina, prosequi semper
debuero, cujus excelsa virtus ac magnitudo animi non tibi
solùm gloriosa, sed mihi etiam tam fausta atque fortunata, &
suspicione me omni atque infamiâ apud alios reges liberavit,
& præclaro ac immortali hoc beneficio tibi in perpetuum de-
20 vinxit. Quàm bene de æquitate tua, déque justitia & sentire
exteri, & sentire & sperare semper tui populi debebunt, qui,
cùm tua res ac majestas ipsa agi videretur, tam nihil turbatam

unconscious of the thing. Happy am I! happy even beyond
my highest hope! (for I boast of no other eloquence than that
persuasion which is inherent in truth itself;) who, when I
had fallen upon those times of my country, in which I was
5 constrained of necessity to engage in a cause at once so arduous
and invidious, that I must seem to impugn all regal right,
have found a witness and an interpreter of my integrity so
illustrious, so truly royal, as to interpret and bear witness for
me, that I have spoken not a syllable against kings, but against
10 the underminers and pests of kings—against tyrants only.
But how magnanimous, Augusta, how secure on all sides must
you be, fortified as you are with a virtue and wisdom clearly
divine! when you could not only peruse with such equanimity,
such calmness, with a candour of mind so unexampled, with
15 a serenity of countenance so perfect, what might have seemed
written against your own right and dignity; but could adopt
an opinion of this nature against your own advocate himself,
so as to be commonly thought even to award the palm to his
adversary! In what honour, in what veneration, must you ever
20 be held by me, when your exalted virtue and greatness of
spirit, not only glorious to yourself, but auspicious and fortunate for me, have freed me, as it respects other kings,
from all suspicion and disgrace, and, by this signal and
immortal benefit, have bound me to you for ever! With
25 what favour must foreigners have thought, with what favour
must your own people have both thought and hoped of
your equity and impartiality, when, at a time in which
your own concerns, in which your majesty itself seemed

te de tuo haud minùs placidè, quàm de populi jure soles, judi-
cantem viderunt. Jam tu quidem haud temerè, tot conquisita
undique volumina, tot literarum monumenta congessisti, non
quasi te illa quicquam docere, sed ut ex illis tui cives te discere,
5 tuæque virtutis ac sapientiæ præstantiam contemplari possint;
cujus ipsa Divæ species, nisi tuo animo penitùs insedisset, &
quasi oculis conspiciendam se tibi præbuisset, haud ullâ profectò librorum lectione, tam incredibiles amores excitâsset in
te sui: quò magìs illum mentis tuæ vigorem planè æthereum &
10 quasi purissimam divinæ auræ partem in illas ultimas regiones
delapsam admiramur; quam neque cœlum illud triste ac nubi-
losum ullis frigoribus extinguere aut gravare, neque solum
illud horridum ac salebrosum, quod & ingenia quoque in-
colarum haud rarò indurat, quicquam in te inæquale aut
15 asperum creare potuit: quin & ipsa terra illa, tot metallis fæ-
cunda, si aliis noverca, tibi certè alma parens, te summis enixa
viribus totam auream produxisse videtur. Dicerem Adolphi
filiam invicti atque inclyti regis unicam prolem, nisi tu illi,
Christina, tantum præluceres, quantum viribus sapientia, belli
20 artibus pacis studia præcellunt. Jam inde profectò regina

to be the subject of contention, they saw you delivering your judgment, with as little emotion, with no less composure, on your own rights, than you had been accustomed to do on the rights of the people! Besides, it was for no idle pur-
5 pose that you collected from all parts such multitudes of choice volumes, so many monuments of learning! It was not that from these things yourself might learn any thing, but that from them your own citizens might learn to know you, that they might be able to contemplate the pre-eminence of your
10 virtue and of your wisdom; and unless the very image of the goddess of wisdom had sat before your inmost spirit, unless she had appeared, as it were, in a visible form before your eyes, she could never have raised in you, by any book-learning, such an ardent love of herself. This makes us admire the more your
15 vigour of mind manifestly ethereal, as if the purest particle of the breath divine had fallen upon those remote regions—a particle, which that melancholy and cloudy sky, with its freezing cold, could neither extinguish nor oppress; nor could that horrid and rugged soil, which is wont to harden also the
20 minds of its inhabitants, create in you any thing unequal or rough; nay, this very land, so fertile in divers metals, though to others a stepmother, being certainly to you a fostering parent, seems to have exerted her utmost powers to produce you entirely of gold. I would address you as the daughter of
25 Adolphus, as the only descendant of that invincible and famous king, if, Christina, you did not outshine him as much as wisdom exceeds strength, as much as the arts of peace surpass the stratagems of war. Henceforward, not the queen of the

Austri haud sola celebrabitur: habet nunc & septentrio reginam suam, & dignam sanè quæ non modò sapientissimum
illum Judæorum regem, aut siquis unquam similis futurus
esset, auditum proficisceretur, sed ad quam alii tanquam ad
5 clarissimum regalium virtutum exemplar, & visendam omnibus Heroinam, undique concurrant: nullúmque in terris fastigium par esse ejus laudibus ac meritis fateantur, in qua
minimum hoc esse videant, quòd sit Regina, tot gentium
monarcha. Non autem hoc minimum, quòd etiam hoc esse
10 decorum suorum minimum ipsa sentiat, aliúdque longé majus atque sublimius meditetur, quàm regnare; hoc ipso nomine innumeris regibus præponenda. Potest itaque, si ea
manet Suecorum gentem calamitas, regnum abdicare, Reginam deponere nunquam potest, non Sueciæ sed totius orbis
15 terrarum dignam se imperio testata.

In has digressum me Reginæ meritissimas laudes, nemo
est, opinor, qui non collaudet, nedum reprehendat; quas ego
quidem sine summa ingratitudinis culpa, vel aliis tacentibus,
prætermittere non potui; qui nescio quâ meâ sorte, sanè feli-
20 cissimâ, aut si quis est occultus vel siderum, vel animorum,
vel rerum consensus aut moderamem, tantam arbitram quam
omnium minimè sperabam, omnium maximè optabam, tam
mihi æquam & faventem in ultimis terris reppererim. Nunc
ad relictum opus, longè quidem diversissimum, redeundum

south alone shall be celebrated in story. The north has now
also his queen, and worthy too, not merely to go and listen to
that wisest king of the Jews, or to any other, should any ever
more arise like him, but to be herself the heroine to be visited
5 by others, flocking from all quarters as to the brightest pat-
tern of royal virtue; and who should confess that there is no
dignity upon earth equal to her praises and merits; of which
they would see that the least is, that she is a queen—the monarch of so many nations. Again, it is not the least, that she
10 herself thinks this the least of her honours, and meditates upon
something far greater and more sublime, than to reign; merit-
ing to be valued, on this very account, above innumerable
kings. Hence, she may abdicate the kingdom, should such a
misfortune await the Swedish nation; but that she, who has
15 proved herself worthy of the empire, not of Sweden only, but
of the world, should divest herself of the queen, can never be
in her power!

There is no one I trust, who, so far from blaming, would
not commend me for this digression to an eulogium of the
20 queen so well deserved; an eulogium which, though others
were silent, I could not omit without a heavy charge of ingratitude; since, I know not by what chance, though certainly
by a most happy one, or whether by some hidden consent or
guidance of the stars, or of spirits, or of things—I, who the
25 least of all men expected, who the most of all wished such a
thing, have found, in the remotest regions, an arbitress so
illustrious, so impartial and favorable to me.

We must now return to the remaining part of the work, of

tamen est. *Infremuisse,* ais, *nos ad Defensionis regiæ famam;* *dispexisse igitur Grammaticastrum aliquem famelicum, qui* *venalem calamum parricidii patrocinio vellet commodare.* Hæc abs te malitiosissimè ficta sunt, ex quo memineras, regios,

5 cum suis mendaciis ac maledicentiæ præconem dispicerent, adiisse Grammaticum, si non famelicum, certè auri plus nimio sitientem Salmasium; qui non solùm præsentem operam suam, sed bonam quoque mentem, si quam priùs habuit, illis libentissimè vendidit; ex quo memineras Salmasium,

10 famâ jam deploratâ atque perditâ, cum dispiceret, qui existimationem afflictam atque obtritam, quoquo modo reparare quiret, te invenisse justo Dei judicio, non, unde excussus es, ministrum Genevensem, sed episcopum Lampsacenum, id est, ex horto Priapum, suæ domûs constupratorem; unde &

15 insulsissimas laudes, tanto cum dedecore emptas aversatus, & ex amico inimicissimus factus, tibi laudatori suo, multa moriens imprecatus est. *Unus inventus est, magnus scilicet* *Heros, quem Salmasio opponerent, Joannes Miltonus.* Ego Heroëm me esse nesciebam, tu Heroïs cujuspiam fortè filius

20 per me sis licèt; totus enim noxa es. Atque unum me esse inventum, qui causam populi Anglicani tuear, si reipublicæ rationes cogito, sanè quàm doleo, si laudem, ejus participem habere me neminem facilè patior. Quis & unde sim dubium

however different a nature. By your account, "we were in the utmost agitation at the news of the royal defence; and looked around for some hungry pedagogue, who would employ his venal pen in defence of parricide." This, in your unrivalled
5 malice, is what has been invented by you, from your recollecting that the royalists, when they looked around for a crier for their lies and their slander, applied to the grammarian Salmasius, who, if not hungry, was at least not a little thirsty of gold; who fairly sold them not merely his present work, but
10 his good intentions, if he ever had any, for the future—from your recollecting that Salmasius, his fame now wept over and gone, when he looked around for some one who should repair, at any rate, his abased and shattered reputation, by the just retribution of God, lighted upon you; who were now no
15 longer the minister of Geneva, from which place you were driven out, but the bishop of Lampsacus—in other words, Priapus from the garden, the defiler of his own house. Whence, loathing such tasteless bepraisings, purchased with so much dishonour, he became, from a friend, an irreconcil-
20 able enemy, and died with many a curse upon you his own eulogist.—"One John Milton, a great hero doubtless, was found, to be opposed to Salmasius." I did not know that I was a hero, though you, for ought I know, may be the son of some frail heroine; for you are one entire mass of corruption. That
25 I was the only one who was found to defend the cause of the people of England, if I consider the interests of the commonwealth, is a subject of real concern to me; if I consider the glory, it is not willingly that I suffer any one to share it with

ais esse. Tam olim erat dubium quis Homerus, quis Demos-
thenes. Equidem tacere diu, & posse non scribere, quod nunquam potuit Salmasius, didiceram; eáque in sinu gestabam
tacitus, quæ si tum proferre libuisset, æquè ac nunc, inclaruisse
5 jamdudum poteram: sed cunctantis famæ avidus non eram,
ne hæc quidem, nisi idoneâ datâ occasione, unquam prola-
turus; nihil laborans etsi alii me quæcunque nôssem scire
nesciebant; non enim famam sed oportunitatem cujusque rei
præstolabar; unde factum est, ut multò ante plurimis essem
10 notus, quàm Salmasius notus esset sibi; nunc Andremone
notior est caballo. *Homóne an vermis.* Equidem malim me
vermem esse, quod fatetur de se etiam rex Davides, quàm
tuum vermem in pectore nunquam moriturum intùs celare.
Aiunt, inquis, *hominem Cantabrigiensi Academiâ ob flagitia*
15 *pulsum, dedecus & patriam fugisse, & in Italiam commi-*
grasse. Vel hinc licebit conjicere quàm veraces illi fuerint, ex
quibus res nostras auditione accepisti; hîc enim & te & illos
impudentissimè mentiri & nôrunt omnes qui me nôrunt, &
statim ampliùs ostendam. Pulsus verò Cantabrigiâ, cur in
20 Italiam potiùs quàm in Galliam aut Hollandiam commigra-
rem? ubi tu tot flagitiis coopertus, Minister evangelii, non

me. Who and whence I am, say you, is doubtful. So also was
it doubtful, in ancient times, who Homer was, who Demos-
thenes. The truth is, I had learnt to be long silent, to be able to
forbear writing, which Salmasius never could; and carried
5 silently in my own breast what if I had chosen then, as well
as now, to bring forth, I could long since have gained a name.
But I was not eager for fame, who is slow of pace; indeed, if
the fit opportunity had not been given me, even these things
would never have seen the light; little concerned, though
10 others were ignorant that I knew what I did. It was not
the fame of every thing that I was waiting for, but the opportunity. Hence, it happened, that I was known to no small
number of persons, before Salmasius was known to himself;
now he is more known than the pack-horse Andremon.—
15 "Whether he is a man or a worm." In very truth, I had rather
be a worm, a confession which king David also makes of himself, than conceal within my breast that worm of yours that
shall never die.—You proceed—"It is said, that the man was
expelled from the university of Cambridge for his debauch-
20 eries, and that, flying from his disgrace and his country, he
shifted his quarters to Italy." It may be conjectured even from
this, what credit is due to those, from whom you received your
information of our affairs: for, that both you and they are
guilty of a most impudent falsehood, in this particular, is well
25 known to all who know me, and shall presently be shown
more at large. Now, after being expelled from Cambridge,
why should I shift my quarters to Italy, rather than to France
or Holland? where you, who are covered with debaucheries

modò impunè vivis, sed concionaris, sed sacra etiam mini-
steria, summo cum illius Ecclesiæ opprobrio, inquinatissimis
manibus conspurcas. Cur verò in Italiam, More? novus credo
Saturnus, ut alicubi laterem, in Latium scilicet profugi. Ve-
5 rùm ego Italiam, non, ut tu putas, facinorosorum latibulum
aut asylum, sed humanitatis potiùs, & civilium doctrinarum
omnium hospitium & noveram antea, & expertus sum. *Re-*
versus librum de divortiis conscripsit. Non aliud scripsi atque
ante me Bucerus de regno Christi copiosè, Fagius in Deutero-
10 nomium, Erasmus in Epistolam primam ad Corinthios deditâ
operâ in Anglorum gratiam, aliíque multi percelebres viri, in
commune bonum scripserunt. Quod in illis nemo reprehen-
dit, cur id mihi præ cæteris fraudi esset, non intelligo: vellem
hoc tantùm, sermone vernaculo me non scripsisse; non enim
15 in vernas lectores incidissem; quibus solemne est sua bona
ignorare, aliorum mala irridere. Téne verò, turpissime, de
divortiis obstrepere, qui cum Pontia ancilla tibi desponsata,
post stuprum eo obtentu illatum, immanissimum omnium
divortium fecisti? Et tamen erat illa Salmasii famula, An-
20 glica, ut fertur fœmina, regiis partibus apprimè dedita;
nempe hoc erat, sceleratè adamâsti ut rem regiam, reliquisti
ut rem publicam, cujus tamen conversionis, quam odisse adeo

out of number, and a minister of the gospel, not only live with
impunity, but preach; but, to the utter disgrace of that church,
defile with your filthy hands even the holy ministeries. Why
then to Italy, More? like another Saturn, I suppose, I fled to
5 Latium, to find a hiding place! But I fled to Italy, not, as you
imagine, as to the skulking corner, or the place of refuge to
the profligate, but because I knew, and had found before, that
it is the retreat of civility and of all polite learning.—"On his
return, he wrote his book on divorce." I wrote nothing more
10 than what Bucer before me wrote at large on the kingdom of
Christ, than what Fagius on Deuteronomy, Erasmus on the
first epistle to the Corinthians—works intended for the particular benefit of Englishmen—than what many other very
celebrated men have written for the good of mankind in gen-
15 eral. Why that should be charged upon me in particular as a
fault, which nobody finds fault with in them, I cannot comprehend. I could wish only that I had not written in the vernacular tongue; for I had not fallen upon vernacular readers,
with whom it is usual to be unconscious of their own good
20 fortune, and to ridicule the misfortune of others. And is it
for you, base seducer, to make a clamour about divorce, who
have been guilty of the most cruel of all divorces with Pontia,
the waiting maid, whom you engaged in marriage, and with
this lure debauched her? And yet this servant of Salmasius
25 was an Englishwoman, as it is said, attached the most warmly
to the royal party; in short, miscreant, you loved her as a royal
thing and left her as a public thing; but take care you are not
found to be the author of her conversion, the thought of which

vis videri, vide ne ipse author fueris; vide, inquam, ne sub-
versâ funditus dominatione Salmasianâ Pontiam ipse in rem
publicam converteris. Et hoc modo multas tu quidem una in
urbe res publicas, regius licet, aut fundasse diceris aut ab aliis
5 fundatas minister publicus administrare. Hæc tua sunt di-
vortia, seu mavis, diverticula, unde in me Curius prodiisti. Ad
mendacia nunc redis. *Cum de regis capite inter conjuratos*
ageretur, scripsit ad eos, & nutantes in malam partem im-
pulit. Ego vero neque ad eos scripsi, neque impellere attine-
10 bat, quibus id omnino agere, sine me, deliberatum jam erat:
verùm ea de re quid scripserim, infrâ dicetur, uti etiam de
Iconoclaste. Nunc quoniam iste, Hominem an dicam hæreo;
purgamentum potiùs hominis, ab ancillarum adulteriis ad
adulterandam omnem veritatem progressus, congestis in me
15 tot unâ serie mendaciis, apud exteros infamem reddere conatus est, peto ne quis rem secùs interpretetur, aut in invidiam
trahat, néve molestè ferat, si de me plura quàm vellem &
dixi suprà, & porrò dicam: ut si oculos à cæcitate, nomen ab
oblivione aut calumnia non possum, vitam tamen possim ab
20 ea saltem obscuritate quæ cum macula sit, in lucem vindicare.
Idque non unam ob causam mihi erit necessariò faciendum.
Primùm ut tot viros bonos atque doctos, qui per omnes vici-

you seem so unable to endure; take care, I say, lest by utterly
overturning Salmasia's sovereignty, you do not convert Pontia
into a republic. In this way, indeed, you are said to have
founded, though yourself a royalist, many republics in the
5 same city, or, to administer them, as public minister, after they
have been founded by others. Such are your divorces, or as you
would rather have it, your diversions, from which you have
come out against me, a very Curius.—You now return to your
lies. "When the decapitation of the king was agitated by the
10 conspirators, he wrote to them, while yet wavering, and urged
them to the horrid deed." Now I neither wrote to them, nor
was it possible that I should urge those, who had already resolved upon the thing, without even an intention of consulting me. But I shall speak of what I wrote upon that subject
15 hereafter, as also of the *Eikonoklastes*.

Since this man (though I am in doubt whether I should
call him a man, or merely the refuse of a man) from his corruption of maid-servants, has proceeded to corrupt all truth,
and by heaping upon me lies without number, has endeav-
20 oured to render my name infamous among foreigners, let me
intreat that I may not be misinterpreted, that I may not excite
ill-will, that I may not give offence, if I have spoken before,
and if I shall speak again more of myself than I could wish;
that, if I cannot rescue my eyes from blindness, my name from
25 oblivion or calumny, I may at least be able, in open day, to
redeem my life from that dimness which is produced by a
stain. This will be necessary for me on more accounts than
one. And first, that so many excellent and learned men,

nas gentes nostra jam legunt, deque me haud malè sentiunt, ne propter hujus maledicta mei pœniteat; verùm ita sibi persuadeant non eum esse me, qui honestam orationem inhonestis moribus, aut liberè dicta serviliter factis unquam dedecorârim; vitámque nostram Deo bene juvante, ab omni turpitudine ac flagitio remotam longè semper fuisse: deinde, ut quos laudandos mihi sumo viros illustres ac laude dignos, hi sciant nihil me pudendum magis existimare, quàm si ad eorum laudes vituperandus ipse ac nequam accederem; sciat denique populus Anglicanus, quem ut defenderem, meum sive fatum sive officium, sua virtus impulit, si vitam pudenter atque honestè semper egi, meam defensionem, nescio an honori aut ornamento, certè pudori aut dedecori nunquam sibi fore: qui igitur, & unde sim, nunc dicam. Londini sum natus, genere honesto, patre viro integerrimo, matre probatissimâ, & eleemosynis per viciniam potissimùm notà. Pater me puerulum humaniorum literarum studiis destinavit; quas ita avidè arripui, ut ab anno ætatis duodecimo vix unquam ante mediam noctem à lucubrationibus cubitum discederem; quæ prima oculorum pernicies fuit: quorum ad naturalem debilitatem accesserant & crebri capitis dolores; quæ omnia cùm discendi impetum non retardarent, & in ludo literario, & sub

throughout the neighbouring nations, who are now reading my writings and are disposed to think favourably of me, may not feel regret and shame on my account; but may be convinced, that I am not such a one, who has ever disgraced fair

5 words by foul deeds, or the language of a free man by the actions of a slave; and that my life, by God's help, has been ever far removed from all baseness and loose behaviour. Secondly, that those praise-worthy and illustrious men, whose eulogies I undertake to pronounce, may know it to be my

10 opinion, that there could be no greater cause for shame, while myself was vicious and deserving of reproof; in fine, that the people of England, to whose defence, whether it was my destiny or my duty, I was impelled by their own virtue, may know, that if I have ever led a life free from shame and dis-

15 honour, my defence (whether it may redound to their honour and ornament I know not) can certainly never prove to them a cause of shame or disgrace. Who, then, and whence I am I will now make known.

I was born at London, of respectable parents. My father

20 was a man of the highest integrity; my mother, an excellent woman, was particularly known throughout the neighbourhood for her charitable donations. My father destined me from a child for the pursuits of polite learning, which I prosecuted with such eagerness, that after I was twelve years old,

25 I rarely retired to bed from my lucubrations till midnight. This was the first thing which proved pernicious to my eyes, to the natural weakness of which were added frequent headaches. But as all this could not abate my instinctive ardour for

aliis domi magistris erudiendum quotidie curavit: ita variis
instructum linguis, & perceptâ haud leviter philosophiæ dul-
cedine, ad Gymnasium gentis alterum, Cantabrigiam misit:
Illîc disciplinis atque artibus tradi solitis septennium studui;
5 procul omni flagitio, bonis omnibus probatus, usquedum
Magistri, quem vocant, gradum, cum laude etiam adeptus,
non in Italiam, quod impurus ille comminiscitur, profugi, sed
sponte meâ domum me contuli, meíque etiam desiderium,
apud Collegii plerósque socios à quibus eram haud mediocriter
10 cultus, reliqui. Paterno rure, quo is transigendæ senectutis
causâ concesserat, evolvendis Græcis Latinísque scriptoribus
summum per otium totus vacavi; ita tamen ut nonnunquam,
rus urbe mutarem, aut coëmendorum gratiâ librorum, aut
novum quidpiam in Mathematicis, vel in Musicis, quibus tum
15 oblectabar, addiscendi. Exacto in hunc modum quinquennio,
post matris obitum, regiones exteras, & Italiam potissimùm,
videndi cupidus, exorato patre, uno cum famulo profectus
sum. Abeuntem, vir clarissimus Henricus Woottonus, qui ad
Venetos Orator Jacobi regis diu fuerat, & votis & præceptis,
20 eunti peregrè sanè utilissimis, eleganti epistolâ perscriptis, me
amicissimè prosequutus est. Commendatum ab aliis nobilis-

learning, he provided me, in addition to the ordinary instruc-
tions of the grammar school, masters to give me daily lessons
at home. Being thus instructed in various languages, and having gotten no slight taste of the sweetness of philosophy, he
5 sent me to Cambridge, one of our two national colleges. There,
aloof from all profligate conduct, and with the approbation of
all good men, I studied seven years, according to the usual
course of discipline and of scientific instruction—till I obtained, and with applause, the degree of master, as it is called;
10 when I fled not into Italy, as this foul miscreant falsely asserts,
but, of my own free will, returned home, leaving behind me
among most of the fellows of the college, who had shown me
no ordinary attention, even an affectionate regret. At my
father's country house, to which he had retired to pass the
15 remainder of his days, being perfectly at my ease, I gave myself up entirely to reading the Greek and Latin writers; ex-
changing, however, sometimes, the country for the town,
either for the purchase of books, or to learn something new
in mathematics, or in music, which at that time furnished the
20 sources of my amusement. After passing five years in this
way, I had the curiosity, after the death of my mother, to see
foreign countries, and above all, Italy; and having obtained
permission of my father, I set out, attended by one servant. On
my departure, I was treated in the most friendly manner by
25 Sir Henry Wotton, who was long ambassador from king James
to Venice, and who not only followed me with his good
wishes, but communicated, in an elegant letter, some maxims
of the greatest use to one who is going abroad. From the rec-

simus vir Thomas Scudamorus vicecomes Slegonensis, Caroli regis Legatus, Parisiis humanissimè accepit; méque Hu-
goni Grotio viro eruditissimo, ab Regina Suecorum tunc temporis ad Galliæ regem Legato, quem invisere cupiebam, suo
5 nomine, & suorum uno atque altero deducente, commendavit: discedenti post dies aliquot Italiam versùs, literas ad mercatores Anglos, quà iter eram facturus, dedit, ut quibus possent officiis mihi præstò essent. Nicæâ solvens, Genuam perveni; mox Liburnum & Pisas, inde Florentiam. Illa in urbe,
10 quam præ cæteris propter elegantiam cum linguæ tum inge-
niorum semper colui, ad duos circiter menses substiti; illic
multorum & nobilium sanè & doctorum hominum familia-
ritatem statim contraxi; quorum etiam privatas academias,
(qui mos illic, cum ad literas humaniores, tum ad amicitias
15 conservandas laudatissimus est) assiduè frequentavi. Tui
enim Jacobe Gaddi, Carole Dati, Frescobalde, Cultelline,
Bonmatthæi, Clementille, Francine, aliorúmque plurium
memoriam, apud me semper gratam atque jucundam, nulla
dies delebit. Florentiâ Senas, inde Romam profectus, post-
20 quam illius urbis antiquitas & prisca fama me ad bimestre
ferè spatium tenuisset (ubi & Luca Holstenio, aliísque viris
cum doctis tum ingeniosis, sum usus humanissimis) Nea-
polim perrexi: Illìc per Eremitam quendam, quîcum Româ
iter feceram, ad Joannem Baptistam Mansum, Marchionem
25 Villensem, virum nobilissimum atque gravissimum, (ad

ommendation of others, I was received at Paris with the utmost courtesy, by the noble Thomas Scudamore, Viscount of Sligo, who of his own accord introduced me, accompanied by several of his suite, to the learned Hugo Grotius, at that time
5 ambassador from the queen of Sweden to the king of France, and whom I was very desirous of seeing. On my setting out for Italy some days after, he gave me letters to the English merchants on my route, that they might be ready to do me any service in their power. Taking ship at Nice, I arrived at
10 Genoa; and soon after at Leghorn and Pisa, thence to Florence. In this last city, which I have always valued above the rest for the elegance of its dialect and of its genius, I continued about two months. Here I soon contracted a familiar acquaintance with many persons eminent for their rank and learning,
15 and regularly frequented also their private academies—an institution which deserves the highest commendation, as calculated to preserve at once polite letters and friendly intercourse: for, the pleasing, the delightful recollection I still retain of you Jacobo Gaddi, of you Carolo Dati, Frescobaldi,
20 Coltellino, Bonmatthei, Clementillo, Francini, and many others, no time will efface. From Florence I pursued my route to Sienna, and then to Rome; and having been detained about two months in this city by its antiquities and ancient renown, (where I enjoyed the accomplished society of Lucas Holsten-
25 ius and of many other learned and superior men) I proceeded to Naples. Here I was introduced by a certain hermit, with whom I had travelled from Rome, to John Baptista Manso, Marquis of Villa, a man of the first rank and authority, to

quem Torquatus Tassus insignis poeta Italus de amicitia
scripsit) sum introductus; eodémque usus, quamdiu illic fui,
sanè amicissimo; qui & ipse me per urbis loca & Proregis
aulam circumduxit, & visendi gratiâ haud semel ipse ad
5 hospitium venit: discedenti seriò excusavit se, tametsi multò
plura detulisse mihi officia maximè cupiebat, non potuisse illa
in urbe, propterea quòd nolebam in religione esse tectior. In
Siciliam quoque & Græciam trajicere volentem me, tristis ex
Anglia belli civilis nuntius revocavit: turpe enim existima-
10 bam, dum mei cives domi de libertate dimicarent, me animi
causâ otiosè peregrinari. Romam autem reversurum, mone-
bant Mercatores se didicisse per literas parari mihi ab Jesuitis
Anglis insidias, si Romam reverterem; eò quod de religione
nimis liberè loquutus essem. Sis enim mecum statueram, de
15 religione quidem iis in locis sermones ultro non inferre; inter-
rogatus de fide, quicquid essem passurus, nihil dissimulare.
Romam itaque nihilo minùs redii: quid essem, si quis inter-
rogabat, neminem celavi; si quis adoriebatur, in ipsa urbe
Pontificis, alteros prope duos menses, orthodoxam religionem,
20 ut antea, liberrimè tuebar: Deóque sic volente, incolumis
Florentiam rursus perveni; haud minùs mei cupientes revi-
sens, ac si in patriam revertissem. Illic totidem, quot priùs,

whom the illustrious Italian poet, Torquato Tasso, addressed
his book on friendship. By him I was treated, while I stayed
there, with all the warmth of friendship: for he conducted me
himself over the city and the viceregent's court, and more
5 than once came to visit me at my own lodgings. On my leaving Naples, he gravely apologized for showing me no more
attention, alleging that although it was what he wished above
all things, it was not in his power in that city, because I had
not thought proper to be more guarded on the point of re-
10 ligion. As I was preparing to pass over also into Sicily and
Greece, I was restrained by the melancholy tidings from England of the civil war: for I thought it base, that I should be
travelling at my ease, even for the improvement of my mind
abroad, while my fellow-citizens were fighting for their lib-
15 erty at home. As I was about to return to Rome, the merchants gave me an intimation, that they had learnt from their
letters, that, in case of my revisiting Rome, the English Jesuits
had laid a plot for me, because I had spoken too freely on the
subject of religion: for I had laid it down as a rule for myself,
20 never to begin a conversation on religion in those parts; but
if interrogated concerning my faith, whatever might be the
consequence, to dissemble nothing. I therefore returned notwithstanding to Rome; I concealed from no one, who asked
the question, what I was; if any one attacked me, I defended
25 in the most open manner, as before, the orthodox faith, for
nearly two months more, in the city even of the sovereign
pontiff himself. By the will of God, I arrived safe again at
Florence; revisiting those who longed no less to see me, than

menses libenter commoratus, nisi quod ad paucos dies Lucam
excucurri, transcenso Apennino, per Bononiam & Ferraram,
Venetias contendi. Cui urbi lustrandæ cum mensem unum
impendissem, & libros, quos per Italiam conquisiveram, in
5 navem imponendos curâssem, per Veronam ac Mediolanum,
& Pæninas Alpes, Lacu denique Lemanno, Genevam delatus
sum. Quæ urbs, cùm in mentem mihi hinc veniat Mori ca-
lumniatoris, facit ut Deum hìc rursus testem invocem, me his
omnibus in locis, ubi tam multa licent, ab omni flagitio ac
10 probro integrum atque intactum vixisse, illud perpetuò cogi-
tantem, si hominum latere oculos possem, Dei certè non
posse. Genevæ cum Joanne Deodato, Theologiæ professore
doctissimo, quotidianus versabar. Deinde eodem itinere, quo
priùs, per Galliam, post annum & tres plus minus menses in
15 patriam revertor; eodem ferme tempore quo Carolus, cum
Scotis, ruptâ pace, bellum alterum quod vocant Episcopale,
redintegrabat; in quo fusis primo congressu regiis copiis, cùm
videret etiam omnes Anglos, & meritò quidem, in se pessimè
animatos, malo coactus, non sponte, Parlamentum haud ita
20 multò post, convocavit. Ipse, sicubi possem, tam rebus tur-
batis & fluctuantibus, locum consistendi circumspiciens, mihi
librísque meis, sat amplam in urbe domum conduxi; ibi ad
intermissa studia beatulus me recepi; rerum exitu Deo im-

if I had returned to my own country. There I willingly stopped as many months as before, except that I made an excursion for a few days to Lucca; when, crossing the Apennine, I made the best of my way, through Bononia and Ferrara, to Venice.

5 Having spent a month in getting a survey of this city, and seen the books shipped which I had collected in Italy, I was brought, by way of Verona, Milan, and the Pænine Alps, and along the lake Lemano, to Geneva. This city, as it brings to my recollection the slanderer More, makes me again call God

10 to witness, that, in all these places where so much licence is given, I lived free and untouched of all defilement and profligate behaviour, having it ever in my thought, that if I could escape the eyes of men, I certainly could not escape the eyes of God. At Geneva I had daily intercourse with John Deodati,

15 the very learned professor of divinity. Then, by the same route as before, I returned through France, to my own country, after an absence of a year and about three months. I arrived nearly at the time that Charles, breaking the pacification, renewed the war, called the episcopal war, with the Scots, in which the

20 royal forces were routed in the first engagement; and Charles, now finding the whole English nation enraged, and justly, to the last degree against him, not long after called a parliament; though not by his own will, but as compelled by his necessities. Looking about me for some place in which I

25 might take up my abode, if any was to be found in this troubled and fluctuating state of affairs, I hired, for me and my books, a sufficiently spacious house in the city. Here I returned with no little delight to my interrupted studies; leav-

primis, & quibus id muneris populus dabat, facilè permisso.
Interea Parlamento rem strenuè gerente, Episcoporum fastus
detumuit. Ut primùm loquendi saltem cæpta est libertas con-
cedi, omnia in Episcopos aperiri ora; alii de ipsorum vitiis,
5 alii de ipsius ordinis vitio conqueri; iniquum esse, se solos ab
ecclesiis omnibus, quotquot reformatæ sunt, discrepare; exemplo fratrum, sed maximè ex verbo Dei, gubernari Ecclesiam
convenire. Ad hæc sanè experrectus, cùm veram affectari
viam ad libertatem cernerem, ab his initiis, his passibus, ad
10 liberandam servitute vitam omnem mortalium, rectissimè
procedi, si ab religione disciplina orta, ad mores & instituta
reipublicæ emanaret, cùm etiam me ita ab adolescentia parâs-
sem, ut quid divini, quid humani esset juris, ante omnia possem non ignorare, méque consuluissem ecquando ullius usus
15 essem futurus, si nunc patriæ, immo verò ecclesiæ tótque fra-
tribus evangelii causâ, periculo sese objicientibus deessem,
statui, etsi tunc alia quædam meditabar, huc omne ingenium,
omnes industriæ vires transferre. Primùm itaque de refor-
manda ecclesia Anglicana, duos ad amicum quendam libros
20 conscripsi: deinde, cum duo præ cæteris magni nominis Episcopi suum jus contra Ministros quosdam primarios assere-

ing without difficulty, the issue of things more especially to God, and to those to whom the people had assigned that department of duty. Meanwhile, as the parliament acted with great vigour, the pride of the bishops began to lose its swell. No

5 sooner did liberty of speech begin to be allowed, than every mouth was open against the bishops. Some complained of their personal vices, others of the vice of the order itself. It was wrong, they said, that they alone should differ from all other reformed churches; that it was expedient the church

10 should be governed by the example of the brethren, and above all by the word of God. I became perfectly awake to these things; and perceiving that men were in the right way to liberty; that, if discipline originating in religion continued its course to the morals and institutions of the commonwealth,

15 they were proceeding in a direct line from such beginnings, from such steps, to the deliverance of the whole life of mortal man from slavery—moreover, as I had endeavoured from my youth, before all things, not to be ignorant of what was law, whether divine or human; as I had considered, whether I

20 could ever be of use, should I now be wanting to my country, to the church, and to such multitudes of the brethren who were exposing themselves to danger for the gospel's sake—I resolved, though my thoughts were then employed upon other subjects, to transfer to these the whole force of my mind and

25 industry. Accordingly, I first wrote *Of the Reformation of the English Church,* in two books, to a friend. Next, as there were two bishops of reputation above the rest, who maintained their own cause against certain leading ministers; and

rent, ratus de iis rebus, quas amore solo veritatis, & ex officii
Christiani ratione didiceram haud pejùs me dicturum quàm
qui de suo quæstu & injustissimo dominatu contendebant, ad
hunc libris duobus, quorum unus de Episcopatu prælatico,
5 alter de ratione Disciplinæ ecclesiasticæ inscribitur, ad illum,
scriptis quibusdam animadversionibus, & mox Apologiâ, respondi; & ministris facundiam hominis, ut ferebatur ægrè
sustinentibus, suppetias tuli; & ab eo tempore, si quid postea
responderent, interfui. Cùm petiti omnium telis Episcopi
10 tandem cecidissent, otiúmque ab illis esset, verti aliò cogi-
tationes; si qua in re possem libertatis veræ ac solidæ rationem
promovere; quæ non forìs, sed intus quærenda, non pugnando,
sed vitam rectè instituendo, rectéque administrando adipiscen-
da potissimùm est. Cùm itaque tres omnino animadverterem
15 libertatis esse species, quæ nisi adsint, vita ulla transigi com-
modè vix possit, Ecclesiasticam, domesticam seu privatam, atque civilem, déque prima jam scripsissem, déque tertia Magistratum sedulò agere viderem, quæ reliqua secunda erat, domesticam mihi desumpsi; ea quoque tripartita, cùm videretur
20 esse, si res conjugalis, si liberorum institutio rectè se haberet, si
denique liberè philosophandi potestas esset, de conjugio non

as I had the persuasion, that on a subject which I had studied
solely for the love of truth and from a regard to Christian duty,
I should not write worse than those who contended for their
own lucre and most iniquitous domination; to one of them I
5 replied in two books, of which one was entitled *Of Prelatical
Episcopacy,* the other *Of the Reason of Church Government;*
to the other, in some *Animadversions,* and soon after, in an
Apology; and thus, as was said, brought timely succour to
those ministers, who had some difficulty in maintaining their
10 ground against the bishops' eloquence: from this time too, I
held myself ready, should they thenceforward make any reply. When the bishops, at whom every man aimed his arrow,
had at length fallen, and we were now at leisure, as far as they
were concerned, I began to turn my thoughts to other subjects;
15 to consider in what way I could contribute to the progress of
real and substantial liberty; which is to be sought for not from
without, but within, and is to be obtained principally not by
fighting, but by the just regulation and by the proper conduct
of life. Reflecting, therefore, that there are in all three species
20 of liberty, without which it is scarcely possible to pass any life
with comfort, namely, ecclesiastical, domestic or private, and
civil; that I had already written on the first species, and saw
the magistrate diligently employed about the third, I undertook the domestic, which was the one that remained. But as
25 this also appeared to be three-fold, namely, whether the affair
of marriage was rightly managed; whether the education of
children was properly conducted; whether, lastly, we were to
be allowed freedom of opinion—I explained my sentiments

solùm ritè contrahendo, verùm etiam, si necesse esset, dissol-
vendo, quid sentirem explicui; ídque ex divina lege, quam
Christus non sustulit, nedum aliam, totâ lege Mosaïcâ graviorem civiliter sanxit; quid item de excepta solùm fornicatione
5 sentiendum sit, & meam aliorúmque sententiam exprompsi, &
clarissimus vir Seldenus noster, in Uxore Hebræâ plùs minùs
biennio pòst editâ, uberiùs demonstrâvit. Frustrà enim libertatem in comitiis & foro crepat, qui domi servitutem viro indig-
nissimam, inferiori etiam servit; ea igitur de re aliquot libros
10 edidi; eo præsertim tempore cùm vir sæpè & conjux hostes inter
se acerrimi, hic domi cum liberis, illa in castris hostium mater-
familias versaretur, viro cædem atque perniciem minitans.
Institutionem deinde liberorum uno opusculo breviùs quidem
tractabam; sed quod satis arbitrabar iis fore, qui ad eam rem,
15 quâ par esset diligentiâ, incumberent; quâ quidem re, nihil
ad imbuendas, unde vera atque interna oritur libertas, virtute
hominum mentes, nihil ad rempublicam bene gerendam, &
quam diutissimè conservandam majus momentum potest af-
ferre. Postremò de typographia liberanda, ne veri & falsi

not only on the proper mode of contracting marriage, but also
of dissolving it, should that be found necessary: and this I did
according to the divine law which Christ has never abrogated;
and much less has he given a civil sanction to any other, that
5 should be of higher authority than the whole law of Moses.
In like manner I delivered my own opinion and the opinion
of others concerning what was to be thought of the single exception of fornication—a question which has been also co-
piously elucidated by our celebrated Selden, in his *Hebrew*
10 *Wife,* published some two years after. Again, it is to little
purpose for him to make a noise about liberty in the legislative
assemblies, and in the courts of justice, who is in bondage to an
inferior at home,—a species of bondage of all others the most
degrading to a man. On this point, therefore, I published
15 some books, and at that particular time, when man and wife
were often the fiercest enemies, he being at home with his
children, while she, the mother of the family, was in the camp
of the enemy, threatening slaughter and destruction to her
husband. I next treated, in one little work, of the education of
20 children, briefly it is true, but at sufficient length, I conceived,
for those, who apply themselves to the subject with all that
earnestness and diligence which it demands—a subject than
which there can be none of greater moment to imbue the
minds of men with virtue, from which springs that true lib-
25 erty which is felt within; none for the wise administration of
a commonwealth, and for giving it its utmost possible duration. Lastly, I wrote, after the model of a regular speech,
Areopagitica, on the liberty of printing, that the determina-

arbitrium, quid edendum, quid premendum, penès paucos
esset, eósque ferè indoctos, & vulgaris judicii homines, librorum inspectioni præpositos, per quos nemini ferè quicquam
quod supra vulgus sapiat, in lucem emittere, aut licet aut libet,
5 ad justæ orationis modum Areopagiticam scripsi. Civilem,
quæ postrema species restabat, non attigeram; quam Magi-
stratui satis curæ esse cernebam: neque de jure regio quicquam à me scriptum est, donec Rex hostis à Senatu judicatus,
bellóque victus, causam captivus apud Judices diceret, capi-
10 tísque damnatus est: Tum verò tandem, cùm Presbyteriani
quidam Ministri, Carolo priùs infestissimi, nunc Independentium partes suis anteferri, & in Senatu plus posse indignantes, Parlamenti sententiæ de Rege latæ, (non facto irati,
sed quod ipsorum factio non fecisset) reclamitarent, & quan-
15 tum in ipsis erat, tumultuarentur, ausi affirmare Protestan-
tium doctrinam, omnésque ecclesias reformatas ab ejusmodi
in reges atroci sententiâ abhorrere, ratus falsitati tam apertæ
palàm eundum obviàm esse, ne tum quidem de Carolo quicquam scripsi aut suasi, sed quid in genere contra tyrannos
20 liceret, adductis haud paucis summorum Theologorum testimoniis, ostendi; & insignem hominum meliora profitentium,

tion of true and false, of what ought to be published and what
suppressed, might not be in the hands of the few who may
be charged with the inspection of books, men commonly
without learning and of vulgar judgment, and by whose
5 licence and pleasure, no one is suffered to publish any thing
which may be above vulgar apprehension. The civil species of
liberty, the last which remained, I had not touched, as I per-
ceived it drew sufficient attention from the magistrate. Nor
did I write any thing on the right of kings, till the king, pro-
10 nounced an enemy by the parliament, and vanquished in war,
was arraigned as a captive before judges, and condemned to
lose his head. But, when certain presbyterian ministers, at first
the bitterest foes to Charles, unable to endure that the inde-
pendent party should now be preferred to them, and that
15 it should have greater influence in the senate, began to
clamour against the sentence which the parliament had pro-
nounced upon the king (though in no wise angry at the deed,
but only that themselves had not the execution of it) and tried
to their utmost to raise a tumult, having the assurance to
20 affirm that the doctrine of protestants, that all the reformed
churches shrunk with horror from the atrocity of such a sentence against kings—then indeed, I thought it behoved me
openly to oppose so barefaced a falsehood. Yet even then, I
neither wrote nor advised any thing concerning Charles; but
25 simply showed, in general, what may be lawfully done against
tyrants; adducing, in confirmation, the authorities of no small
number of the most eminent divines; inveighing, at the same
time, almost with the zeal of a preacher against the egregious

sive ignorantiam sive impudentiam propè concionabundus
incessi. Liber iste non nisi post mortem Regis prodiit, ad com-
ponendos potiùs hominum animos factus, quàm ad statuen-
dum de Carolo quicquam quod non meâ, sed Magistratuum
5 intererat, & peractum jam tum erat. Hanc intra privatos pari-
etes meam operam nunc ecclesiæ, nunc reipublicæ gratìs dedi;
mihi vicissim vel hæc vel illa præter incolumitatem nihil; bonam certè conscientiam, bonam apud bonos existimationem,
& honestam hanc dicendi libertatem facta ipsa reddidere:
10 commoda alii, alii honores gratìs ad se trahebant: me nemo
ambientem, nemo per amicos quicquam petentem, curiæ fo-
ribus affixum petitorio vultu, aut minorum conventuum vesti-
bulis hærentem nemo me unquam vidit; domi fere me con-
tinebam, meis ipse facultatibus, tametsi hoc civili tumultu
15 magna ex parte sæpe detentis, & censum ferè iniquiùs mihi
impositum, & vitam utcunque frugi tolerabam. His rebus
confectis, cùm jam abundè otii existimarem mihi futurum,
ad historiam gentis, ab ultima origine repetitam, ad hæc
usque tempora, si possem, perpetuo filo deducendam me con-
20 verti: quatuor jam libros absolveram, cum ecce nihil tale cogi-
tantem me, Caroli regno in rempublicam redacto, Concilium

ignorance or impudence of those men, who had promised
better things. This book was not published till after the death
of the king, being intended rather to compose the minds of
men, than to settle any thing relating to Charles; that being
5 the business of the magistrates instead of mine, and which,
at the time I speak of, had been already done. These services
of mine, which were performed within private walls, I gratu-
itously bestowed at one time upon the church, at another,
upon the commonwealth; while neither the commonwealth
10 nor the church bestowed upon me in return any thing beyond
security. It is true, that I gained a good conscience, a fair
repute among good men, and that the deeds themselves rendered this freedom of speech honorable to me. Some men
however gained advantages, others honours, for doing noth-
15 ing; but no man ever saw me canvassing for preferment, no
man ever saw me in quest of any thing through the medium
of friends, fixed, with supplicatory look to the doors of the
parliament, or clung to the vestibules of lower assemblies. I
kept myself commonly at home, and supported myself, how-
20 ever frugally, upon my own fortune, though, in this civil
broil, a great part was often detained, and an assessment
rather disproportionate, imposed upon me. Having dispatched
these things, and thinking that, for the future, I should now
have abundance of leisure, I undertook a history of the nation
25 from its remotest origin; intending to bring it down, if I
could, in one unbroken thread to our own times. I had already finished four books, when lo! (Charles's kingdom being reduced to a commonwealth) the council of state, as it

Statûs, quod dicitur, tum primùm authoritate Parlamenti constitutum, ad se vocat, meâque operâ ad res præsertim externas uti voluit. Prodiit haud multò post attributus Regi liber, contra Parlamentum invidiosissimè sane scriptus: huic
5 respondere jussus, Iconi Iconoclasten opposui; non *regiis manibus insultans,* ut insimulor, sed reginam veritatem regi Carolo anteponendam arbitratus; immo cum præviderem hanc calumniam cuivis maledico in promptu fore, ipso exordio, & sæpe aliàs, quoad licuit, à me istam invidiam sum
10 amolitus. Prodiit deinde Salmasius; cui quis responderet, adeò non diu, quod ait Morus, dispiciebant, ut me in concilio tum etiam præsentem statim omnes ultro nominarent. Hactenus ad obturandum os tuum, More, & mendacia redarguenda bonorum maximè virorum in gratiam, qui me aliàs
15 non nôrint, meî rationem reddidi. Tu igitur, More, tibi dico immunde, φιμώθητι, obmutesce inquam; quo enim magis mihi maledixeris, eo me rationes meas uberiùs explicare coëgeris; ex quo aliud lucrari nihil poteris, quàm ut tibi mendaciorum opprobrium adhuc gravius concilies, mihi ad integ-
20 ritatis commendationem eo latiùs viam aperias. Reprehenderam ego Salmasium, quòd extraneum se & alienigenam rebus nostris immiscuisset: Tu instas, *ad eos qui ad Angliam non pertinent, hanc defensionem maximè pertinere.* Quid

is called, now first constituted by authority of parliament, invited me to lend them my services in the department more particularly of foreign affairs—an event which had never entered my thoughts! Not long after, the book which was 5 attributed to the king made its appearance, written certainly with the bitterest malice against the parliament. Being ordered to prepare an answer to it, I opposed the *Iconoclast* to the *Icon;* not, as is pretended, "in insult to the departed spirit of the king," but in the persuasion, that queen truth ought 10 to be preferred to king Charles; and as I foresaw that some reviler would be ready with this slander, I endeavoured in the introduction, and in other places as far as it was proper, to ward off the reproach. Next came forward Salmasius; and no long time, as More reports, was lost in looking about for 15 some person to answer him, so that all, of their own accord, instantly nominated me, who was then present in the council. —It is chiefly, More, for the sake of those good men, who have otherwise no knowledge of me, that, to stop your mouth and to confound your lies, I have so far given an account of 20 myself. I tell you, then, foul priest, hold your peace, I say: for the more you revile me, the more fully will you compel me to explain my own conduct; from which you could gain nothing yourself, but the reproach, already too heavy, of being a liar; and would lay open for me a still wider field for the 25 commendation of my own integrity.

I had censured Salmasius, as being of another country, and of foreign extraction, for intermeddling with our affairs. You insist, "that this defence concerns those most, who have no

enim? *possint,* inquis, *Angli existimari studio partium acriùs agere; Gallos verò consentaneum est rei, non hominum, rationem habuisse.* Ad hæc eadem quæ priùs regero; externum & longinquum, qualis tu es, in alienas res præsertim turbatas, immersurum se neminem nisi corruptum; Salmasium prius demonstravi mercede conductum; te constat per Salmasium & Arausionenses professoriam cathedram petiisse; deinde, quod fædius est, exagitas Parlamentum, & subagitas Pontiam. Quam autem affers rationem, cur hæc ad exteros potius pertinerent, deridicula prorsus est; si enim Angli partium studiis feruntur, quid vos aliud, qui illos solos sequimini, quàm eorum affectus duntaxat in vos transfertis? adeò ut, si Anglis illis credendum in sua causa non est, vobis profectò sit multò minus; qui rerum nostrarum nihil intelligitis, aut saltem creditis, nisi quas ab ipsis accepistis quibus, vestrâ quoque sententiâ, vix est credendum. Hìc rursum effundis te in laudem magni Salmasii: magnus sanè tibi fuit, quem tu quasi pro lenone habuisti ancillæ suæ; laudas tamen; at is te non laudat, immo ante mortem palàm est abominatus, séque ipse millies incusavit, quòd Spanhemio gravissimo Theologo, de te, quàm

concern with England." And why? "Englishmen (you say) may be supposed to be strongly actuated by the spirit of faction; whereas, it is likely, that the French took more account of the thing, than of the men." To this I make the same re-

5 tort as before; that no man, who is a foreigner and at a great distance, like yourself, will embroil himself with the affairs of another country, especially when those affairs are in a state of distraction, unless he is corrupted. I have before shown that Salmasius was bribed; it appears that yourself, through the

10 medium of Salmasius and of the Orange faction, made interest for a professorial chair; and what is still worse, you are next falling foul of the parliament, while you are playing foul with Pontia. But the reason you give why these things rather concerned foreigners is perfectly ridiculous: for if the English

15 are carried away by party feelings, what is it that you, who follow them exclusively, transfer to yourselves, if not their passions only? Hence, if those Englishmen are not to be believed in their own cause, surely much less are you to be believed, who know nothing of our affairs, or at least believe nothing, but

20 what you have received from these very persons, and who, even in your own judgment, are scarcely worthy of credit.— Here again you break out in encomiums upon the great Salmasius. To you he was great indeed, you having employed him as a sort of pimp to procure his servant girl. You praise

25 him nevertheless; but he praises not you; nay, before his death it was well known that he held you in abomination, and reproached himself a thousand times for not giving credit to that venerable divine Spanheim, who warned him of your impiety.

impius esses, non credidisset. Nunc totus in rabiem versus rationi quasi renuntias; *Jamdudum rationi* scilicet *defunctus est Salmasius.* Tu clamandi tantum & furendi partes tibi deposcis, & tamen primas in maledicendo etiam tribuis Sal-

5 masio; *non quia verbis sævit, sed quia Salmasius.* Ὦ σπερμο-λόγε! has nempe argutias morigeranti debemus Pontiæ. Hinc clamor tuus argutari atque etiam minurizare didicit; hinc minitabundus quoque, *experiemini,* inquis, *aliquando, fædissimæ belluæ, quid styli potuerint.* Téne experiemur, ancil-

10 lariole, téne mœche, aut stylum tuum, ancillis tantummòdo metuendum? cui si quis raphanum aut mugilem solùm intenderit, actum mehercule præclarè tecum putes, si nate non fissa & incolumi stylo isto salaci tuo queas aufugere. *Equidem non adeo sum,* inquis, *vacui capitis ut provinciam à Salmasio*

15 *susceptam aggrediar:* quam ille quidem sine capite admodum vacuo, nunquam aggressus fuisset; festivè tu quidem vacuitate capitis magnum Salmasium tibi anteponis. *At regii sanguinis clamorem ad cœlum tollere* quod *ineruditi* etiam *debent:* hoc nempe tuum esse ais. Clama, vociferare, boa; perge hypo-

20 critari, sancta verba usurpare, & Priapeïa vivere: Exurget, mihi crede, aliquando quem inclamas toties ultionum Deus,

—Now you have worked yourself up into a fury, as if bidding adieu to reason: "Salmasius," it seems "has been dead long ago in reason"; you ask for yourself the part only of crying and raving; and yet you give the first in reviling also to

5 Salmasius; "not because he is outrageous in his language, but because he is Salmasius." Babbler! for these smart things I suppose we are indebted to the more-bearing Pontia. It is hence your cry has learnt to be witty, as well as to lament in whining tone; it is hence also, in your bullying way, you

10 thus threaten us: "The time shall come, ye foul beasts, when ye shall be made to feel what the style can do." Shall we be made to feel you, maid-hunting miscreant—shall we be made to feel you, lecher, or your style, which is formidable only to maid-servants? When, if any one should only show

15 you a radish-root or a mullet, by Hercules, you would think yourself well off, to escape without having your breech cut in sunder, and without the loss of that salacious style of yours.— "Indeed (you remark) my head is not so empty as to attempt a task which had been undertaken by Salmasius": a task,

20 however, which he had never undertaken, unless his head had been deplorably empty. It is truly amusing, for you to rank the great Salmasius before yourself in emptiness of head.— "To raise the cry of the royal blood to heaven," "it being the duty" even "of the illiterate"—you mean, I suppose, is your

25 duty. Cry, vociferate, bellow; go on to play the hypocrite, to have words of sanctity in your mouth, to live in the worship of Priapus! Be assured, the time shall come, when the God of vengeance, to whom you so often cry, shall arise; he shall

exurget, téque imprimis eradicabit, diaboli ministrum, &
reformatæ ecclesiæ infandum dedecus & luem. Inculpantibus
Salmasii maledicentiam quamplurimis, respondes, *Sic cum
parricidis monstrorum omnium turpissimis, fuisse agendum.*
5 Laudo; telis enim nos instruis: & quo te pacto, tuósque perdu-
elles tractari conveniat, commodus doces, nósque ipse ab-
solvis. Nunc quando ratione nihil potes, ne audes quidem
occupatum ab Salmasio jus omne regium, & quicquid est in
eo rationis causatus, à contumeliis & rabie ad narrationes
10 quasdam miserabiles conversus, expers rationis, institutos ab
initio clamores tantùm persequeris: quas partim Salmasianas
recoxisti, partim ex elencho illo ἐλεγχίστῳ anonymo, qui
non patriâ solùm, sed nomine etiam profugit, descriptas inter-
polâsti: quarum ad præcipua capita, vel in Iconoclaste, vel in
15 Salmasianis ita jam respondi, ut citra modum Historiæ, re-
sponderi ampliùs posse non putem. Sempérne ego ut iden-
tidem eandem orbitam teram, & ad Balatronis cujusque stri-
dorem dicta toties cogar iterare? non faciam; neque meâ sic
abutar vel operâ vel otio. Si quis conductitios ejulatus, &
20 compositos vænalissimi hominis ploratus, si quis declama-
tiunculas, quas etiam ancillaris concubitus adulterinas eduxit

arise, and it shall be his first care to root out you, minister of
the devil! the unutterable disgrace and pest of the reformed
church. To the multitudes who condemn the abuse of Salmasius, you reply,—"It is thus that parricides, of all monsters
5 the most abominable, deserve to be treated." I commend you;
for you furnish us with weapons; and instruct us opportunely
in what way it is proper that yourself as well as your adversaries should be dealt with; at the same time that you absolve
us from blame. Finding you can do nothing with reason,
10 afraid to venture upon the general ground of the right of
kings, which had been pre-occupied by Salmasius, and having alleged every thing that has relation to reason to be found
in him, you now tack about from contumely and fury to some
wretched narratives, though being destitute of any rational
15 purpose, you merely continue the same clamour with which
you set out. These narratives you have partly dressed up from
Salmasius, and partly copied from that anonymous and most
refutable view, the author of which has forsaken not his country only, but his name; to their chief points having already
20 replied at sufficient length, either in *Eikonoklastes,* or in
my answer to Salmasius, I cannot, I think, well say more,
at lesser length than a regular history. Shall I for ever be
compelled, every now and then, to tread the same round,
and, at the noise of every low fellow, to repeat what I have so
25 often said before? I will not do it; I will not make so ill a use
either of my labour or of my time. If any one thinks these mer-
cenary cries, these ready-made lamentations of a hireling
mourner, these contemptible speechifyings, the spurious

& spurias, Morilli nothi gemellas, fide satis locupletes arbi-
tratur esse, ad me quod attinet, nihil quidem moror, quo
minùs ita existimet; neque enim est ut ab ejusmodi credulo ac
temerario metuendum nobis quicquam sit: attingam tamen
5 pauca, multorum instar, ex quibus tam quis ipse, quàm quid
dicat, & quid de reliquo judicandum sit, summatim intelli-
getis. Postquam de camera plebis & camera procerum, ad
unam redigenda, multa exoticus deblateravit, (quod postu-
latum nemo sanus reprehenderet) *ut æqualitate,* inquit, *in*
10 *rempublicam invectâ, ad eandem in ecclesiam introducendam*
procederetur; tunc enim adhuc stabant episcopi: hic nisi sit
purus putus Anabaptismus, nihil video. Quis hoc à Theologo
& ministro Gallico sperâsset unquam? sanè qui Anabaptismus
quid sit, nisi hoc sit, non videt, eum ego crediderim haud ma-
15 gìs videre quid sit Baptismus. Sed si res propriis vocabulis
appellare malimus, æqualitas in republica non est Anabaptismus, sed Democratia longè antiquior; in ecclesia præsertim constituta, est disciplina Apostolica. At enim *stabant*
episcopi. Fatemur, stabant & Genevæ; cum illa civitas &
20 episcopum & eundem legitimum principem religionis causâ
expulit; quod illis laudi, cur id nobis probro ducitur? scio

progeny of concubinage with a waiting maid, and born at a litter with the little bastard More—if any one thinks these things of sufficient account to be believed, I, for my own part, shall make no attempt to hinder him from thinking so still;
5 indeed, from any one so credulous and thoughtless, I can in truth have nothing to fear. I will touch, however, upon a few things, which will answer the purpose of many, from which you will learn in a few words of what description the author is, as well as what he says; and likewise what is to be thought
10 of the rest.

    This alien having talked a good deal of nonsense about the reduction of the Lords and Commons to a single house (a demand which no man in his senses would blame) remarks, "that, having established equality in the state, they might pro-
15 ceed to introduce the same into the church: for at the time I speak of, the bishops yet remained: if this be not rank ana-baptism, I do not see what is." Who could ever have expected this from a divine and a minister of the Gallic church? He who sees not what anabaptism is, unless this be it, I should
20 really think can see as little what baptism is. But, if we would call things by their right names, equality in the state is not anabaptism, but democracy, a thing far more ancient; and as established in the church, is the discipline of the apostles. But "the bishops remained." Granted; they remained too at
25 Geneva, when that city expelled, on account of religion, its bishop, who was at the same time its legitimate prince. Why should that be considered as disgraceful in us, which in them was regarded as honourable? I am not at a loss, More, to

quid tibi vis, More, Genevensium suffragia ultum is; quibus dimissus cum ignominia, an ejectus ex illa ecclesia fueris, in dubio est. Te ergo cum Salmasio tuo ab evangelico hoc instituto descivisse, & ad episcopos transfugisse, si modò refert quo tu transfugeris, apparet. *Deinde ad ministrorum,* inquis, *nostratium æqualitatem respublica transiit, ut palàm sit eundem spiritum tunc viguisse qui octavo demum anno nefando regis parricidio rem peregit.* Ergo idem ut videtur spiritus & ministros constituit vestrates, & parricidium peregit: Perge ut occepisti, quas par est apostatam, eructare insanias. *Non plures,* inquis, *tribus libellis supplicibus confecerunt, qui in regem animadverti postulabant.* Quod notum est, & ipse memini, falsissimum esse. Sanè qui has res apud nos memoriæ mandarunt, non tres tantummodo libellos istiusmodi, sed multos ex diversis Angliæ provinciis, exercitúsque legionibus unius ferè mensis spatio, tres uno die allatos fuisse memorant. Vides quanta cum gravitate hac de re deliberaverit Senatus, cujus cunctationem Populus lenitatis nimiæ suspectam tot supplicibus libellis eximendam putavit. Quot reris millia hominum fuisse idem sentientium, qui Senatum ad id hortari, quod jam tum seriò agitabat, vel importunum existimarent

know what you would be at; you would revenge the votes of
the Genevese, by which it is yet a question, whether you were
dismissed with ignominy, or ejected from the Genevese
church. That you, therefore, as well as Salmasius, are become
5 a renegado from this evangelical institution, and are gone over
to the bishops, (if it be of any consequence whither you go) is
manifest.—"Then the state passed (you say) to the equality
of the ministers of our persuasion: for it is known to every
body, that the same spirit then prevailed, which at last, in the
10 eighth year, put an end to the business by the atrocious parricide of the king." It appears, then, that the same spirit by
which the ministers of your persuasion were constituted, also
executed the parricide. Go on as you have begun, to belch out
your ravings, which comport well with an apostate.

15   "There were only three petitions (you say) which demanded punishment on the king": which is well known, and
which I myself remember, to be utterly false. Indeed, those
among us who have charged their memories with these circumstances, remember not three petitions only of this kind,
20 but many from different counties of England; and that, for
the space of nearly a month, three a day were presented by the
regiments of the army. You see what grave deliberation the
parliament must have bestowed upon this subject, when
the people, suspecting them of excess of lenity, thought it
25 right, by their numerous petitions, to put an end to their lin-
gering. How many thousands were there, do you suppose,
who were unanimous in thinking it officious or superfluous
to urge the parliament to a measure, which was then under

vel supervacaneum? quorum ex numero & ipse fui, qui tamen quid voluerim obscurum non est. Quid si conticuissent
omnes rei magnitudine perculsi, eóne minùs habuisset Senatus in re tanta quod statueret, expectandúsne populi nutus
5 erat, ex quo tantorum exitus consiliorum penderet? enimverò
supremum gentis Concilium, ab universo populo ea mente
adhibitum, ut impotentem regis dominatum coerceret, postea-
quam efferatum & repugnantem bello cepisset, si recurrere
ad jussa populi deberet, velit jubeátne de captivo hoste suppli-
10 cium sumi, profectò qui rempublicam fortissimè recuperas-
sent, quid aliud fecisse viderentur quàm in laqueos tyranni à
populo, si fors ita ferret, absoluti sese præcipites dedisse? aut
si acceptâ maximis de rebus decernendi summâ potestate, de
iis quæ præsertim vulgi captum superant, non dico ad popu-
15 lum (nam cum hac potestate ipsi populus jam sunt) sed ad
multitudinem rursus referre cogerentur quæ imperitiæ suæ
conscia ad eos prius omnia retulerat, quis ultro citróque refe-
rendi finis esset? quis tandem in hoc Euripo consistendi locus?
quod firmamentum inter libellos istiusmodi tot capitum levis-
20 simorum, quæ salus quassatis rebus hominum foret? quid si

their serious consideration? Of this number I myself was one, though what was my wish it is not hard to divine. What if all men had been silent, in amazement at the magnitude of the thing? Would the senate have been more at a loss how to 5 decide in so great a matter? Was the nod of the people to be waited for, on which to hang the issue of counsels so important? In truth, if the supreme council of the nation, which is employed by the whole body of the people as a check upon the wild domination of the king, after having made the king a 10 prisoner of war, he being found in open violence and resistance, were obliged to recur to the commands of the people, and to ask their orders to punish a captive enemy—what else would those men, who with so much courage had rescued the commonwealth, have appeared, in fact, to have done, but, 15 with the countenance of the people, if they had haply obtained it, to have rashly thrown themselves into the toils of the tyrant? Or if, after having accepted the sovereign power to decide on things of the highest moment, on things especially which are above the capacity of the vulgar, they had been 20 compelled again to refer, I do not say to the people, (for though invested with this power, they are themselves still the people) but to the multitude, who, from feeling their own ignorance, had before referred every thing to them—what would have been the end of this referring forward and back- 25 ward? In fine, what resting place had there been in this Euripus? Amidst these petitions proceeding from so many fantastical heads, what settlement, what safety could there have been for the shaken fabric of society? What if they had de-

restituendum regno Carolum postulassent? cujusmodi libellos
extitisse aliquot non supplices sed minaces fatendum est sedi-
tiosorum hominum, quorum nunc odium, nunc miseratio
æquè stulta aut malitiosa esse solebat; horúmne ratio habenda
5 fuit? qui *ut cum Rege colloquium institueretur, ingenti,* inquis, *numero pagis relictis ad Parlamenti fores accurrebant;
quorum Senatores, immisso milite, plurimos trucidarunt.* Et
Surrienses dicis paganos, qui nescio aliorum è malitia, agrestes
ipsi, an suâ improbitate impulsi, cum libello supplice bene
10 poti, & comessabundi potiùs, quam aliquid petituri, per urbem ibant; mox curiæ fores facto agmine ferociter obsederunt;
collocatos ibi milites stationibus deturbârunt, unum ad ipsas
curiæ fores occiderunt, priusquam illos vel dicto vel facto
quisquam lacessisset: inde meritò pulsi ac malè multati, haud
15 ultra duos trésve occisi, vinolentiam potiùs quàm *libertatem
spirantes.* Passim concedis *potiores fuisse Independentium
partes, non numero, sed consilio & virtute militari.* Unde ego
& jure & merito superiores quoque fuisse contendo: nihil
enim est naturæ convenientius, nihil justius, nihil humano
20 generi utilius aut melius, quàm ut minor majori, non nu-

manded that Charles should be restored to the kingdom?
That there were some petitions of this description, not however, of a petitionary but of a menacing nature, must be confessed, from seditious persons, whose hatred one while, and
5 whose complaining another, was, for the most part, equally
absurd and malicious: and were such to obtain notice? who
according to your account, "to procure a conference with the
king, left their villages and flocked to the doors of the parliament house in great numbers; of whom very many were
10 cruelly murdered by the military, who were admitted by the
members." You mention also the country people of Surrey—
mere peasants, who, whether instigated by the malice of others, or by their own licentious inclinations, I am not informed,
paraded through the city with a petition, being in a state of
15 intoxication, and more prepared for carousing than for peti-
tioning. Soon, in a body they beset the doors of the parlia-
ment-house in a riotous manner; turned the soldiers who were
stationed there from their posts; killed one at the very parliament doors, without having received the slightest provocation
20 by word or deed; and "breathing" drunkenness rather than
"liberty," they were very properly driven thence and roughly
handled, though not more than two or three of them were
killed.—You every where concede that "the Independents
were the most powerful, not in number, but in counsel and mil-
25 itary virtue." And I contend, that they were hence also justly
and deservedly superior: for there is nothing more agreeable
to nature, nothing more just; nothing more useful or more for
the interest of man, than that the less should yield to the

merus numero, sed virtus virtuti, consilium consilio cedat;
qui prudentiâ, qui rerum usu, industriâ, atque virtute pollent,
hi meâ quidem sententiâ, quantumvis pauci, quantovis numero, plures erunt, & suffragiis ubique potiores. Multa spar-
5 sim inseris de *Cromuello,* quæ cujusmodi sint infra videbimus; de reliquis responsum jampridem Salmasio est. Judicium quoque Regis non prætermittis, quamvis & illud à
magno tuo rhetore miserabiliter sit declamatum. Proceres,
id est, Regis purpuratos, & ministros ferè aulicos, à judicando
10 Rege ais abhorruisse: Nos id parùm referre, altero libro
ostendimus. *Deinde curiarum judices erasos; quippe qui re-*
sponderant esse contra Angliæ leges, Regem judicio sisti.
Nescio quid tunc responderint, scio quid jam approbent atque
defendant: non est novum, Judices, quos minimè decet, me-
15 ticulosos esse. *Præficitur ergo sordidæ & sceleratæ curiæ, par*
Præses, obscurissimus & petulantissimus nebulo. Te verò
tot vitiis & sceleribus obstrictum, immo meram spurcitiem,
merum scelus, usque adeo obduxisse menti & sensibus callum,
nisi tua mens potiùs tota callus est, ut in Deum atheus, & sac-
20 rorum contaminator, in homines inhumanus, cujusque optimi

greater; not number to number, but virtue to virtue, and counsel to counsel. Those who excel in prudence, in their experience in business, in industry and virtue, will, in my opinion, however few, prove to be the majority, and will prevail
5 more in the suffrages of mankind than any number, however great.

You intersperse a good many things about Cromwell, and of what description we shall see hereafter. As to the rest, we have long since replied to them as urged by Salmasius. You do
10 not forget also the judgment passed upon the king, notwithstanding this has been pitifully declaimed over by your great rhetorician. The nobles (you say) that is, the king's courtiers, and courtly ministers, as most of them were, shrunk with horror from judging the king. That this is of little weight, we
15 have shown in another work.—"Next, the judges of the courts were struck out: for they when appealed to had returned for answer, that it was contrary to the laws of England, that the king should be put upon his trial." I know not what they then answered; but I know what they now approve and defend. It
20 is no new thing for judges to be timorous, though in them of all men it is the least becoming.—"For this despicable and accursed court there was chosen a suitable president—an obscure and insolent scoundrel." Now for you who have been guilty of so much impurity and wickedness—for you
25 who are nothing but one mass of foulness and of crimes, to have brought such a callus upon your mind and senses (if your mind be not rather one entire callosity) as towards God to be an atheist and a defiler of the sacred rites, towards man a

calumniator esse ausis, quid aliud est esse quàm germanum
Iscariotam atque diabolum? Quamvis autem tua vituperatio
laus summa sit, tamen præstantissimo viro cui oblatras, nec
non amico mihi semper plurimùm colendo, nequaquam
5 deero; quo minus ab improbissimis perfugarum & Mororum
linguis, quas nisi causâ reipublicæ nunquam sensisset, vin-
dicem. Est *Joannes Bradscianus* (quod nomen libertas ipsa,
quacunque gentium colitur, memoriæ sempiternæ celebran-
dum commendavit,) nobili familiâ, ut satis notum est, ortus;
10 unde patriis legibus addiscendis, primam omnem ætatem
sedulò impendit; dein consultissimus causarum ac disertissi-
mus patronus, libertatis & populi vindex acerrimus, & magnis
reipublicæ negotiis est adhibitus, & incorrupti Judicis munere
aliquoties perfunctus: Tandem uti Regis judicio præsidere
15 vellet, à Senatu rogatus, provinciam sanè periculosissimam
non recusavit. Attulerat enim ad legum scientiam ingenium
liberale, animum excelsum, mores integros ac nemini ob-
noxios; unde illud munus omni prope exemplo majus ac for-
midabilius, tot Sicariorum pugionibus ac minis petitus, ita
20 constanter, ita graviter, tanta animi cum præsentia ac dignitate gessit atque implevit, ut ad hoc ipsum opus, quod jam
olim Deus edendum in hoc populo mirabili providentiâ decre-

savage, a calumniator of the undertakings of every man of eminent character,—what is it but to be near of kin to Iscariot and to the devil? But though your censure is the highest praise, yet, far be it from me to be so wanting to that pre-
5 eminent personage, at whom you are barking, and who is a friend of my own, of all others, the most deserving of my reverence, as not to defend him from the audacious tongues of the fugitives and the Mores, which but for the commonwealth he never had felt.

10 John Bradshaw (a name which liberty herself, wherever she is respected, has commended for celebration to everlasting memory) was sprung, as is well known, from a noble family; and hence, spent the early part of his life in the diligent study of the laws of his country. Becoming afterwards a skil-
15 ful and eloquent pleader, a zealous defender of liberty and of the people, he was admitted to the higher offices in the state, and several times discharged the function of an incorrupt judge. At length, on a request from the parliament that he would preside on the trial of the king, he refused not the dan-
20 gerous office: for to skill in the law, he added a liberal mind, a lofty spirit, with manners unimpeached, and beholden to no man. This office, therefore, which was great and fearful almost surpassing all example, marked out as he was by the daggers and threats of so many ruffians, he executed and filled
25 with such steadiness, such gravity, with such dignity and presence of mind, that he seemed destined and created by the deity himself for this particular act—an act which God in his stupendous providence had pre-ordained should be exhibited

verat, ab ipso Numine designatus atque factus videretur;
& Tyrannicidarum omnium gloriam tantum superaverit,
quantò est humanius, quantò justius, ac majestate plenius,
Tyrannum judicare, quàm injudicatum occidere. Alioqui
5 nec tristis, nec severus, sed comis ac placidus, personam tamen quam suscepit tantam, æqualis ubique sibi, ac veluti
consul non unius anni, pari gravitate sustinet, ut non de tri-
bunali tantùm, sed per omnem vitam judicare Regem diceres.
In consiliis ac laboribus publicis maximè omnium indefessus,
10 multísque par unus; domi, si quis alius, pro suis facultatibus
hospitalis ac splendidus, amicus longè fidelissimus, atque in
omni fortuna certissimus, bene merentes quoscunque nemo
citiùs aut libentiùs agnoscit, neque majore benevolentiâ pro-
sequitur; nunc pios, nunc doctos, aut quavis ingenii laude
15 cognitos, nunc militares etiam & fortes viros ad inopiam re-
dactos suis opibus sublevat; iis si non indigent, colit tamen
libens atque amplectitur; alienas laudes perpetuò prædicare,
suas tacere solitus; hostium quoque civilium si quis ad sani-
tatem rediit, quod experti sunt plurimi, nemo ignoscentior.
20 Quod si causa oppressi cujuspiam defendenda palam, si gratia
aut vis potentiorum oppugnanda, si in quenquam bene meritum, ingratitudo publica objurganda sit, tum quidem in illo
viro, vel facundiam vel constantiam nemo desideret, non

among this people—and he so far surpassed the glory of all
tyrannicides, as it is more humane, more just, more full of
majesty, to try a tyrant, than to put him to death without trial.
He was otherwise neither gloomy nor severe, but mild and
5 gentle. Yet, at all times equal to himself—the consul, as it
were, not of a single year—he supported the high character
which he took upon him with a becoming gravity; so that you
would think him sitting in judgment upon the king, not on
the tribunal only, but every moment of his life. He is above
10 all men indefatigable in counsel, and in exertions for the public—he alone is equal to a host. At home, he is, according to
his means, hospitable and splendid; the most faithful of
friends, and, in every change of fortune, the most to be relied
upon. No one sooner or more willingly discovers merit, wher-
15 ever it is to be seen, or acts towards it with greater favour. At
one time he aids the pious, at another the learned, or men
known for any species of skill; now he relieves, from his private fortune, brave men of the military profession who have
been reduced to want; and if they are not in want, he yet re-
20 ceives them with a willing courtesy, a friendly welcome. It
is his constant practice to proclaim the praises of others, and
to conceal his own: and among his political enemies, if any
has happened to return to his right senses, which has been the
case with many, no man has been more ready to forgive. But
25 if the cause of the oppressed is to be openly defended; if the
favour and the power of the mighty is to be resisted; if the
public ingratitude against any meritorious character is to be
reproved; then indeed, no one could find in this man any

patronum, non amicum, vel idoneum magis & intrepidum,
vel disertiorem alium quisquam sibi optet; habet, quem non
minæ dimovere recto, non metus aut munera proposito bono
atque officio, vultúsque ac mentis firmissimo statu dejicere
5 valeant. Quibus virtutibus, & plerisque meritò charus, &
inimicissimis non contemnendus, gestarum egregiè rerum in
republica laudem, dirupto te, More, tuíque similibus, apud
omnes tum exteros tum posteros, in omne ævum propagabit.
Sed pergendum, Rex capite damnatus est: *contra hanc vesa-*
10 *niam Londini pulpita fere omnia detonare.* Ligneo isto to-
nitru haud multum terres; istos Salmoneas nihil veremur, qui
fictitium illud fulmen & arrogatum sibi, aliquando luent;
graves profectò authores & synceri, qui paulò ante ex iisdem
pulpitis contra Pluralistas & Nonresidentes strepitu æquè
15 horribili detonabant; paulò post, raptis hic sibi ternis, ille
quaternis Prælatorum sacerdotiis, quos tonando abegerant,
atque inde nonresidentes necessariò facti, eodem ipsi crimine
tenebantur in quod detonabant, & sui quisque tonitrus biden-
tal factus est: neque ullus adhuc pudor; nunc in vendicandis
20 sibi decimis toti sunt; & sanè si decimarum tanta sitis est,

want of eloquence or of firmness; no one could even desire an advocate, or a friend, more able, more intrepid, more eloquent: for he has found one, whom no threats can turn aside from rectitude, whom neither intimidation nor bribes can
5 bend from his duty and virtuous purpose, can move from an unshaken steadiness of mind and of countenance. By these virtues, he has made himself deservedly dear to most men, and not to be despised by his greatest enemies. And when you, More, and those who are like you, shall be utterly confounded,
10 he shall spread the renown of his country's noble deeds among all foreign nations, and with posterity to the end of time.

But we must proceed. The king was condemned to lose his head. "Against this outrage, almost all the pulpits in London began to thunder." You will not fright us much with this
15 wooden thunder; we are nothing afraid of these Salmoneuses; the time will come when they will suffer for this counterfeit thunder, which they have had the presumption to wield. Now these are authorities truly grave and sincere, when but a little before, and from the very same pulpits, they thundered
20 with a noise equally horrific against pluralists and non-residents; and soon after, one seizing upon three, another upon four, to his own share, of the benefices of the prelates, whom with their thundering they had driven out, and thus of necessity becoming non-residents themselves, they were guilty of
25 the same crime as that against which they thundered; so that each was struck with the lightning which proceeded from his own thunderclap. Nor do they yet feel any shame. Now they are struggling tooth and nail in defence of tithes; and if their

censeo affatim decimandos: non terræ fructus tantùm, sed &
maris fluctus sibi habeant decumanos. Iidem primò bellum
suadebant in Regem, ut in hostem exitio devotum; mox capto
hosti, & imputatæ à semetipsis toties cædis ac sanguinis effusi
5 damnato, parci volebant utpote regi. Ita in pulpitis tanquam
in taberna quadam meritoria, quæ volunt mercimonia, quæ
volunt scruta, vendunt popello; & quod miserius est, quæ jam
vendidere, quoties volunt reposcunt. At *Scoti regem sibi reddi*
flagitabant, commemorant Senatus promissa quando Anglis
10 *regem tradiderant.* Atqui ego vel Scotos etiam fatentes habeo,
nulla omnino promissa publica intercessisse, cùm rex tradere-
tur; & turpe sanè fuisset Anglis, regem suum à Scotis in
Anglia conductitiis, reddendum non fuisse nisi per condi-
tiones: quid? quod ipsa Parlamenti responsio ad Scotorum
15 cartulas Id. Mart. 1647. edita, ullam hac de re interpositam
ab se fidem, quo pacto rex tractandus esset, dilucidè negat; indignum quippe censuisse, non nisi eâ lege sua jura obtineri à
Scotis potuisse. Attamen *regem reddi sibi flagitabant.* Mites,

thirst of tithes is so great, why I would let them have tithes
enough in all conscience; they should have not the tenth only
of the fruits of the earth, but the tenth waves of the sea. The
same persons were the first to advise war against the king, as
5 against an enemy devoted to destruction: by and by, when we
had gotten the enemy into our hands—an enemy who had
been so often condemned by themselves as the cause of the
slaughter and bloodshed, they would spare him forsooth as
being a king. Thus, in their pulpits, as if in a tradesman's
10 shop, they sell whatever wares, whatever trumpery they
please, to the poor, silly people; and what is worse, they re-
claim what they have sold as often as they think proper.—
Again—"The Scots earnestly demanded that the king should
be set at liberty; they mention the promises of the parliament
15 after they had delivered up the king to the English." Now I
can prove from the confession of the Scots themselves, that
there were no public promises at all, when the king was delivered up; and disgraceful indeed had it been to the English,
if their own king was not to be given up by the Scots, who
20 were mercenaries in the pay of England, unless on conditions:
nay, the very answer itself of the parliament to the stipula-
tions of the Scots, which answer was made public on the 15th
of March 1647, clearly denies that any assurance had been
given as to the point, how the king was to be treated. Indeed,
25 the parliament thought it a disparagement of their dignity,
that they should be unable to obtain their right of the Scots,
but on such a condition.—But "they earnestly demanded that
the king should be set at liberty." The gentle souls began no

credo, homines frangebantur animo, desiderium sui regis
ferre diutius non poterant: immoverò iidem illi, cum ab initio
horum in Britannia motuum, de jure regio haud semel in
Parlamento retulissent, essétque ab omnibus assensum, ob tres
5 maximas causas regem privari regno posse, si tyrannus existat,
si fundum regium alienet, si suos deserat, circa annum 1645.
Parlamento Perthæ habito sententias rogare cæperunt, sitnè
rex quem sanctis infestum esse constet, communione ecclesiæ
interdicendus? verum antequam ea de re quicquam decer-
10 neretur, Montrossius ad eam urbem cum copiis accedens conventum disturbavit. Iidem in suo quodam ad Cromuellum
Imperatorem responso, an. 1650. fatentur punitum jure
regem, juris tantummodo formam fuisse vitiosam, eo quòd
ipsi in illius judicii consortium non vocarentur. Hoc ergo
15 facinus sine illis atrox, cum illis egregium fuisset, ex eorum
quippe nutu fas atque nefas pendebat, justum atque injustum
definiendum erat: quid isti, obsecro, rege sibi reddito lenius
in eum statuissent? At *Delegati Scotici à Senatu Anglico responsum hoc prius tulerant, nolle se regni Anglicani formam*

doubt to relent; they could no longer bear the yearning of their spirits towards their king: and yet, from the beginning of these commotions in Britain, these same men had more than once brought forward a motion in parliament on the subject
5 of the right of kingship, and had unanimously resolved, about the year 1645, that there were three main reasons for which a king may be deprived of his kingdom—his proving to be a tyrant, his alienation of the royal demesnes, and his desertion of his people. In the parliament held at Perth, they proceeded
10 to collect the sentiments of the house on the question, whether a king, who was plainly an enemy to the saints, might not be interdicted from the communion of the church? But before they came to any determination on this point, the assembly was thrown into confusion by the approach of Montrose to
15 that city at the head of his forces. The same men, in their answer to general Cromwell, in the year 1650, acknowledge that the king was justly punished; that the form only of the trial was reprehensible, and because themselves were not invited to act a part in it. This transaction, then, having taken
20 place without them, is atrocious; if themselves had had a share in it, it would then have been glorious; as if right and wrong depended upon their nod, and just and unjust must be defined agreeably to their dictate. Suppose the king had been set at liberty, would themselves, let me ask, have been more lenient
25 in their resolutions respecting him?—But "the Scottish delegates had received for answer before from the parliament of England—that it was not their intention to alter the form of the English government; though they afterwards answered,

immutare, postea tamen respondere se tunc noluisse, nunc
velle, prout salus reipublicæ postularet. Et rectè quidem re-
sponderunt: quid tu hinc? *hæc stropha,* inquis, *omnia fœdera,*
commercium, ipsumque sensum communem evertit. Tuum
5 quidem evertit, qui nescis inter libera promissa, & pactam
fæderis fidem quid intersit: Angli de forma reipublicæ suæ
futura, cujus rationem Scotis reddere necesse non erat, quod
tum ipsis videbatur, liberè quidem respondent; nunc salus
reipublicæ aliud suadebat; si fidem, si jusjurandum populo
10 datum violare nollent. Utrum sanctiùs obligare putas, libe-
rúmne de forma reipublicæ futura datum Scoticis legatis responsum, an necessarium de salute reipublicæ procuranda datum suo populo jusjurandum & summam fidem? Licere
autem Parlamento vel Senatui, prout expedit, consilia mutare,
15 quoniam quicquid nos affirmamus, anabaptisticum tibi est &
monstrosum, malo ex Cicerone audias pro Plancio. Stare
omnes debemus tanquam in orbe aliquo reipublicæ; qui quoniam versetur, eam deligere partem debemus, ad quam nos
illius utilitas salúsque converterit. Et statim. Neque enim in-
20 constantis puto, sententiam, tanquam aliquod navigium atque
cursum, ex reipublicæ tempestate moderari. Ego verò hæc

that they had no intention at that time; but that now they had such an intention, as the safety of the state required it." And they answered well. But what is your remark upon this? "This subterfuge, you say, overturns all treaties, intercourse,
5 and common sense itself." It overturns your common sense, it seems, since you know not the difference between an unconditional promise, and the obligation of a treaty. Concerning the form of the future government, a view of which it was unnecessary to present to the Scots, the English gave a frank
10 reply, according to the best of their judgment at the time. Now, the safety of the state calls for different measures, if they would not forfeit their faith and solemn oath to the people. Which do you imagine to be of the most sacred obligation, an unconditional promise given the Scottish commissioners con-
15 cerning the future form of the government, or an oath originating in necessity, and an assurance of the most solemn kind given their own countrymen, that they would provide for the safety of the state? But that a parliament or senate is at liberty, according to expediency, to change its counsels, I would have
20 you learn, since every affirmation of ours is, in your eyes, anabaptistical and monstrous, from Cicero's oration for Plancius. "We should all take our stand as it were in some circle of the commonwealth; and since this circle turns round, we should make choice of that particular point of it, to which we may
25 be directed by its advantage and safety." He proceeds to say that he does not consider it any mark of inconstancy, for a man to regulate his opinion, as if a sort of ship and a ship's course, by the political atmosphere. "Indeed, I have learnt, I

didici, hæc vidi, hæc scripta legi, hæc de sapientissimis &
clarissimis viris & in hac republica, & in aliis civitatibus monumenta nobis literæ prodiderunt, non semper easdem sententias, ab iisdem, sed quascunque Reipublicæ status, inclinatio
5 temporum, ratio concordiæ postularet, esse defendendas. Hæc
Marcus Tullius: sed tu More Hortensium mavis; hæc illæ
ætates quæ civili maximè prudentiâ floruerunt; quæ si sequun-
tur anabaptistæ, meâ quidem sententiâ sapiunt. Quàm multa
alia possem proferre, quæ à ministerculis hisce & suo Salmasio,
10 si res non verba spectemus, planè indocto, pro anabaptisticis
damnantur. At *nihilo,* inquis, *plus potuerant potentissimi
Belgii fœderati ordines, qui per oratores suos & prece & pretio oblato strenuè allaborarunt sacrum Regis caput redimere.*
Velle profectò justitiam sic redimere, idem erat atque regem
15 salvum nolle: verùm didicerunt, non omnes esse mercatores;
non adeò vendacem esse Senatum Anglicanum. Quod autem
ad judicium regis, *ut plurima,* inquis, *Christo similia Carolus
pateretur, milites in eum ingeminant ludibria.* Plura quidem
passus est similia Christus maleficis, quàm Carolus Christo;
20 & multa istiusmodi jactabantur vulgò ab iis quibus ad invidiam facti majorem excitandam, quidvis fingere aut fictum
referre studium erat: Fac tamen gregarios milites insolentiùs

have observed, I have read—the writings of the wisest and
most illustrious men in this republic and in other states have
recorded for our use, that the same men are not always bound
to defend the same opinions, but such as may be required by
5 the state of the nation, the bent of the times, and by a regard
to union." Thus Marcus Tullius; but you, More, would prefer
Hortensius. Such are the maxims of those ages, which flourished most in civil prudence—maxims, which, if the anabap-
tists follow, they are in my judgment, wise. How many more
10 could I produce, which, by these trashy ministers and their
Salmasius, a man absolutely without learning, if we consider
things rather than words, are condemned as anabaptistical!—
Again, you say, "the most potent, the united states of Holland
could do no more: for they struggled hard, through the me-
15 dium of their ambassadors, both by entreaty and rewards, to
ransom the sacred head of the king." Now to wish thus to
bribe justice, was the same thing as not to wish that the king
might be saved. But they have found, that all men are not
merchants; that the parliament of England is not so eager to
20 sell.—Upon the sentence of the king you remark, "In how
many respects did Charles, in his sufferings, resemble Christ!
the soldiers made their incessant mocks at him." In truth,
Christ resembled malefactors in his sufferings more than
Charles resembled Christ; and many things of this sort were
25 every where bandied about by those who, on account of this
act, made it their business to stir up the greater malice, to in-
vent all manner of falsehood, and to retail what they found
invented to their hands. But suppose the common soldiers did

se gessisse; non id continuò in causam est conferendum. *Mac-*
tatum vero esse quempiam ad pedes regis prætereuntis, appre-
cantem ut Deus ejus misereretur, nec antea audivi unquam,
nec convenire quenquam adhuc potui qui audivisset: quin
5 immo tribunum ipsum, qui toto illius judicii tempore custo-
diis præfuit, regísque à latere vix discessit, interrogandum hac
de re curavi: is denique nec audisse se hoc antea, & pro certo
scire falsissimum id esse, constanter asseverabat. Ex quo intelligi potest tuarum narrationum fides, etiam in reliquis quàm
10 firma sit. Nam in benevolentia quoque & adoratione, si posses, Carolo post mortem procuranda, quàm in odio nobis vel
iniquissimè conflando haud multo veracior invenieris. *Audi-*
tum ais *fuisse Regem in fatali pegmate episcopo Londinensi*
ingeminantem, memento, memento. Id regis Judices anxios
15 nempe habuit, quid illa ultimum iterata vox sibi voluisset;
accersitur, ut ais, episcopus, & illud geminum *memento* quid
sibi quæsivisset, additis minis, enuntiare jubetur. Is primò,
(sic enim fingi expediebat) ex composito nimirum delicias
fecit; &, quasi arcanum quoddam, prodere recusavit. Cum
20 illi vehementiùs instarent, id quasi metu sibi expressum, &
nolenti extortum, ægrè tandem edidit, quod re vera quovis

behave with insolence; it does not immediately follow, that
this is to be placed to the account of the cause. "That some man
was actually murdered at the feet of the king, as he was passing
along, for praying that God would have mercy on him," is
5 what I never heard before; nor could I ever yet meet with any
one who had heard it: nay, I caused an inquiry to be made, as
to this matter, of the colonel who commanded the guards
during the whole time of the execution, and who scarcely
moved a step from the king's side; and he positively affirmed
10 that he had never heard this before, and that he knew for certain that it was wholly without foundation. From this we may
learn what credit is due to your narratives; nay, what foundation there is for credit even in the other parts of your work: for
in soliciting for favour and even for adoration, if you can ob-
15 tain it, for Charles after his death, you will be found to have
paid not much more regard to truth, than in your iniquitous
attempts to kindle hatred against us.—"The king (you say)
on the fatal scaffold, was heard to say twice to the bishop of
London, remember! remember!" This, to be sure, made the
20 king's judges anxious to know, to what last request this word,
thus repeated, could have reference; and the bishop was sent
for, as you report, and ordered, with threats, to declare what
this reiterated "remember" meant. He, it seems, was at first
squeamish, as had been pre-concerted (for a fiction of this
25 sort was expedient) and refused to disclose it, as if it had been
some great secret. But upon their becoming more urgent with
him, he at length, with much ado, made known, but in such
a manner as if it had been wrested from him by intimidation

pretio divulgatum vellet; *Jusserat me,* inquiens, *rex, ut si possem ad filium pervenire, hoc supremum morientis patris mandatum ad eum perferrem, ut regno & potestati suæ restitutus, vobis suæ necis authoribus ignosceret: hoc me me-*
5 *minisse, rex iterum atque iterum jussit.* O magis, regémne dicam pietatis, an episcopum rimarum plenum! qui rem tam secretò in pegmate suæ fidei commissam ut effutiret tam facilè expugnari potuit. At ô taciturne! jampridem Carolus hoc idem inter alia præcepta filio mandaverat, in illa Icone Ba-
10 silica; quem librum ideo scriptum satis apparet, ut omni cum diligentia nobis vel invitis secretum illud, qua ostentatione simulatum erat, eâdem paulo pòst evulgaretur. Sed video planè decrevisse vos Carolum quendam absolutissimum, si non Stuartum hunc, at saltem hyperboreum aliquem & fabu-
15 losum, fucatis quibuslibet coloribus depictum, imperitis rerum obtrudere: ita fabellam hanc velut acroama quoddam, diverbiis & sententiolis pulchrè distinctum, nescio quem ethologum imitatus, ad inescandas vulgi aures putidè concinnasti. Ego verò, ut non negaverim interrogatum fortasse obiter ab uno
20 vel altero consessorum hac de re episcopum, ita accersitum, deditâ operâ vel à concilio vel ab illo judicum collegio, quasi

and against his will, what in reality, he would have had di-
vulged at any price. "The king (said he) ordered me, if I
could ever get to his son, to carry him this last command of a
dying father, that, should he ever be restored to his kingdom
5 and his power, he would pardon you the authors of his death:
this is what the king charged me again and again to remember." Shall I say now, that the king was the more pious, or
that the bishop was the more leaky, when he could so easily be
won upon, to blab a thing entrusted to him with so much
10 secrecy on the scaffold! But O miracle of taciturnity! Charles
had long ago entrusted this very same thing to his son, among
other precepts, in the *Icon Basilike;* which book, it sufficiently
appears, was written, for the express purpose of divulging to
us a little after, with all diligence, even against our wish, that
15 secret, and with the same parade with which it had been
counterfeited. But I see plainly that you are determined
to impose upon the inexperienced, if not this Stuart, at least
some Charles Stuart who is the mirror of all excellence,
some hyperborean and fabulous Charles, whom you draw
20 in whatever false colours may happen to hit your fancy. Thus
you have fantastically got up this fable, as if for scenic repre-
sentation, bravely embellished, after what mimic I know
not, with dialogue and pithy sentences, as baits for vulgar
ears. Now I do not mean to deny that the bishop might have
25 been incidentally questioned, as to this point, by some one
or another of the commissioners; but I do not find that he was
sent for, that either the council or that body of judges paid
any particular attention to it, as if they had been at all appre-

id omnes curassent, aut sollicitè quæsivissent non comperio.
Sed demus inde quæ vis: dederit in pegmate suprema hæc
episcopo mandata, ut suæ necis authoribus ignosceretur, per-
ferenda ad filium Carolus: quid tam egregium aut singulare
5 præter cæteros eò loci deductos fecit? quotusquisque est mo-
rientium in pegmate, qui peracturus jam vitæ fabulam, cùm
hæc mortalia quàm vana sint videt, non idem faciat; & inimicitias, iras, odia, tanquam ex scena quadam jam exiturus,
libens non deponat, aut saltem simulet, ut vel misericordiam,
10 vel innocentiæ opinionem suæ in animis hominum relinquat?
Simulâsse Carolum, neque unquam ex animo, & sincero
mentis proposito tale mandatum dedisse filio, *ut suæ necis
authoribus ignosceret,* vel si hoc palàm, aliud tamen clanculum mandâsse, argumentis non levibus demonstrari potest:
15 nam filius, alioqui plus satis patri obsequens, patris gravissimo
atque ultimo præcepto tam religiosè sibi per episcopum tra-
dito, haud dubiè paruisset: quî autem paruit, cujus vel jussu
vel authoritate duo Legati nostri, alter in Hollandia, alter in
Hispania, & hic ne suspicione quidem ulla regiæ necis reus,
20 trucidati sunt? qui denique haud semel scripto publico edixit

hensive on that account, or that they made any anxious inquiry about the matter. But let us now give your account of
the business. Charles, on the scaffold, gave these last commands to the bishop, to be carried to his son, that he should
5 pardon the authors of his death. And in this, what has he done
that is so extraordinary, so different from what others have
done who have been brought to the same situation? Who is
there among those who die on a scaffold, who when about to
finish the drama of life, and seeing the vanity of things mor-
10 tal, would not act in the same way? and willingly lay aside,
or at least pretend so to do, his enmities, his angers, his hatreds,
as if now making his exit from the stage, that he may leave
behind him in the minds of men a feeling of compassion, or a
conviction of his innocence? That Charles dissembled; that
15 he never from his heart, from the sincere purpose of his mind,
gave such a command to his son, as "that he should pardon
the authors of his death"; or that if he gave this command in
public, he gave a different in private, may be proved by no
light arguments: for there can be no doubt that the son, who
20 was, in other respects, over-obsequious to the father, would
have paid obedience to the last and the most solemn of his
father's injunctions, delivered to him with such religious care
by the bishop. But in what manner has he paid obedience to
it, when either by his order or by his authority, two of our
25 ambassadors, one in Holland, the other in Spain, have been
murdered; the latter without even the slightest suspicion of
being accessary to the king's death? When, in fine, he has
more than once, by a public declaration in writing, made

atque omnibus palam fecit, se nolle patris sui interfectoribus ullo pacto veniam concedere? Hanc igitur narratiunculam tuam vide an veram esse velis; quæ quo magis collaudat patrem, eo magis vituperat filium. Nunc instituti oblitus, non
5 regii sanguinis ad cœlum, sed populi ad Senatum clamores ementiris, odiosissimus post Salmasium in republica aliena pragmaticus & ardelio, qui tam fœdè præsertim res tuas domi agas. Tuáne voce, impurissime, populus pro se utatur, cujus halitum ipsum oris lue venereâ fœtidum, purus omnis aver-
10 saretur? tu verò perfugarum ac perditorum voces populo attribuis; & quod agyrta peregrinus ad coronam solet, vilissimorum duntaxat animalium voces imitaris. Quis autem negat ea posse tempora sæpiùs accidere, in quibus civium longè major numerus improborum sit; qui Catilinam vel Anto-
15 nium, quàm saniorem Senatus partem sequi malint; neque idcirco boni cives obniti contra, & fortiter facere non debebunt, sui magis officii, quàm paucitatis rationem ducentes: tuam ergo tam bellam pro nostro populo oratiunculam, ne charta omnino pereat, in annales Volusi suadeo inseras; nobis
20 rhetorculo tam hircoso atque olido, non est usus. Dehinc injuriarum in ecclesiam postulamur. *Exercitus est omnium hæresewn lerna.* Qui non maledicunt, exercitum nostrum ut for-

known to all men, that it is not his intention, on any account, to pardon those who put his father to death? It is for you to consider, therefore, whether you could wish this pretty narrative of yours to be true, when in proportion as it applauds
5 the father, it condemns the son.

You now lose sight of your main object, and feign cries, not of the royal blood to heaven, but of the people against the parliament—you, who, next to Salmasius, are the most odious of meddlers in other people's affairs, while at home no man
10 manages his own so shamefully. Shall the people employ your voice in their defence, you mass of impurity, from whose very breath, tainted with venereal corruption, every clean person would turn with loathing? You take the voice of the beggarly refugees for the voice of the people; and like a foreign
15 mountebank to the crowd, imitate the voices only of the vilest of animals. Now who denies that times may often occur, when a large majority of the citizens may be unprincipled— citizens, who would make choice of Catiline or Antony for their leader, in preference to the sounder part of the senate;
20 but it will not less behove good citizens to strive against them on that account, and to do bravely, more regardful of their duty, than of the smallness of their number. This dainty piece of declamation therefore, of yours, in behalf of our people, I would advise you, that the paper might not be wholly wasted,
25 to insert in the annals of Volusius. As for ourselves, we do not stand in need of so paltry, so goatish, so rank a rhetorician.

We are next accused of injuries to the church. "The army is the Lerna of all heresies." Those who do not calumniate our

tissimum, ita modestissimum ac religiosissimum esse confi-
tentur: aliis in castris ferè potatur, variis libidinibus indulge-
tur, rapitur, aleâ luditur, juratur & perjuratur; in his nostris
quod datur otii, disquirendæ veritati impenditur, sacræ Scrip-
5 turæ invigilatur; nec quisquam pulchrius existimat hostem
ferire, quàm se atque alios cœlestium cognitione rerum eru-
dire, aut bellicam magis quàm evangelicam militiam exercere.
Et sanè si proprium belli usum consideramus, quid aliud
magis deceat milites? qui ideo constituti sunt atque con-
10 scripti, ut essent legum defensores, paludati justitiæ satellites,
ecclesiæ propugnatores: quid illis, non ferocius aut trucu-
lentius, sed civilius aut humanius esse oporteat? qui non bellum serere ac metere, sed pacem & incolumitatem humano
generi arare, vero ac proprio fine laborum suorum debent.
15 Quòd siquos ad hæc præclara instituta aspirantes vel alienus
error, vel sua animi infirmitas transversos abducit, in eos, non
ferro sæviendum, sed rationibus ac monitis, precibus quoque
ad Deum fusis enitendum, cujus est solius omnes animo erro-
res dispellere, & cœlestem veritatis lucem, cui volet imper-
20 tire. Hæreses quidem, sic verè dictas, nos nullas approbamus,
ne omnes quidem toleramus; extirpatas etiam volumus, sed
quibus convenit modis, præceptis nimirum & saniore doc-

army, acknowledge it to be not only the bravest of armies, but the most modest and religious. Other camps are usually distinguished for drunkenness, for indulgence in various lusts, for rapine, gaming, swearing, and perjury: in ours, the leisure 5 which is allowed is spent in the search of truth, in diligent attention to the holy scripture; nor is there any one who thinks it more honorable to smite the foe, than to instruct himself and others in the knowledge of heavenly things—more honorable to engage in the warfare of arms, than in the warfare of 10 the gospel. And indeed, if we consider the proper use of war, what can be more becoming in soldiers, who are enlisted and embodied for the express purpose of being the defenders of the laws, the guardians of justice in martial uniform, the champions of the church? What is there which can make it 15 more incumbent upon men to be, not ferocious and barbarous, but courteous and humane, whose duty it is not to sow and reap war, but to cultivate peace and safety for the race of man, as the true and proper end of their labours? But if any of those who aspire to these noble designs should be led astray by the 20 errors of others, or by their own infirmity, we should not in savage rage proceed against them with the sword, but should struggle against them with reason, with admonition, and with prayer poured forth to God, with whom alone it rests to dispel all errors from the mind, and to impart to whom he wills the 25 heavenly light of truth. Nevertheless, we approve no heresies which are justly so called; nor do we even tolerate all; we wish them extirpated, but by such means as are suitable—that is, by precept and sounder doctrine: for as they are seated in the

trina, ut in mente sitas, non ferro ac flagris quasi ex corpore evellendas. *Altera,* inquis, *par nostra injuria est in temporali, quod vocant, ecclesiæ fundo.* Percontare Belgas vel etiam Germaniæ superioris protestantes, numquid ab ecclesiæ bonis
5 abstinuerint; in quos Cæsar Austriacus quoties bellum movet, vix alium quærit belli titulum, quàm ut bona ecclesiæ restitui jubeat. Verùm illa profectò non ecclesiæ, sed ecclesiasticorum duntaxat bona fuere, qui hoc maximè sensu clerici, vel etiam holoclerici, ut qui sortem totam invasissent, rectiùs nomi-
10 nari poterant; immo lupi veriùs plerique eorum, quàm aliud quidvis erant dicendi; luporum autem bona, vel congestas potiùs prædas majorum ex superstitione partas, quam per tot sæcula quæstui habuerunt, in usus transferre belli à se-metipsis conflati, nefas non erat, quando aliud non erat
15 reliquum, unde sumptus belli tam gravis ac diuturni sup-peterent. Atqui *expectabatur, ut episcopis ereptæ opes in pastores ecclesiarum erogarentur.* Expectabant, scio, illi, & avebant omnia in se transfundi: nulla enim est vorago tam profunda, quæ non expleri citiùs quàm clericorum avaritia
20 possit. Aliis fortasse in locis, haud æquè ministris provisum; nostris jam satis superque bene erat; oves potiùs appellandi quàm pastores, pascuntur magis quàm pascunt; pinguia illis

mind, they are not to be cut out with the sword and lash, as if their seat had been in the body.—Again; "Another and no less injury of ours is in the temporal foundation of the church." Ask the Dutch, or even the protestants of Upper
5 Germany, whether they have ever abstained from the property of the church, when the Emperor of Austria seeks for no other pretence for making war against them, than that he may order the possessions of the church to be restored. But the truth is, that those possessions were not the property of the
10 church, but of the ecclesiastics only, who in this sense especially may be called clergy, or more properly, holoclergy, inasmuch as they had seized upon the whole patrimony. Indeed, most of them deserve to be called wolves, rather than any thing else; and what crime was there in transferring the
15 property of wolves,——or rather the accumulated plunder, obtained from the superstition of preceding times, of which for so many ages they had made their advantage,—to the purposes of a war kindled by themselves, when there was nothing else left to supply the heavy and daily expences of that war?
20 But, "it was expected that a law would be made for bestowing the wealth wrested from the bishops upon the pastors of the churches." I know that they expected and coveted that all should be poured upon themselves: for there is no gulf so deep which may not sooner be filled than the avarice of the clergy.
25 In other places perhaps the provision for the ministers is inadequate; ours were already provided for well enough and more than enough. They should be called sheep rather than shepherds: for they are fed more than they feed. With them

plerumque omnia, ne ingenio quidem excepto; decimis enim
saginantur, improbato ab aliis omnibus ecclesiis more; Deóque sic diffidunt, ut eas malint per magistratum atque per vim
suis gregibus extorquere, quàm vel divinæ providentiæ, vel
5 ecclesiarum benevolentiæ & gratitudini debere; atque inter
hæc tamen & apud discipulos & apud discipulas, tam crebrò
convivantur, ut quid domicœnium sit, aut domiprandium
penè nesciant: hinc itaque luxuriant plerique, non egent;
liberíque eorum & conjuges luxu & lautitiis, cum divitum
10 liberis atque conjugibus certant: hanc novis latifundiis ada-
uxisse luxuriam, idem prorsus fuisset, ac siquis novum vene-
num, (quam olim pestem sub Constantino vox missa cœlitùs
deflevit) in ecclesiam infudisset. Proximum est ut de injuriis
in Deum, quarum tres maximè nominantur, de fiducia nimi-
15 rum divinæ opis, *de precibus etiam atque jejuniis,* reddenda
nobis ratio sit. Verùm ex ore tuo, hominum corruptissime, te
redarguo; illúdque Apostoli abs te prolatum in te retorqueo,
Quis es tu qui *alienum servum judicas?* coram Domino nostro
sine stemus vel cadamus. Illud insuper addam Davidis pro-
20 phetæ, Cùm flens affligo jejunio animam meam, tum hoc
vertitur in summum probrum mihi. Cæteras hac de re tuas
garritiones febriculosas, quas nemo bis legat, minutim persequi si vellem, haud leviùs profectò ipse peccem. Nec minus
aliena sunt quæ de successibus prolixè oscitas: Cave tibi,

all things are usually full of fatness, their intellects even not
excepted: for they are pampered with tithes, a custom which
is disallowed by all other churches, and are so distrustful of
God, as to choose rather to extort them from their flocks by
5 the magistrate and by force, than to owe them either to divine
providence, or to the kindness and gratitude of the churches.
And besides all this, they are so often feasting with their dis-
ciples both male and female, that they scarcely know what it
is to dine or sup at home. Hence most of them live in luxury,
10 rather than in want; and their children and wives vie, in extrav-
agance and finery, with the children and wives of the rich. To
have increased this luxury by new and large possessions would
have been precisely the same thing, as if some new poison had
been poured into the church—a pest, which of old under
15 Constantine was deplored by a voice from heaven.—The next
thing is for us to give an account of the injuries towards God,
of which three are specified, namely, our confidence in the
divine aid, "our prayers, and our fastings." Now out of thine
own mouth, most corrupt of mortals, will I condemn thee;
20 and that expostulation of the apostle, which thou hast produced, I will retort against thee: who art thou that "judgest
another man's servant?" Before our own master let us stand
or fall. I will add that passage also from David the prophet:
"When I wept and chastened my soul with fasting, that was
25 to my reproach." Were I to follow in detail your other deli-
rious gabblings on this subject, which no one can read twice,
I should myself be chargeable with no light offence.—Nor
is what you so tediously prate about our successes, less foreign

More, & vide, ne post Pontianos sudores, gravedinem fortè
contraxeris aut polypum; metuendum, ne, ut Salmasius ille
magnus nuper, Thermas refrigeres. Equidem de successu sic
paucis respondeo; causam successu neque probari bonam,
5 neque argui malam: nos causam nostram non ex eventu, sed
eventum ex causa judicari postulamus. Jam rationes politicas
desumis tibi tractandas, mancipium cathedrarium, immo
cathedralitium; injurias nimirum nostras in omnes reges ac
populos. Quas? nobis enim nihil tale propositum erat; res
10 nostras tantummodo egimus, aliorum missas fecimus; siquid
ad vicinos ab exemplo nostro boni redundavit, haud invide-
mus; si quid secùs, non nostrâ id culpâ, sed abutentium evenire credimus. Reges aut populi, te Balatronem suarum injuriarum interpretem, quinam tandem constituerunt? certè
15 oratores eorum ac legatos, alii in Senatu, ipse in concilio cum
audirentur sæpè audivi non solùm de suis injuriis nihil que-
rentes, sed amicitiam nostram ac societatem ultrò petentes;
quinetiam regum suorum ac principum nomine, de rebus
nostris nobis gratulantes, etiam bene precantes, pacem ac
20 diuturnitatem, atque eosdem felices successus, in perpetuum

to the purpose. Take care, More, take care, that after your
Pontian sweats, you do not contract a gravedo in your head
or a polypus in your nose. It is to be feared, that, like the once
great Salmasius, you may chill the warm baths. Now as to
5 our success, I reply in these few words; that a cause is neither
proved to be good, nor shown to be bad, by success: we demand not that our cause should be judged of by the event; but
the event by the cause.—You now undertake to handle political considerations, chaired slave as you are, and even cathe-
10 dralized our injuries, against all kings and people. What
injuries? for nothing of this sort had been laid to our charge.
We have merely done our own business; we have not meddled
with other people's business. If any good has overflown upon
our neighbours from our example, we have no invidious feel-
15 ings on that account; or if any thing of a different description,
we do not believe it has happened by our fault, but by the fault
of those who have abused us. And after all, who made you,
such a pitiful fellow as you, interpreter of the injuries whether
of king or people? Certain it is, that when their ambassadors
20 and lieutenants-general have had audience in the council, so
far from complaining of their injuries, I have often heard
them, as others have heard them in the senate, soliciting, of
their own accord, our friendship and alliance; congratulating
us besides, in the name of their kings and princes, on our
25 affairs; and even praying for our prosperity, and wishing us
peace and length of duration, and a continuance of the same
auspicious success. These are not the words of enemies; these
are not, as you report, the words of those who hated us: it

exoptantes. Non inimicorum hæ voces, non eorum qui odissent, ut tu prædicas; aut tu mendacii, quod in te levissimum est, aut reges ipsi fraudum ac malarum artium, quod illis inhonestissimum foret, damnentur necesse est. Verùm scripta nostra objectas confitentium, *Dedisse nos exemplum populis omnibus salutare, tyrannis omnibus formidandum.* Immane crimen profectò narras; idem ferè atque si dixisset quispiam,

Discite justitiam moniti, & non temnere Divos.

Numquid dici potuit perniciosius? *hæc Cromuellius ad Scotos post Dumbarrense prælium scripsit.* Et se quidem & illâ nobili victoriâ dignè. *Ejusmodi sesamo & papavere conspersæ sunt infames Miltoni paginæ.* Illustrem tu quidem collegam semper mihi adjungis, & in hoc facinore parem planè facis, nonnunquam & superiorem; quo ego nomine cohonestari me maximè abs te putem, siquid à te honestum posset proficisci. *Crematæ vero,* inquis, *sunt istæ paginæ à carnifice Parisiensi supremi Senatus authoritate.* Nequaquam id comperi à Senatu factum, sed ab officiario quodam urbico, locum tenente civili nescio an incivili, cui clerici quidam, ignavissima animalia, authores fuere; tam ex dissito atque longinquo, abdomini suo, quod aliquando precor evenire possit, augurantes. Censes non potuisse nos vicissim Salmasii defensionem regiam cremasse? potuissem sanè vel ipse à magistratibus nostris hoc

follows then of necessity, that either you are convicted of a lie, which in you is a very trifling matter, or kings themselves of deceit and wicked arts, which in them would be most dishonorable. But you object to our writings, since in them we
5 confess, "that we have set an example salutary to all people, to be dreaded by all tyrants." You tell of a mighty crime no doubt; pretty much the same thing, as if any one had said:

Advised, learn justice, and revere the Gods.

Could any thing be said more pernicious? "This is what
10 was written by Cromwell to the Scots, after the battle of Dunbar." And which was worthy of himself and of that noble victory. "The infamous pages of Milton are strewn with sesamum and poppy of a like description." You always join me with some illustrious colleague, and in this affair, you
15 make me evidently Cromwell's equal, sometimes even his superior—a name by which, above all others, I think you honour me most, if any thing honorable can proceed from you.—"But those pages (you say) were burnt by the hangman at Paris, by order of the parliament." So far from this
20 being the work of the parliament, I find it was done by one of the city officers, (and whether he held a civil or an uncivil office I know not) at the instigation of some of the clergy, those laziest of animals, who, from scattered and distant auguries, prognosticated for their own bellies, what I pray
25 may one day fall upon them. Do you imagine that we also could not have burnt, in our turn, the royal defence of Salmasius? If I had thought such an insult deserving of any other

facilè impetrasse, nisi illam contumeliam contemptu potiùs
ulciscendam existimassem: Vos ignem igne properantes extinguere, Herculeum præbuistis rogum, unde clarior exur-
gerem; nos consultiùs, Defensionis Regiæ frigus calfacien-
5 dum non censuimus. Illud miror, tam esse Majorum dissi-
miles factos Tolosates (nam & Tolosæ combustos nos accepi-
mus) ut qua in urbe sub Raimundis comitibus, & libertas &
religio defensa olim tam insigniter est, in ea nunc & libertatis
& religionis Defensio combureretur. *Utinam & Scriptor,*
10 inquis. Itane ergastulum? at ego parem ne reddam tibi salutem, More, tu egregiè cavisti; ut qui nigrioribus multò ignibus
jamdudum pereas: urunt te adulteria tua, urunt stupra, urunt
perjuria, quorum ope desponsatam tibi stupro fœminam perfidus excussisti; urunt perditissimi furores, qui impulerunt
15 te, ut sacrosancta munia facinorosus concupisceres, & imper-
spectum Domini corpus incestis manibus sacerdos pollueres;
sanctitatem etiam simulans, in sanctitatis simulatores, dira
omnia hoc tuo clamore denuntiares; tuúmque execrabile
caput, tuámet ipsius damnatum sententiâ irretires: his tu
20 sceleribus & infamiis totus flagras, his tu flammis furialibus
dies atque noctes torreris, dásque nobis pœnas quibus gravi-

revenge than contempt, I could myself have easily obtained
this from our magistrates. In your hurry to put out one fire by
another, you have raised an Herculean pile, from which I may
rise up in greater brightness. We have more wisely thought
5 that the chilliness of the royal defence should not be warmed.
But this I wonder at, that the people of Toulouse should have
become so unlike their ancestors (for I find I have been also
burnt at Toulouse) as now to burn the defence of liberty and
religion in the very city, in which, under the counts of Rai-
10 mond, both liberty and religion had been before so signally
defended. "Would! (you exclaim) that the writer also had
been burnt!" And is this indeed your wish, slave? You have
taken especial care, that I shall not return you a like compli-
ment, as you have been long since consuming in far blacker
15 flames. You are burnt by your adulteries, you are burnt by
your fornications, you are burnt by your perjuries, by the aid
of which perjuries you perfidiously shook off the woman who
became betrothed to you by the sacrifice of her honour; you
are burnt by your outrageous madness, which has impelled
20 you, miscreant as you are, to covet the holiest of functions, and
as a priest, to pollute with adulterous hands the undiscerned
body of the Lord. Under the pretence of sanctity also, you
would denounce, in this cry of yours, every thing that is dire-
ful against pretenders to sanctity, though **you** must bring your
25 own accursed head into the snare, as being condemned even
by your own sentence. With these crimes, with these infamies
are you all on fire; in these furious flames are you scorching
day and night, and suffering a punishment for us, than which

ores imprecari tibi nullus hostis potest. Me interim concre-
mationes vestræ non lædunt, non tangunt, & istis ignominiis
habeo complura quæ opponam grata meo animo atque ju-
cunda. Una me curia, unus fortè lictor Parisiensis, malarum
5 avium impulsu, combussit; at quamplurimi per totam Galliam viri boni atque docti nihilo minus legunt, approbant,
amplectuntur; quamplurimi per immensum Germaniæ
totius tractum, libertatis ferè domicilium, per cæteras quoque
regiones, quâcunque ejus vestigia ulla adhuc manent; quin
10 & ipsa Græcia, ipsæ Athenæ Atticæ, quasi jam redivivæ, no-
bilissimi alumni sui Philaræ voce, applausere. Hoc etiam verè
possum dicere, quo primùm tempore nostra Defensio est edita,
& legentium studia incaluere, nullum vel principis vel civitatis legatum in urbe tum fuisse, qui non vel fortè obvio mihi
15 gratularetur, vel conventum apud se cuperet vel domi in-
viseret. Tuos verò nefas sit præterire manes, Adriane Pauui,
qui legatus ad nos summo cum honore missus, Hollandiæ
decus atque ornamentum, summam in me ac singularem
benevolentiam tuam, etiamsi videre nunquam contigerit,
20 multis sæpè nuntiis significandam curasti. Hoc verò etiam
sæpius recolere memoria juvat, quod sine Dei propitio numine
accidere arbitror nunquam potuisse; mihi, qui contra reges,
ut videbatur, scripseram, majestatem ipsam regiam placidè

no enemy could imprecate on you one more grievous. Meanwhile, these burnings of yours injure not, they touch not me;
and against such disgraces I have many things to oppose which
are grateful, which are delightful to my spirit. Under the
5 influence of bad auspices, I have been burnt by one court,
perhaps by a single Parisian executioner. But, in spite of this,
how many excellent and learned men are there, throughout
all France, who read, approve, embrace? How many throughout the spacious tracts of Germany, the domicile, as it were,
10 of liberty, and in other regions, wherever any traces of liberty
are yet visible: and even Greece herself—Athens the eye of
Greece, revived as it seems once more, has contributed her
applause by the voice of one of her sons—the noble Philaras.
This, moreover, I can truly say; at the time when our defence
15 was first published, and readers were all glowing with attention to it, there was not an ambassador from any prince or
state at that time in the city, who did not congratulate me
either on an accidental meeting, who did not desire my com-
pany at his own house, or who did not visit me at mine. But
20 it were an injury to forget your departed spirit, Adrian Paul,
who, with the high dignity of ambassador to us, and the glory
and ornament of Holland, were solicitous to make known to
me by frequent messages, though I never happened to see you,
your great and distinguished kindness towards me. It is also
25 pleasing to me to dwell frequently upon the circumstance, and
which, it is my belief, could never have happened without the
especial favour of God, that I, who, as it seemed, had been
writing in opposition to kings, have obtained the approving

annuisse; meæque integritati, nec non sententiæ, ut veriori, testimonium divino proximum perhibuisse. Quid enim verear hoc dicere, quoties augustissimam reginam illam, quantis cum laudibus in ore omnium versetur, mecum cogito? Equi-
5 dem Atheniensem illum sapientissimum, cui me tamen non confero, ne ipsius quidem Pythii testimonio, quàm me illius judicio ornatiorem existimem. Quòd si mihi quidem hæc scribere adolescenti contigisset, & oratoribus idem quod poetis liceret, haud dubitassem profectò sortem meam deorum sorti
10 nonnullorum anteferre: quippe illos de forma duntaxat aut de musica, deos, humano sub judice contendisse; me homi-nem in certamine longè omnium præclarissimo, deâ judice, superiorem discessisse. Sic me cohonestatum, nemo nisi car-nifex ignominiosè audeat tractare, tam qui jusserit quàm qui
15 fecerit. Hîc vehementer laboras, ut ne facta nostra Belgico-rum pro libertate facinorum exemplo tueri queamus; quod à Salmasio quoque frustra laboratum est: cui quod tunc re-spondi, idem tibi nunc responsum volo; Falli qui nos opinatur cujusquam exemplo niti; Belgarum pro libertate facinora
20 adjuvisse sæpius ac fovisse, æmulari necesse nunquam ha-buisse; siquid pro libertate fortiter faciendum est, authores ipsi

nod even of royal majesty itself, and its testimony, only not divine, to my integrity, and to the superior truth of my opinion. And why should I scruple to say this as often as I think of that most august queen, whose high praises are the
5 theme of every tongue? Indeed, not even that wisest Athenian, between whom and myself, however, I make no comparison, can I think more graced by the testimony of the Pythian himself, than me by her opinion. And if I had happened to have written what I have, when a young man, and
10 the same liberty were allowed to orators as to poets, I should in truth not have hesitated to prefer my fortune to that of some among the gods; forasmuch as they, being gods, contended only for beauty, or in music, before a human arbiter; and I, being a man, with a goddess for my arbitress, have come off
15 victorious in the noblest far of all contests. Thus highly honoured, no one but an executioner would dare to treat me with disrespect, whether by ordering it to be done, or by doing it himself.

Here you labour hard to prevent our defending what we
20 have done by the example of the exploits of the Dutch in favour of liberty—a point which has been fruitlessly laboured also by Salmasius. I would return the same answer to you now, as I did then to him: that he who thinks our struggles have been occasioned by the example of any one, is mistaken;
25 that, of necessity, we, who have often aided and encouraged the exploits of the Dutch in favour of liberty, could never have been their rivals; and that, if any thing is to be done bravely for liberty, we, being our own masters, are accus-

nobis sumus, præire, non sequi alios assueti. Tu verò etiam ad
bellum contra nos tressis orator, stultissimis argumentis, &
te verberone dignis, Gallos hortaris: *Nostros,* inquis, *legatos
excipere Gallicus spiritus nunquam sustinebit.* Sustinuit quod

5 plus est, suos jam ter & amplius ad nos ultrò mittere: Galli
igitur generosi, ut solent, tu degener & spurius, politicarum
rationum rudis ac falsus deprehenderis. Hinc id agis ut de-
monstres, *à fœderatis ordinibus ex composito rem in longum
duci, eosque nobiscum nec fœdus nec bellum velle.* Atqui

10 interest profectò ipsorum ordinum, non pati consilia sua sic
nudari, &, ut ita dicam, vitiari à Genevensi perfuga apud se
stabulante, qui si diutiùs toleretur, non ancillis modò, sed
consiliis etiam publicis stuprum videtur illaturus; cùm ipsi
fraterna atque sincera omnia præ se ferant; nunc pacem, quæ

15 vota sunt bonorum omnium, perpetuam nobiscum redinte-
graverint. *Jucundum erat,* inquit, *videre, quibus ludibriis,
quibus periculis furciferi illi legati,* Anglorum scilicet, *quotidie conflictarentur, non modo ab Anglis regiis, &c. sed
maximè omnium à Batavis.* Nisi exploratum nobis jam diu

20 esset quibusnam & prioris legati Dorislai cædes, & duorum
postea acceptæ injuriæ referendæ sint, en delatorem, qui hospites & altores suos etiam falsò deferat: Hunccine apud vos,

tomed to lead the way, not to follow others. But you, vile orator, by the absurdest of arguments, worthy of a paltry fellow like you, also incite the French to war against us: "The spirit of the French, (you say) will never bear to receive our
5 ambassadors." But, what is more, the spirit of the French has already borne to send their own, three or four times, and of its own accord, to us. The French, then, are generous as usual; while you, degenerate and spurious, are found to be ignorant and mistaken as to your political considerations.—You next
10 try to make it appear, that the negotiation was purposely spun out to a great length by the United States; and that they were desirous neither of a treaty nor of a war with us. Surely it concerns the States not to suffer their counsels to be thus exposed, and, as I may say, falsified by a Genevese fugitive who is got
15 housed among them, and who, if tolerated much longer, will not merely, as it seems, bring prostitution upon their servant maids, but upon their public counsels: for they themselves are all sincerity and brotherly kindness, and have now, agreeably to the wish of every good man, renewed with us a perpetual
20 peace. "It was amusing (says he) to see, with what scoffs, with what perils, those gallows ambassadors," namely of the English, "had daily to contend, not only from the English royalists, &c. but most of all from the Dutch." If we had not long since discovered on whom was to be charged the murder
25 of Dorislaus our first ambassador, and the injuries received by our two succeeding ambassadors, here would be an informer, who accuses even falsely his hosts and supporters. And do you suffer this man, Hollanders, to be fostered among you, who

Batavi, non modò venereum in ecclesia ministrum, sed san-
guinarium etiam, nec violandi solùm juris omnis hortatorem,
sed violati quoque falsum indicem ac proditorem ali?

Ultimus accusationum titulus est *nostra injuria in Refor-*
5 *matas ecclesias.* At verò quî magis nostra in illas quàm illarum
in nos? si exemplo instes, certè si ab ipsis Valdensibus & Tolo-
sanis, ad Rupellanam usque famem monumenta repetas, nos
omnium ecclesiarum ultimi reperiemur contra tyrannos arma
sumpsisse. At primi capite damnasse. Sanè quia nobis hoc
10 primis in manu adhuc fuit: quid illi, si data similis facultas
fuisset, fuissent facturi, opinor ne ipsos quidem satis nôsse.
Equidem in ea sum sententia, contra quem bellum gerimus,
eum, siquis rationis aut judicii usus sit, hostem à nobis judicari; hostem autem tam interficere quàm oppugnare, eodem
15 semper jure licuisse: Tyrannus igitur cùm non noster solùm,
sed totius propè generis humani publicus hostis sit, eum quo
jure armis oppugnari, eodem posse & interfici. Nec verò hæc
mea unius sententia est, aut nova, eandem & aliis olim sive
prudentia sive sensus communis dictavit. Hinc pro Rabirio
20 M. Tullius: Si interfici Saturninum nefas fuit, arma sumpta
esse contra Saturninum sine scelere non possunt; si arma jure

is not merely a debauchee-minister of the church, but a san-
guinary instigator to the violation of all right, and the false
and traitorous informer, when the violence has been committed?

5   The last title of the accusations is—"Our injury towards
the reformed churches." Now how have we injured them,
more than they have injured us? If you urge, by our example,
I reply, that if you examine into records, beginning from the
Waldenses, and people of Toulouse, and proceeding down-
10 wards to the famine of Rochelle, we shall be found to be the
last of all the churches who have taken up arms against tyrants, though the first who have condemned one to a capital
punishment: and in truth, because we were the first who had
it in our power. What they would have done, if they had had
15 the same power, is not very well known, I apprehend, even
to themselves. In short, my opinion is, that (if a man has any
use of his reason) he, against whom we make war, is considered by us as an enemy; that, to put an enemy to death has
always been lawful, by the same right as we oppose him; and
20 as a tyrant is not simply our enemy, but the general enemy as
it were of the whole human race, that, by the same right as
he may be resisted by arms, may he likewise be put to death.
Nor is this my opinion alone, or any new opinion; the same
was suggested, whether by prudence or common sense, to
25 others in ancient times. Hence Marcus Tullius for Rabirius:
"If it was unlawful for Saturninus to be put to death, arms
could not, without a crime, have been taken up against Saturninus; if you admit that arms were justly taken up, you nec-

sumpta concedis, interfectum jure concedas necesse est. Plura
hac de re & suprà dixi, sæpè aliàs, & per se res obscura non est.
Ex quibus quid Galli etiam, eâdem datâ occasione fuissent
facturi, ipse queas divinare. Addo & hoc amplius, quicunque
5 armis tyrannum oppugnant, iidem, quantum in se est, & in-
terficiunt: immo, quicquid vel sibi vel aliis ineptè satis persua-
dere cupiunt, jam interfecere. Sed & doctrina hæc nobis haud
magis quàm Gallis, quos tu hoc piaculo cupis eximere, debe-
tur: unde enim Francogallia illa, nisi ex Gallia, unde vindiciæ
10 contra tyrannos? qui liber etiam Bezæ vulgò tribuitur; unde
alii quorum meminit Thuanus? tu tamen, quasi ego solus,
id satagit, inquis, *Miltonus, cujus ego piacularem vesaniam*
pro meritis excepissem. Tu excepisses, furcifer? cujus nefaria
flagitia si ecclesia illa Middelburgensis, te pastore infamis &
15 infelix, pro meritis excepisset, jamdudum te Satanæ man-
dasset; si pro meritis excepisset magistratus, jamdudum adulteria patibulo pendens luisses: Et luiturus propediem sanè
videris; evigilavit enim, ut audio nuper, tua illa ecclesia Middelburgensis, suæque famæ consuluit, téque caprimulgum
20 pastorem, immo hircum potius olentissimum ablegavit ab se
in malam crucem; hinc & magistratus Amsterodamensis pul-

essarily admit that he was justly put to death." I have said
more on this subject above, and often elsewhere; besides, the
thing is not dark in itself. Whence, you may judge what the
French themselves would have done, if the same opportunity
5 had been given them. I moreover add: those who oppose a
tyrant with arms, do all they can to put him to death; nay,
they have already put him to death, whatever they may absurdly wish to persuade themselves or others. But this doctrine belongs no more to us, than to the French, whom you
10 would willingly exempt from this heinous crime: else, whence
that Francogallia, if not from Gaul? Whence those *Vindica-
tions against Tyrants*—a book commonly ascribed to Beza
himself? Whence other books mentioned by Thuanus? And
yet you say, "This is the point which Milton is labouring with
15 such busy zeal," as if I were the only one, "and whose atrocious fury I would have received as it deserved." You would
have received, you villain? whose nefarious profligacies if the
church of Middelburg which has the misfortune and infamy
of having you for a pastor, had received as they deserved, it
20 had long ago have sent you to the devil; if the magistrates had
received as they deserved, you would long ago have expiated
your adulteries on a gallows. To tell the truth, you seem very
likely to make an expiation ere it be long: for, as I am lately
informed, your church of Middelburg has watched you nar-
25 rowly, has consulted its own reputation, and has sent you
about your business, that you may go and be hanged—goat-
herd of a pastor as you are, nay, the rankest of goats. Hence
too, the magistrates of Amsterdam laid an interdict for you

pitum quoque interdixit tibi, orchestram tuam; tuúmque
illud os impudicum eo ex loco ad summam omnium bonorum
offensionem conspici, illam impiam vocem vetuit in sacro
publicè audiri: restat jam tibi sola Græcarum literarum pro-
5 fessio; & hæc quoque brevi eripienda, præter unam illam
literam, cujus non professor, sed discipulus mox pensilis
meritò futurus es. Neque hæc iratus tibi ominor, sed duntaxat
jus dico: maledicis enim tantum abest ut talibus offendamur
qualis tu es, ut tales semper nobis vel exoptemus; immo divinâ
10 planè benevolentiâ fieri arbitremur, ut qui in nos acerrimè
clamitarunt, tales potissimùm semper extiterint; qui maledicendo non infamant, sed honestant, sed laudant, nam lau-
dando certè maledixissent. Sed irruentem modò quid te retinuit tam fortem homuncionem? *Nisi mihi,* inquis, *religio*
15 *fuisset in magni Salmasii provinciam excurrere, cui solida de*
magno scilicet adversario victoria relinquetur. Siquidem &
ille & ego nunc magnus tibi videor, eo difficilior provincia,
præsertim mortuo, fortassis ero; de victoria, modò veritas
vincat, parum sollicitus. Interim tu clamitas; *parricidium in*
20 *doctrinam vertunt, eámque reformatarum ecclesiarum con-*
sensione cupiunt quidem, non audent aperto ore defendere;
fuit, inquit Miltonus, etiam summorum hæc sententia Theo-
logorum, qui ipsi reformandæ ecclesiæ authores fuere. Fuit,

on the pulpit, which is your stage; and forbad that shameless face of yours to be seen from that place, to the utter scandal
of all good men; forbad that impious voice to be heard in
public on a sacred subject. At this time, your professorship of
5 Greek alone remains; and this also is soon to be taken away,
all but that single letter, of which, however, you will not be
the professor, but ere long deservedly the disciple pensile from
the top. Nor do I forebode these things for you in anger, but
simply speak what is right: for, so far from being offended at
10 such revilers as you, we could even wish to have always such;
and are persuaded that it is through the divine favour it has
happened, that those who have raised the most virulent clam-
ours against us, have always been eminently such, whose
abuse is no infamy, but honour, but applause: for certain it
15 is, that their praise would have been a reproach. But as you
are so courageous a fellow, what has checked your late violence? "Unless (you say) I had been religiously scrupulous
not to invade the province of the great Salmasius, to whom
shall be left the substantial part of the victory over his great
20 adversary, forsooth." Since you now seem to think *me* great
as well as him, I shall perhaps be found to be a province the
more difficult to be invaded, especially as he is dead. I am
little solicitous about the victory, provided only truth be the
victor.—Meanwhile, you pursue your clamour: "They con-
25 vert parricide into a doctrine; and this they would fain do,
with the consent of the reformed churches; they dare not defend it openly. This was the opinion also, says Milton, of the
most eminent divines, the very authors of the reformation in

inquam, & id fusiùs docui in eo libro qui nostro idiomate
Tenor sive Tenura regum & magistratuum inscriptus est,
secundùm editus, & alibi: nunc actum toties, agendi fastidium
cepit: illic ex Luthero, Zuinglio, Calvino, Bucero, Martyre,
5 Paræo, citantur ipsa verbatim loca; ex illo denique Cnoxo,
quem *unum,* me, *Scotum* ais *innuere, quemque hac in re
reformatos omnes, præsertim Gallos, illâ ætate condemnasse.*
Atqui ille contrà, quod ibi narratur, se illam doctrinam no-
minatim à Calvino, summísque aliis eâ tempestate theologis,
10 quibuscum familiariter consueverat, hausisse affirmat: plura
etiam illic nostrorum, regnante Mariâ & Elizabethâ, sinceri-
orum theologorum in eandem sententiam deprompta reperies.
Tu verò tandem conceptis ad Deum precibus malè prolixis
peroras impius abominandis; & os illud adulterum, obduratus
15 cœlo offers: sino te facilè, neque interpello; major enim cu-
mulus ad impietatem tuam accedere non potuit. Revertor nunc
ad id quod suprà pollicitus sum, & objecta Cromuello præcipua crimina quæ sunt, in medio hic ponam; ut sparsa quàm
fuerint levia possit intelligi, quæ collecta nullum pondus in se
20 habent. *Coram pluribus testibus pronunciavit sibi in animo
esse, monarchias omnes evertere, reges omnes exitio dare.*
Quæ tua sit narrationum fides, jam aliquoties vidimus; dixit
fortasse tibi perfugarum aliquis Cromuellum ita dixisse: ex

the church." It was, I say; and this I have shown abundantly
in the book, in our own tongue, entitled *The Tenure of Kings
and Magistrates,* second edition; and in other places. What I
have done so often, I feel a reluctance to do again. In that
5 work, I have cited word for word the very passages from
Luther, Zuinglius, Calvin, Bucer, Martyr, Paræus, and lastly
from that Knox, "the only Scot (you say) I have of my side,
and who was condemned, as to this matter, by all the Protestants of that age, especially by the French." On the con-
10 trary, he himself affirms, as is there related, that he drew this
doctrine expressly from Calvin, and from other eminent theo-
logians of that time, with whom he had familiar intercourse.
You will there find also more upon the same subject taken
from the sincerer part of our divines, in the reigns of Mary
15 and Elizabeth. But at length you impiously conclude in a
tedious ready-made prayer to God, deserving of execration;
and hardened in iniquity, offer up that adulterous mouth to
heaven. I have no difficulty in suffering you to proceed without interruption: for your impiety could receive no accession.
20   I now return to what I promised above, and will here bring
forward to public view the chief crimes which are laid to the
charge of Cromwell; that it may be seen how light they must
have been when scattered, when, in a body, they have no
weight against him. "He declared it, before numerous wit-
25 nesses, to be his intention to overturn all monarchies, to ex-
terminate all kings." What credit is due to your narratives, we
have often seen already. One of the refugees, perhaps, told
you that Cromwell had said so; of those numerous witnesses,

illis multis testibus nullum nominas: quod itaque sine authore
maledicis, suopte vitio ruit. Non is est Cromuellus, quem de
suis jam factis ullus unquam vaniloquum audierit; tantùm
abest ut infecta quæ sunt, támque difficilia, de iis insolentius
5 quicquam promittere ac minitari consueverit: sanè ista tibi
qui narrarunt, nisi voluntate atque naturâ magis quàm consilio mendaces essent, hoc saltem quod ab ingenio ejus alienis-
simum est, non affinxissent. Regibus autem, quos ut sibi
caveant frequenter mones, licebit cum saluti prospexerint suæ,
10 spreto te monitore tam imperito, non sermunculos ex trivio
arripere, sed rationes se dignas inire, quibus quid suâ intersit
faciliùs perspexerint. Alterum est crimen persuasisse regi
Cromuellum, *ut in insulam Vectim clanculum se subduceret.*
Constat regem Carolum rem suam multis aliàs rebus, ter fugâ
15 perdidisse; primùm cum Londino Eboracum fugit, deinde
cum ad Scotos in Anglia conductitios, postremò cum ad insulam Vectim. At hujus postremæ suasor erat Cromuellus.
Optimè; sed tamen ego regios illos primùm miror, qui Carolum toties affirmare non dubitant fuisse prudentissimum, &
20 eundem simul vix unquam suæ spontis; sive apud amicos sive
inimicos, in aula vel in castris, in aliena ferè potestate semper
fuisse; nunc uxoris, nunc episcoporum, nunc purpuratorum,

you name not one; so that, that abuse of yours which is without authority, falls by its own default. Cromwell is not a man who has been ever heard, by any one, to boast of the achievements he has actually performed; and equally far is he from
5 making insolent promises and threats, as to those he intends to perform, especially achievements of such difficulty. Indeed, those who told you all this, if they had not been wilfully and naturally liars, rather than from deliberation, would at any rate, not have invented a forgery, which is totally foreign to
10 his character. But when kings, whom you frequently admonish to take care of themselves, look out for their own safety, they will not be obliged to snatch at any trivial tittle-tattle, but will be at liberty to despise so ignorant an adviser as you, and to listen to plans of policy worthy of themselves, and by
15 which they may more easily discern their true interests.—Another crime is, that Cromwell persuaded the king "to retire privately to the Isle of Wight." It is well known, that king Charles had rendered his affairs desperate from various other causes, and three times by flight: first, when he fled from
20 London to York; secondly, when he fled to the Scotch mercenaries in England; and lastly, when he fled to the Isle of Wight. But it was Cromwell who persuaded him to this last flight. Very well; and yet, in the first place, I cannot but admire those royalists, who persist in affirming, that Charles
25 was a paragon of prudence, when he scarcely ever had a will of his own: when, whether among his friends or enemies, in the court or in the camp, he was almost always at the disposal of others; at one time of his wife, at another of the bishops,

nunc militum, denique hostium; pejora plerúmque consilia,
& pejorum fermè sequutum; Carolo persuadetur, Carolo im-
ponitur, Carolo illuditur, metus incutitur, spes vana osten-
ditur, velut præda omnium communis, tam amicorum quàm
5 hostium, agitur & fertur Carolus. Aut hæc è scriptis suis
tollant, aut sagacitatem Caroli prædicare desistant. Fateor
deinde, quamvis prudentiâ atque consilio præstare pulcrum
sit, tamen ubi respublica factionibus laborat, suis incommo-
dis haud carere; & consultissimum quemque eo magis ob-
10 noxium calumniis utriusque partis reddere: hoc sæpè Cromuello obfuit; hinc Presbyteriani, inde hostes quicquid in se
durius fieri putant, non id communi Senatus consilio, sed
Cromuello soli imputant; immo siquid per imprudentiam
ipsi malè gerunt, id dolis & fraudibus Cromuelli assignare
15 non erubescunt; culpa omnis in eum derivatur, omnis in eum
faba cuditur. Et tamen certissimum est, fugam ad Vectim
regis Caroli, absenti tum aliquot millibus passuum Cromuello, tam novum accidisse & inopinatum, quàm cuilibet ex
Senatu tum in urbe versanti, quem ut de re inopinatissima
20 sibi recèns allata per literas certiorem fecit. Res autem ita se
habuit; exercitus universi vocibus rex territus, qui eum nullis

now of the courtiers, then of the military, and lastly of his
enemies: when, for the most part, he followed the worst counsels, and those commonly of the worst men; and Charles is
persuaded, Charles is imposed upon, Charles is played upon,
5 he is smitten with fear, he is deluded with vain hopes; when
Charles was driven and carried about, the common prey, as
it seemed, of all; of friends as well as of enemies. Let them
take away these things from their writings, or cease to extol
the sagacity of Charles. Again, though it is an excellent thing
10 to excel in prudence and in counsel, yet, when the commonwealth is torn with factions, it is not without its inconven-
iences; and renders the man of the greatest capacity and experience the more obnoxious to the calumnies of both parties.
This is what has frequently happened to Cromwell. Hence
15 the presbyterians, his enemies, for that reason, impute not to
the parliament in general, but to Cromwell alone any measure
which they may think harsh towards themselves; and even,
when themselves, through their own inprudence, conduct
any business unsuccessfully, they have the effrontery to ascribe
20 this also to the wiles and artifices of Cromwell. Every fault is
fathered upon him; it is he who must bear the blame of every
thing. And yet, it is beyond all doubt, that King Charles's
flight to the Isle of Wight, happened as suddenly and unex-
pectedly to Cromwell, he being at the time some miles dis-
25 tant, as to the member of parliament then in the city, to whom
he communicated it as a thing the most unexpected in the
world, of which he had just been informed by letter. The truth
of the matter is this: the king, terrified at the outcry of the

officiis suis aut pollicitis factum meliorem, ad supplicium poscere jam tunc cœperat, statuit cum duobus tantummodo consciis nocturnâ fugâ sibi consulere: verùm fugiendi certior, quam quo fugeret, per comitum suorum vel imperitiam vel
5 timiditatem, inops consilii quo se reciperet, Hamundo Vectis insulæ præsidi se ultro dedidit; ea spe, facilem sibi ex ea insula, parato clam navigio, transitum in Galliam aut in Belgium fore. Hæc ego de fuga regis in Vectim ex iis comperi, quibus rem totam pernoscendi quàm proxima facultas erat. Sed &
10 hoc quoque criminosum est, quòd per Cromuellum, *Angli ingentem de Scotis parti sunt victoriam.* Non *parti sunt,* More, sed sine solæcismo claram sibi pepererunt; tu verò cogita, quàm Scotis cruentum illud prælium fuerit, cujus tu mentionem tantummodo facere nequivisti, quin instabile præ
15 metu professorium caput tuum ad Prisciani pluteum nutando allideres. Sed videamus porro quantum flagitium Cromuelli fuerit, Scotos irrumpentes, imperium sibi in Anglos jam pollicentes, nobilissimo post multas ætates prælio vicisse. *Inter has turbas, dum Cromuellus cum exercitu abest:*
20 Immò dum hostem in Angliæ viscera jam progressum, jam Parlamento ipsi imminentem Cromuellus, etiam deficientes

whole army, (who, as he failed to alter his conduct for the better in consequence of any offices or promises of theirs, began, even at the time I speak of, to demand his punishment,) resolved to provide for his own safety by flying in the night, with two attendants, the only persons privy to his escape. But more determined to fly than rightly knowing whither—at a loss where to seek refuge through the inexperience or timidity of his attendants, he made a voluntary surrender of himself to Hammond, governor of the Isle of Wight, in hopes of being able to procure a ship privately, in which he might get an easy passage from that island into France or Holland. I had this account of the king's flight to the Isle of Wight from those who had the best possible opportunity of being acquainted with the whole affair thoroughly.—And it is likewise a crime, it seems, that, through Cromwell, "the English gained a great victory over the Scots." Not *parti sunt,* More; but, without the solecism, *pepererunt,* gained for themselves a splendid victory. Imagine now, what a bloody battle that must have been to the Scots, when you could not even mention it, without knocking your professorial head, made giddy by fear, against Priscian's desk! But further; let us see what great crime it was in Cromwell to have conquered, in the noblest battle which had been fought for many ages, the Scots who were meditating an irruption, and already promised themselves the supreme sway over the English. "Amidst this confusion, while Cromwell is absent with his army": Yes, while Cromwell, seeing the enemy advanced into the heart of England, threatening even the parliament, was conquering and

Cambros ad fidem reducendo, & obsidione longâ defessus, ut
vidit, ut vicit, ut gloriosissimè fudit, Presbyterianos *tædium
Cromuelli ceperat:* Hîc verum dicis; dum is communem hostem cum vitæ discrimine propulsat, hi militantem pro sese
5 & in acie fortiter dimicantem confictis criminibus accusant
domi; & Huntingtonum centurionem quendem in ejus caput
subornant. Quis tantæ ingratitudinis fœditatem sine fremitu
vel audire possit? Eorundem instinctu, nequissimum genus
homuncionum ac petulantissimum, tyrones tabernarum ma-
10 ximo numero curiæ fores obsident; Senatum, quicquid ipsis
videtur, (quo quid indignius?) clamore suo ac minis cogunt
decernere: jámque reducem à Scotis victorem fortissimum,
aut exulantem, aut pœnas indignissimas dantem vidissemus
Camillum nostrum; nisi Fairfaxius imperator, invictissimi
15 Legati sui tantum dedecus perferendum non censuisset; nisi
cunctus exercitus, & is quoque satis ingratè habitus, tam
atrocia prohibuisset. Urbem itaque ingressus, urbicos nullo
negotio repressit; Scotorum hostium partibus addictos meritò
Senatu movit: pars reliqua insolentiis tabernariorum jam
20 liberata, colloquium Vectense, contra Senatus consultum edic-
túmque publicum, cum rege initum rescindit: Huntingtonus

gloriously dispersing that enemy; while he was harassing
himself in reducing the revolted Welsh to obedience, and by
a long siege—the presbyterians "began to be tired of Cromwell." Here you speak the truth. While he is repelling the
5 common enemy at the hazard of his life, while he is engaged
in war for themselves and bravely fighting in the field, these
men are accusing him at home of fabricated crimes, and suborn one captain Huntingdon, to charge him with a capital
offence. Who can even listen with patience to such baseness
10 of ingratitude! At the instigation of the same persons—a most
worthless and insolent set of fellows—the apprentices from
the shops in great numbers beset the doors of the parliament-
house; and with their clamour and threats, compel the parliament to resolve whatever they choose to dictate; and what
15 could be a greater indignity than this? And when returned,
the bravest of conquerors, from the Scots, we should have seen
our Camillus sent into banishment, or suffering the most unmerited of punishments, if general Fairfax had not thought
it was not to be borne that such disgrace should be inflicted
20 on his invincible lieutenant; if the whole army, which was
likewise treated with sufficient ingratitude, had not put a stop
to conduct so atrocious. Cromwell, therefore, having entered
the city, soon reduced the citizens to order, and deservedly
turned out of the parliament the partisans of the hostile Scots;
25 the rest, now freed from the insults of the shopkeepers, re-
scinded the treaty which in contradiction to the vote of parliament, and a public declaration, had been entered into with
the king, in the Isle of Wight. His accuser Huntingdon, left

autem ille accusator, impunis & sui juris relictus, tandem
pœnitentiâ ductus, ipse suâ sponte à Cromuello veniam petiit,
& à quibus esset subornatus ultro fassus est. Hæc ferè sunt
quæ fortissimo patriæ liberatori, nisi ad quæ supra respondi,
5 crimina objiciuntur; quæ quid valeant videtis. Verùm ego
tantum virum, déque hac republica tam insignitè meritum,
si duntaxat nihil mali commisisse defendam, nihil egero; cum
præsertim non reipublicæ solùm, sed & meâ quoque intersit,
ut qui eâdem infamiâ tam prope sim conjunctus, quàm opti-
10 mum eum, atque omni laude dignissimum, gentibus, quoad
possum, omnibus atque sæculis demonstrare. Est *Oliverius
Cromuellus* genere nobili atque illustri ortus: nomen republicâ olim sub regibus benè administratâ clarum, religione
simul orthodoxâ vel restitutâ tum primùm apud nos vel sta-
15 bilitâ clarius: Is maturâ jam atque firmatâ ætate, quam &
privatus traduxit, nullâ re magis quàm religionis cultu puri-
oris, & integritate vitæ cognitus, domi in occulto creverat;
& ad summa quæque tempora fiduciam Deo fretam & ingentem animum tacito pectore aluerat. Parlamento ab rege ulti-
20 mùm convocato, sui municipii suffragiis lectus Senatorium
munus obtinuit; illic rectissimis sententiis consiliísque firmis-

in impunity and to his own disposal, at length repented, and of his own accord asked forgiveness of Cromwell, and without solicitation, confessed by whom he had been suborned. These are the chief crimes, with the exception of those to which I
5 have replied above, with which this magnanimous deliverer of his country has been reproached; and of what weight they are you now see.

But I shall have done nothing, if I only make it appear that this great man, who has deserved so highly of the common-
10 wealth, has done nothing wrong; when it concerns not the commonwealth alone, but myself in particular, conjoined as I am so closely with him in the same infamy, to show forth to the nations, and as far as I am able, to all ages, his transcendent merit, his sovereign worthiness of all praise. — Oliver
15 Cromwell was sprung from a noble and illustrious family. The name was famous of old under the kings for skill in the administration of public affairs; and it grew more famous in consequence of the orthodox or reformed religion being at the same period established among us for the first time. He
20 grew up in the privacy of his own family, and till his age was quite mature and settled, which he also passed in private, was chiefly known for his strict attendance upon the purer worship, and for his integrity of life. He had cherished his confidence in God, he had nursed his great spirit in silence, for
25 some extraordinary times. When a parliament was at last called by the king, he was returned member for his own town; and immediately became conspicuous for the justness of his opinions, and the firmness of his counsels. When the

simis statim innotuit: Ubi ad arma deventum est, delatâ suâ
operâ, equitum turmæ præficitur; sed bonorum virorum concursu, ad ejus signa undique confluentium, auctus copiis, &
gestarum rerum magnitudine & celeritate conficiendi sum-
5 mos ferè duces brevi superavit. Nec mirum; sui enim noscendi
exercitatissimus miles, quicquid intus hostis erat, spes vanas,
metus, cupiditates, apud se prius aut deleverat, aut subactas
iam habuerat; in se priùs imperator, sui victor, de se potissimùm triumphare didicerat; itaque ad externum hostem quo
10 primùm die in castra venit, veteranus, & in illa omni castrensi
militia consummatus accessit. Non est ut in his possim orationis carceribus, tot urbes captas, tot prælia & quidem maxima,
in quibus nunquam victus aut fusus, Britannicum orbem totum continuis victoriis peragravit, pro dignitate rerum exequi;
15 quæ justæ sanè historiæ grande opus, & iterum quasi cam-
pum quendam dicendi, & exæquata rebus narrandi spatia de-
siderant. Sufficit hoc unicum singularis & prope divinæ
virtutis indicium, tantam in eo viguisse sive animi vim atque
ingenii, sive disciplinæ non ad militarem modò, sed ad Chris-
20 tianam potiùs normam & sanctimoniam institutæ, ut omnes
ad sua castra tanquam ad optimum non militaris duntaxat
scientiæ, sed religionis ac pietatis gymnasium, vel jam bonos

appeal was made to arms, he was appointed, by his own choice, to a troop of horse; and as his force was augmented by the eager zeal of the good, who flocked from all quarters to his standard, he soon surpassed almost the greatest generals in 5 the grandeur of his achievements, and in the rapidity with which they were executed. Nor is this to be wondered at: for, he was a soldier, above all others the most exercised in the knowledge of himself; he had either destroyed, or reduced to his own control, all enemies within his own breast—vain 10 hopes, fears, desires. A commander first over himself, the conqueror of himself, it was over himself he had learnt most to triumph. Hence, he went to encounter with an external enemy as a veteran accomplished in all military duties, from the day he first entered the camp. It would not be possible for 15 me, within the limits of this discourse, to follow him with all suitable dignity, through so many captured cities, so many battles, and those of the greatest order, in none of which was he ever conquered or put to flight; but he traversed the whole circle of Britain in one continued series of victories—victories, 20 which demand the great work of a regular history; another field, as it were, on which they may be told; a space for narration equal to the things to be described. To evince his extraordinary, his little less than divine virtue, this mark will suffice; that there lived in him an energy whether of spirit 25 and genius, or of discipline, established not by military rule only, but by the rule of Christ and of sanctity, that he drew all to his camp, as to the best school both of military science, and of religion and piety—nay those who were already good and

& fortes undique attraheret, vel tales, ipsius maximè exemplo, efficeret: eósque toto belli, pacis etiam nonnunquam inter-mediæ tempore, per tot animorum & rerum vicissitudines, non largitionibus & militari licentiâ, sed authoritate & solo

5 stipendio, adversantibus licèt multis, in officio contineret & adhuc contineat: quâ quidem laude neque Cyro, neque Epa-minondæ, neque antiquorum ulli excellentissimo Imperatori laus ulla major attribui solet. Hinc enim exercitum, quo nemo minori spatio majorem aut instructiorem, sibi com-

10 paravit, & per omnia dicto audientem, & civibus gratum atque dilectum; & hostibus, armatis quidem formidolosum, pacatis admirabilem, quorum in agris atque sub tectis ita non gravis, & sine omni maleficio versabatur, ut cum regiorum suorum vim, vinolentiam, impietatem atque libidines, cogi-

15 tarent, mutatâ sorte læti, non nunc hostes, sed hospites ad-venisse crederent; præsidium bonis omnibus, terrorem malis, virtutis etiam omnis & pietatis hortatores. Sed neque te fas est præterire, *Fairfaxi,* in quo cum summâ fortitudine summam modestiam, summam vitæ sanctitatem, & natura & divinus

20 favor conjunxit: Tu harum in partem laudum evocandus tuo jure ac merito es; quanquam in illo nunc tuo secessu, quan-tus olim Literni Africanus ille Scipio, abdis te quoad potes;

brave, from all parts, or made them such principally by his own example; and although there were many who opposed him, retained them in their duty, (and yet retains,) during the whole period of the war, sometimes even of an intervening peace, through so many changes of minds and of circumstances, not by largesses and military licence, but by his authority and their pay alone: and greater praise than this we are not wont to bestow either upon Cyrus, Epaminondas, or upon any of the first generals of antiquity. Hence it is, that no one ever raised for himself a larger or better disciplined army in shorter time, obedient in all things to the word of command, welcome to the citizens and beloved by them; to its enemies in arms terrible indeed, but when reduced to peaceable subjection, the objects of their admiration: for so far from being oppressive and mischievous, when quartered in their fields, and their houses, when those enemies recollected the violence, the drunkenness, the impiety and lust of their own royalists, they were happy at the change, and now thought themselves visited not by enemies, but by guests; a protection to the good, a terror to the evil, the encouragers to all virtue and piety.

Nor must I forget you, Fairfax, in whom nature and the divine favour have conspired to unite the greatest modesty, the most exemplary sanctity of life, with the highest courage. Your merit and your right entitle you to be called forth to receive your share of these eulogies; though in your present secession, like that Scipio Africanus of old at Liternum, you hide yourself, as much as possible, from the public view. It is

nec hostem solùm, sed ambitionem, & quæ præstantissimum quemque mortalium vincit, gloriam quoque vicisti; tuísque virtutibus & præclarè factis, jucundissimum & gloriosissimum per otium frueris, quod est laborum omnium & humanarum actionum vel maximarum finis; qualíque otio cùm antiqui Heroes, post bella & decora tuis haud majora, fruerentur, qui eos laudare conati sunt poetæ, desperabant se posse aliâ ratione id quale esset dignè describere, nisi eos fabularentur, cœlo receptos, deorum epulis accumbere. Verùm te sive valetudo, quod maximè crediderim, sive quid aliud retraxit, persuasissimum hoc habeo, nihil te à rationibus reipublicæ divellere potuisse, nisi vidisses quantum libertatis conservatorem, quàm firmum atque fidum Anglicanæ rei columen ac munimentum in successore tuo relinqueres. Te enim salvo, Cromuelle, ne Deo quidem satis confidit, qui rebus Anglorum, satis ut salvæ sint, metuat; cùm videat tam faventem tibi, tam evidenter opitulantem ubique Deum. Verùm tibi tum soli decertanda alia bellorum palæstra erat.

Quid autem multa? res maximas, quâ tu celeritate soles, eâdem si possum brevitate expediam. Amissâ Hiberniâ præter unam urbem totâ, tu, exercitu transmisso, uno statim

not the enemy alone, you have conquered; you have conquered ambition, and what itself conquers the most excellent
of mortals, you have conquered glory; and are now enjoying,
in the most delightful and glorious of retirements, your vir-
5 tues and illustrious deeds, which is the end of all labours, of
the greatest even of human actions—a retirement, which
when the ancient heroes enjoyed after their battles and famous
exploits no greater than yours, the poets who attempted their
eulogies, despaired of being able to describe with appropriate
10 dignity, but by fabling that they were received up into heaven,
and sat at table with the gods. But whether you have with-
drawn on account of your health, which I am most inclined
to think, or whether from any other motive, of this I am fully
persuaded, that nothing could have torn you from the service
15 of the commonwealth, if you had not seen what a protector
of liberty, what a firm and faithful pillar, what a rampart of
England's prosperity you have left in your successor. For,
while you, Cromwell, are in safety, he shows not a sufficient
confidence in the supreme, who has any fears for the prosper-
20 ity of England; seeing, as he must, that God so manifestly
favours you, that, in all things he is your helper. But you were
now left to yourself, and had to engage in a fresh struggle of
battles.

But what need of many words? I will recount your prin-
25 cipal exploits as briefly, if I can, as you are accustomed to
achieve them rapidly. All Ireland was lost, with the exception
only of one city, when you transported an army, and immediately, in a single battle, broke the power of the Irish. What

prælio Hibernicorum opes fregisti; reliqua indies confi-
ciebas; cùm repentè ad bellum Scoticum revocaris. Hinc
contra Scotos irruptionem cum rege suo in Angliam parantes,
indefessus proficisceris; regnum illud, quod omnes reges
5 nostri octingentis annis non poterant, uno circiter anno per-
domuisti, & Anglorum ditioni adjecisti; reliquas eorum
copias, validissimas tamen & expeditas, per summam despe-
rationem in Angliam tum ferè præsidiis nudatam, inopinâ
impressione factâ, Vigornium usque progressas, magnis iti-
10 neribus assecutus, uno prælio delevisti; captâ penè totâ gentis
nobilitate. Hinc alta pax domi: tum te, sed neque tum primùm, non minùs consiliis, quàm belli artibus valere sensi-
mus: id quotidiè in senatu agebas, vel ut cum hoste pacta fides
servaretur, vel uti ea, quæ ex republicâ essent, maturè decerne-
15 rentur. Cum videres moras necti, privatæ quemque rei, quam
publicæ, attentiorem, populum queri delusum se suâ spe, &
potentiâ paucorum circumventum esse, quod ipsi toties moniti nolebant, eorum dominationi finem imposuisti. Parlamentum aliud convocatur novum; concessâ iis duntaxat,
20 quibus par erat, eligendi potestate; conveniunt electi; nihil

remained to be done you were dispatching daily, when you
were suddenly recalled to the war in Scotland. Quitting Ireland you advance, unwearied, against the Scots, who, with
their king, were preparing for an irruption upon England;
5 and in about one year, reduced, and added to the dominion of
England a kingdom, which all our kings, during a period of
eight hundred years, had been unable to subdue. The remains
of their forces, which however were in high condition and
well-equipped, marched, in their utmost despair into Eng-
10 land, which at that time was almost destitute of garrisons.
You pursued them with forced marches, and overtaking them
when they had advanced as far as Worcester, fell upon them
suddenly, and destroyed them in a single battle; taking the
chief part of their national nobility prisoners. There was now,
15 at home, a profound peace: and it was then we felt, but not
then for the first time, that your power was not less in counsel
than in the arts of war. In the parliament, it was your daily
care to see, either that the faith of the treaty entered into with
the enemy should be maintained, or that without delay such
20 resolutions should be adopted as might be for the benefit of
the state. But perceiving that delays were artfully contrived;
that every one was more attentive to his private interest than
to the interest of the public; that the people complained they
were disappointed in their expectations, and circumvented by
25 the power of a few, you put an end to their arbitrary authority, which they, though so often advised to it, had refused to
do. A new parliament is called; the privilege of voting is allowed to those only, to whom it was proper to allow it; the

agunt; cùm se invicem dissidiis & altercationibus diu defati-
gassent, animadvertentes plerique se rebus tantis exequendis,
neque pares esse, neque idoneos, ipsi sese dissolvunt. Deseri-
mur Cromuelle; tu solus superes, ad te rerum summa nostra-
5 rum rediit; in te solo consistit; insuperabili tuæ virtuti cedi-
mus cuncti, nemine vel obloquente, nisi qui aut æquales inæ-
qualis ipse honores sibi quærit, aut digniori concessos invidet,
aut non intelligit nihil esse in societate hominum magis vel
Deo gratum, vel rationi consentaneum, esse in civitate nihil
10 æquius, nihil utilius, quàm potiri rerum dignissimum. Eum
te agnoscunt omnes, Cromuelle, ea tu civis maximus & glo-
riosissimus, dux publici consilii, fortissimorum exercituum
Imperator, pater patriæ gessisti: sic tu spontaneâ bonorum
omnium & animitùs missâ voce salutaris: alios titulos te dignos
15 tua facta non norunt, non ferunt, & superbos illos, vulgi licet
opinione magnos, meritò respuunt. Quid enim est titulus,
nisi definitus quidam dignitatis modus? tuæ res gestæ cùm
admirationis, tum certè titulorum modum omnem excedunt;
& velut pyramidum apices cœlo se condunt, populari titulo-
20 rum aurâ excelsiores. Sed quoniam summis etiam virtutibus,

elected meet; do nothing; and having harassed one another for a while with their dissentions and altercations, and most of them being of opinion that they were unfit persons, and not equal to undertakings of such magnitude, they dissolve them-
5 selves. Cromwell, we are deserted; you alone remain; the sovereign authority of the state is returned into your hands, and subsists only in you. To your invincible virtue we all give place, all but such, who without equal ability are desirous of equal honours; who look with envy upon the honours be-
10 stowed upon others more worthy than themselves, or who know not, that there is nothing in human society more pleasing to God, or more agreeable to reason; that there is nothing more just in a state, nothing more useful, than that the most worthy should possess the sovereign power. That you are such,
15 Cromwell, that such have been your deeds, is acknowledged by all—you, who are the greatest and most glorious of our citizens, the director of the public counsels, the leader of the bravest of armies, the father of your country: for by this title do all good men hail you with spontaneous voice sent forth
20 from the heart. Other titles, though merited by you, your actions know not, endure not; and those proud ones, deemed great in vulgar opinion, they deservedly cast from them. For what is a title, but a certain definite mode of dignity? Your achievements surpass every degree even of admiration, and
25 much more do they surpass every title;—they rise above the popular atmosphere of titles, as the tops of pyramids hide themselves in the clouds. But though it can add nothing to dignity, yet as it is expedient, for virtues even the most ex-

qui honos habetur, humano quodam fastigio finiri ac termi-
nari, non dignum est, sed tamen expedit, assumpto quodam
titulo patris patriæ simillimo, non evehi te quidem, sed tot
gradibus ex sublimi descendere, & velut in ordinem cogi,
5 publico commodo, & sensisti & sustinuisti; regium nomen
majestate longè majore aspernatus. Et meritò quidem: quod
enim nomen, privatus sub jugum mittere, & ad nihilum planè
redigere potuisti, eo si tantus vir factus caperere, idem penè
faceres, atque si gentem aliquam Idololatram Dei veri ope
10 cùm subegisses, victos abs te coleres deos. Tu igitur, Cromuelle, magnitudine illâ animi macte esto; te enim decet; tu
patriæ liberator, libertatis auctor, custosque idem & conser-
vator, neque graviorem personam, neque augustiorem susci-
pere potes aliam; qui non modò regum res gestas, sed He-
15 roum quoque nostrorum fabulas factis exuperasti. Cogita
sæpiùs, quàm caram rem, ab quàm cara parente tua, libertatem à patriâ tibi commendatam atque concreditam, apud te
depositam habes: quod ab electissimis gentis universæ viris,
illa modò expectabat, id nunc à te uno expectat, per te unum
20 consequi sperat: Reverere tantam de te expectationem, spem
patriæ de te unicam; reverere vultus & vulnera tot fortium
virorum, quotquot, te duce, pro libertate tam strenuè decer-
târunt; manes etiam eorum qui in ipso certamine occubue-

alted to be finished and terminated by a sort of human summit, which is counted honour, you thought it right, and suffered yourself, for the public benefit, to assume something
like a title, resembling most that of *pater patriæ,* the father of
5 your country; you suffered yourself not to be raised indeed,
but to descend so many degrees from on high, and to be forced
as it were into the ranks; despising the name of king for majesty far more majestic. And justly so: for if, after becoming so
great, you should be captivated with a name, which, as a
10 private man, you were able to subjugate, to reduce to a cipher,
it would be all one, as if, after subduing, by the help of the
true God, an idolatrous nation, you were to worship as gods
those whom you had brought under subjection. Go on therefore, Cromwell, in your wonted magnanimity; it fits you
15 well. Your country's deliverer, the founder of our liberty, and
at the same time its protector, you can assume no other character more dignified or more august; for your exploits have
surpassed not merely those of kings, but even those which
have been fabled of our heroes. Consider often, how precious
20 a thing you hold deposited with you, and by a parent how
dear—liberty, commended and entrusted to your care by your
country! who, what she before expected from the choicest men
of the whole nation, now expects, and hopes to attain through
you alone. Respect this high expectation of you, this only
25 hope of your country. Respect the countenances and the
wounds of so many brave men who, under your conduct,
have fought so zealously for liberty, and the departed spirits
of those, who have fallen in the struggle. Respect also what

runt: reverere exterarum quoque civitatum existimationem
de nobis atque sermones; quantas res de libertate nostra, tam
fortiter partâ, de nostrâ republicâ, tam gloriosè exortâ sibi
polliceantur: quæ si tam citò quasi aborta evanuerit, profectò
5 nihil æquè dedecorosum huic genti, atque pudendum fuerit:
teipsum denique reverere, ut pro quâ adipiscendâ libertate,
tot ærumnas pertulisti, tot pericula adiisti, eam adeptus, vio-
latam per te, aut ullâ in parte imminutam aliis, ne sinas esse.
Profectò tu ipse liber sine nobis esse non potes; sic enim naturâ
10 comparatum est, ut qui aliorum libertatem occupat, suam ipse
primus omnium amittat; séque primum omnium intelligat
servire: atque id quidem non injuriâ. At verò, si patronus
ipse libertatis, & quasi tutelaris deus, si is, quo nemo justior,
nemo sanctior est habitus, nemo vir melior, quam vindicavit
15 ipse, eam postmodùm invaserit, id non ipsi tantùm, sed universæ virtutis ac pietatis rationi perniciosum ac lethale propemodum sit necesse est: ipsa honestas, ipsa virtus decoxisse
videbitur, religionis angusta fides, existimatio perexigua in
posterum erit, quo gravius generi humano vulnus, post illud
20 primum, infligi nullum poterit. Onus longè gravissimum
suscepisti, quod te penitùs explorabit, totum te atque intimum
perscrutabitur atque ostendet, quid tibi animi, quid virium
insit, quid ponderis; vivatne in te verè illa pietas, fides, justitia, animíque moderatio, ob quas evectum te præ cæteris

foreign nations think and say of us; what great things they
promise themselves from our liberty, which has been won
with so much bravery, from our commonwealth, which has
sprung up with so much glory; and which, if it should vanish
5 as soon as it has arisen, no equal disgrace and shame could fall
upon this nation. Last of all, respect yourself, and suffer not
that liberty, which you have gained with so many hardships,
so many dangers, to be violated by yourself, or in any wise im-
paired by others. Indeed, without our freedom, you yourself
10 cannot be free: for such is the order of nature, that he who
forcibly seizes upon the liberty of others, is the first to lose his
own, is the first to become a slave: and nothing can be more
just than this. But if the patron himself of liberty, and as it
were, her tutelary genius—if he, than whom none is esteemed
15 a more just, a holier, or a better man, should at last offer violence to her whom he has defended, this must, of necessity, be
destructive and deadly not to himself alone, but, in a manner,
to the very cause of all virtue and piety. Honour and virtue
themselves will appear to have faded away; henceforward,
20 religious faith will be narrowed; reputation will be a poor
thing indeed; and a deeper wound than this, after that first,
it would not be possible to inflict upon human kind. You
have taken upon you by far the heaviest burden, which will
try you thoroughly; it will search you through and through,
25 and lay open your inmost soul; it will show what is the pre-
dominant disposition of your nature, what is your strength,
what is your weight; whether there is indeed in you that
living piety, that faith, justice, and moderation of mind, for

Dei numine ad hanc summam dignitatem credimus. Tres Nationes validissimas consilio regere, populos ab institutis pravis ad meliorem, quàm antehac, frugem ac disciplinam velle perducere, remotissimas in partes sollicitam mentem, 5 cogitationésque immittere, vigilare, prævidere, nullum laborem recusare, nulla voluptatum blandimenta non spernere, divitiarum atque potentiæ ostentationem fugere, hæc sunt illa ardua, præ quibus bellum ludus est; hæc te ventilabunt atque excutient, hæc virum poscunt divino fultum auxilio, divino 10 penè colloquio monitum atque edoctum. Quæ tu, & plura, sæpenumero quin tecum reputes atque animo revolvas, non dubito: uti & illud, quibus potissimùm queas modis & illa maxima perficere, & libertatem salvam nobis reddere & auctiorem. Quod meo quidem judicio, haud aliâ ratione 15 rectiùs effeceris, quam si primùm quos laborum atque discriminum comites habuisti, eosdem, quod facis, consiliorum socios cum primis adhibueris; viros sanè & modestissimos, & integerrimos, & fortissimos; quos tot mortes conspectæ, tot strages ante ora editæ, non ad crudelitatem, aut duriciem 20 animi, sed ad justitiam, & numinis reverentiam, & humanæ sortis miserationem, ad libertatem denique eo acriùs retinendam erudierunt, quo gravioribus ejus causâ periculis ipsi suum caput objecêre: Non illi quidem ex colluvione vulgi,

which we have thought that you above all others deserved,
by the will of God, to be elevated to this sovereign dignity.
To rule by your counsel three most potent nations; to be desirous of leading the people from corrupt institutions to a bet-
5 ter plan of life and of discipline than they had before; to send
out your anxious mind, your thoughts, to the remotest parts;
to watch, to foresee, to cavil at no toil, to despise all the blan-
dishments of pleasure, to shun the pomp of wealth and of
power,—these are those arduous things, in comparison of
10 which war is a play-game; these will drive against you like a
mighty wind, and shake your steadiness; these require a man
who is upheld by divine help, who is admonished and taught
by little less than divine converse. All these things and more,
I doubt not, you frequently meditate, and revolve in your
15 mind; as likewise, by what means you may give effect to those
momentous considerations, and restore to us our liberty safe,
and augmented. This, in my judgment, you could in no way
be more likely to accomplish, than by associating those, as you
do, among the first, in your counsels, whom you had first as
20 companions of your labours and of your dangers—men distinguished alike for their modesty, their integrity, and their
courage; whom the sight of such multitudes of deaths, such
multitudes of slaughters, has not taught cruelty or hardness
of heart, but justice, and reverence of God, and compassion
25 for the lot of humanity; but, in fine, to be tenacious of their
liberty in proportion to the danger to which they have exposed
their lives for her sake. These men were not taken from the
refuse of the people, or of foreigners; they are no mob of men,

aut advenarum, non turba collectitia, sed melioris plerique
notæ cives, genere vel nobili, vel non inhonesto, fortunis vel
amplis, vel mediocribus; quid si ipsâ paupertate aliqui com-
mendatiores? quos non præda convocavit, sed difficillima
5 tempora, rebus maximè dubiis, sæpè adversis, ad liberandam
tyrannide rempublicam excitarunt; non in tuto aut curiâ sermones inter se atque sententias tantùm, sed manus cum hoste
conserere paratos. Quòd nisi spes semper infinitas, atque
inanes persequemur, in quibus tandem mortalium sisti aut
10 confidi possit non video, si his horúmque similibus fides non
habebitur. Quorum fidelitatis, certissimum pignus, & indu-
bitatum habemus, quòd pro republica vel mortem oppetere,
si ita sors tulisset, non recusarint; pietatis, quòd implorato
suppliciter dei auxilio, totiésque ab eo insigniter adjuti, à quo
15 auxilium petere, eidem gloriam tribuere omnem rerum pro-
sperè gestarum consueverint; justitiæ, quòd etiam regem in
judicium adduxerint, damnato parci noluerint; moderationis,
quòd & eam experti jam diu sumus, &, quam ipsi sibi pepe-
rere pacem, si eorundem per injuriam rumpatur, quæ mala
20 inde oritura sunt, ipsi primi sint persensuri, ipsi prima vulnera suis corporibus excepturi, déque suis omnibus fortunis
atque ornamentis felicitèr jam partis rursus dimicaturi; for-

but most of them citizens of the better note, either of a noble
origin, or of an origin not disreputable; possessed, some of
ample, others of moderate fortunes. And what if some be rec-
ommended even by their poverty? These were not called to-
5 gether by the hope of plunder, but were excited to the deliverance of the commonwealth from tyranny, by the difficulty
of the times, when the situation of affairs was eminently crit-
ical, often adverse; prepared not only to talk and interchange
opinions, in a place of safety, or in the parliament, but to join
10 in close fight with the enemy. And unless we are to be for ever
in pursuit of vague and idle hopes, I see not in what men we
can at last rest and confide, if we are not to have confidence in
these, and such as these. Of their fidelity we have a certain,
an undoubted pledge, in their not refusing to meet even death,
15 if such should be their destiny, for the public good: of their
piety, in their having been accustomed, after humbly imploring the assistance of God and being often signally assisted by
him, to ascribe all the glory of their success to him whom they
had asked for succour: of their justice, in their having brought
20 even the king to judgment, and refused to spare him when
condemned; of their moderation, since this we have ourselves
long experienced; besides, if the peace which they have obtained for themselves should be broken, through their own
fault, they themselves would be the first to feel the evils which
25 would thence arise, would receive on their own bodies the
first wounds, would have to fight again for all those fortunes
and ensigns of dignity which they had so happily won before:
last of all, of their courage; for, in the recovery of their liberty,

titudinis denique, quòd nulli unquam libertatem feliciùs aut
fortiùs recuperaverint; ne arbitremur ullos alios posse dili-
gentiùs conservare. Gestit clarorum virorum nomina com-
memorare oratio mea: te primum, Fletuode, quem ego ab
5 ipsis tyrociniis ad hos usque militiæ honores, quos nunc ob-
tines à summis proximos, humanitate, mansuetudine, benignitate animi eundem novi; hostis fortem & imperterritum,
sed & mitissimum quoque victorem sensit: Te, Lamberte,
qui vix modicæ dux manûs, ducem Hamiltonum juvenis,
10 totius Scoticæ juventutis flore ac robore circumseptum, & pro-
gredientem retardasti, & retardatum sustinuisti: Te, Des-
boroe, Te, Hualei, qui atrocissimas hujus belli pugnas vel
audienti mihi vel legenti, inter hostes confertissimos expec-
tati semper occurristis: Te, Overtone, mihi multis abhinc
15 annis, & studiorum similitudine, & morum suavitate, concor-
diâ plusquam fraternâ conjunctissime; te Marstonensi prælio
illo memorabili, pulso sinistro cornu nostro, respectantes in
fugâ duces stantem cum tuo pedite, & hostium impetus pro-
pulsantem inter densas utrinque cædes vidêre: Scotico deinde
20 bello, ut primùm Cromuelli auspiciis, tuo marte occupata Fifæ
littora, & patefactus ultra Sterlinium aditus est, te Scoti occi-

no men ever showed greater courage, or had greater success:
and let us not suffer ourselves to think that there are any who
can preserve it with greater diligence.

My speech is impatient to commemorate the names of men
5 who have risen to distinction: and first you Fleetwood, whom
I have known to have been always the same in the humanity,
gentleness, and benignity of your disposition, from the time
you first entered upon the profession of a soldier to your ob-
tainment of these military honours, the next only to the first;
10 and whom the enemy has found of dauntless valour, but the
mildest of conquerors: and you Lambert, who, when a young
man, at the head of a mere handful of men, checked the
progress of the duke of Hamilton, attended with the flower
and strength of the Scottish youth, and kept him at check:
15 you, Desborow, and you, Whalley, whom, whenever I heard
or read of the fiercest battles of this war, I always expected, and found, among the thickest of the enemy: you
Overton, who have been connected with me for these many
years in a more than brotherly union, by similitude of stud-
20 ies, and by the sweetness of your manners: in that mem-
orable battle of Marston Moor, when our left wing was
routed, the chief officers looking back in their flight beheld
you keeping your ground with your infantry, and repelling
the attacks of the enemy, amid heaps of slain on both sides:
25 and afterwards, in the war in Scotland, no sooner were the
shores of Fife occupied, under the auspices of Cromwell, with
your troops, and the way opened beyond Stirling, than both
the western and the northern Scots acknowledged you for the

dentales, te Boreales humanissimum hostem, te Orcades ex-
tremæ domitorem fatentur. Addam & nonnullos, quos togâ
celebres & pacis artibus, consiliarios tibi advocasti, vel ami-
citiâ vel famâ mihi cognitos; Huitlochium, Picheringum,
5 Striclandium, Sidnamum, atque Sidneium (quod ego illustre
nomen nostris semper adhæsisse partibus lætor) Montacuti-
um, Laurentium, summo ingenio ambos, optimisque artibus
expolitos; aliosque permultos eximiis meritis cives, partim
senatorio jampridem munere, partim militari operâ insignes.
10 His & ornatissimis viris & spectatissimis civibus libertatem
nostram proculdubio rectè commiseris; immò quibus tutiùs
committi possit aut concredi, haud facilè quis dixerit. Deinde
si ecclesiam ecclesiæ reliqueris, téque ac magistratus eo onere,
& dimidio simul & alienissimo, prudens levaveris; nec duas
15 potestates longè diversissimas, civilem & ecclesiasticam, siveris
inter se scortari; séque invicem promiscuis ac falsis opibus in
speciem quidem firmare, re autem verâ labefactare ac demum
subvertere: si vim omnem ab ecclesia sustuleris; vis autem
nunquam aberit, quandiu pecunia, ecclesiæ toxicum, veritatis
20 angina, enuntiandi evangelii merces, vi etiam ab nolentibus

humanest of enemies, and the farthest Orcades for their civi-
lizing conqueror. I will yet add some, whom, as distinguished
for the robe and arts of peace, you have nominated as your
counsellors, and who are known to me either by friendship or
5 reputation: Whitlocke; Pickering; Strickland; Sydenham;
and Sidney (an illustrious name, which I rejoice has steadily
adhered to our side); Montague; Lawrence—both men of
the first capacity, and polished by liberal studies: besides
numberless other citizens, distinguished for their rare merits,
10 some for their former senatorial exertions, others for their
military services.

To these accomplished men and chosen citizens you doubtless might properly commit the care of our liberty; indeed, it
is not easy to say, to whom it could more safely be committed
15 or confided. After this, I could earnestly wish that you should
leave the church to itself, and have the prudence to relieve
yourself and the magistrates from that burden, which is one
half, and at the same time, most remote from your own province; and that you should not suffer the two powers, the ec-
20 clesiastical and the civil, which are so totally distinct, to commit whoredom together, and, by their intermingled and false
riches, to strengthen indeed, in appearance, but in reality to
undermine, and at last to subvert one another. I could wish,
that you should take away all power from the church—and
25 power will never be wanting as long as there shall be money,
the poison of the church, the quinsy of truth; as long as there
shall be hire for preaching the gospel, coercively collected
even from those who have no disposition to pay it; that you

coacta, erit; ejeceris ex ecclesia nummularios illos, non co-
lumbas sed columbam, sanctum ipsum spiritum cauponantes.
Tum si leges non tot rogaveris novas, quot abrogaveris vete-
res; sunt enim sæpè in republica, qui multas leges ferendi, ut
5 versificatores multa carmina fundendi impetigine quadam
pruriunt: sed leges quo sunt plures, eo ferè sunt deteriores;
non cautiones sed cautes, tu necessarias duntaxat retinueris,
alias tuleris, non quæ bonos cum malis eodem jugo subjiciant,
aut quibus, dum improborum fraudes præcaventur, quod
10 bonis liberum esse debet, vetatur, sed quæ in vitia tantum
animadvertant, res per se licitas abutentium ob noxam, non
prohibeant. Leges enim ad frænandam malitiam solùm sunt
comparatæ, virtutis libertas formatrix optima atque auctrix
est. Deinde si juventutis institutioni ac moribus meliùs pro-
15 spexeris, quàm est adhuc prospectum, nec dociles juxta atque
indociles, gnavos atque ignavos, impensis publicis ali æquum
senseris, sed jam doctis, jam benè meritis doctorum præmia
reservaveris. Tum si liberè philosophari volentibus permise-
ris, quæ habent, sine magistelli cujuspiam privato examine,

should cast out from the church those money-changers, who
sell not doves, but the dove, the holy spirit itself. Again, I
could wish, that you should introduce fewer new laws, than
you abrogate old ones: for there are often to be found in a
5 state men, who have a sort of diseased itching for the enaction
of a multiplicity of laws, like that of versifiers for the fabri-
cation of a multitude of verses; but laws are commonly bad,
in proportion as they are numerous—acting not as warnings
to men, but as rocks on which they must split. You should
10 retain only those which are necessary; should enact others;
yet not such as would bring the good and the bad under the
same yoke, or such as, while they provided against the knavery
of the unprincipled, should, at the same time, prohibit what,
to honest men, should be free from all restraint; but such as
15 should punish only actual crimes, and not forbid things, in
themselves lawful, for the fault of those who abuse them: for
laws have been provided only to restrain malignity; to form
and increase virtue, the most excellent thing is liberty. Next,
I could wish you should make a better provision for the edu-
20 cation and morals of youth, than has been yet made; and that
you should feel it to be unjust, that the teachable and unteach-
able, the diligent and the idle, should be maintained at the
public charge; and that you should reserve the rewards of the
learned for those who are already proficients in learning, for
25 those whose merit is already established.—Again, it is my
earnest wish, that you would give permission to those who are
inclined to freedom of inquiry, to publish what they have to
communicate at their own peril, without the private inquisi-

suo periculo in lucem proferre: ita enim maximè veritas efflo-
ruerit; nec semidoctorum semper sive censura, sive invidia,
sive tenuitas animi, sive superstitio aliorum inventa, omném-
que scientiam suo modulo metietur, suóque arbitrio nobis im-
5 pertiverit. Postremò si ipse neque verum neque falsum, quicquid id est, audire metueris: eos autem minimè omnium audi-
eris, qui sese liberos esse non credunt, nisi aliis esse liberis, per
ipsos non liceat; nec studiosiùs aut violentiùs quicquam agunt,
quàm ut fratrum non corporibus modò sed conscientiis quo-
10 que vincula injiciant; pessimámque omnium tyrannidem, vel
pravarum consuetudinum vel opinionum suarum & in rempublicam & in ecclesiam inducant; tu ab eorum parte semper
steteris, qui non suam tantummodo sectam aut factionem, sed
omnes æquè cives, æquali jure liberos esse in civitate arbitran-
15 tur oportere. Hæc sicui satis libertas non est, quæ quidem à
magistratibus exhiberi potest, is mihi ambitionis atque tur-
barum, quam libertatis ingenuæ studiosior videtur; præsertim cum agitatus tot factionibus populus, ut post tempestatem,
cùm fluctus nondum resederunt, statum illum rerum opta-
20 bilem atque perfectum, ipse non admittat.

Nam & vos, ô cives, quales ipsi sitis ad libertatem vel acqui-
rendam vel retinendam haud parvi interest: nisi libertas vestra
ejusmodi sit, quæ neque parari armis, neque auferri possit,

tion of any magisterial censor: for nothing could contribute
so much to the growth of truth; nor would all science be for
ever measured out to us in the bushel, and be bestowed at the
good pleasure of the half-learned, whether arising from their
5 censure, their envy, their narrow-mindedness, or from their
having detected superstition in others. Lastly, it is my fervent
wish, that you should not be afraid to listen either to truth or
falsehood, of whatever description that may be; but that you
should listen the least of all to those, who never fancy that
10 themselves are free, unless they deprive others of their freedom; who labour at nothing with so much zeal and earnestness, as to enchain not the bodies only, but the consciences of
their brethren; and to introduce into church and state the
worst of all tyrannies—the tyranny of their own misshapen
15 customs and opinions. May you ever take part with those,
who think it just, that not their own sect or faction alone, but
all the citizens alike should have an equal right to be free.
Should any one think this liberty, which may be dispensed by
the magistrates, to be not enough, such a man seems to me to
20 have his thoughts employed more about ambition and dis-
turbance, than a generous liberty; and the more, as, notwithstanding the people have been agitated with so many factions,
as after a tempest before the waves have yet subsided, he
refuses to admit so desirable and perfect a state of things.

25   And as for you, citizens, it is of no small concern, what
manner of men ye are, whether to acquire, or to keep posses-
sion of your liberty. Unless your liberty be of that kind, which
can neither be gotten, nor taken away by arms; and that alone

ea autem sola est, quæ pietate, justitiâ, temperantiâ, verâ denique virtute nata, altas atque intimas radices animis vestris egerit, non deerit profectò qui vobis istam, quam vi atque armis quæsivisse gloriamini, etiam sine armis citò eripiat.

5 Multos bellum auxit, quos pax minuit: si perfuncti bello, pacis studia neglexeritis, si bellum pax vestra, atque libertas, bellum tantummodò vestra virtus est, vestra summa gloria, invenietis, mihi credite, ipsam pacem vobis infestissimam; pax ipsa vestrum bellum longè difficillimum, & quam putâstis 10 libertatem, servitus vestra erit. Nisi per veram atque sinceram in Deum atque homines pietatem, non vanam atque verbosam, sed efficacem & operosam, superstitiones animis, religionis veræ ac solidæ ignoratione ortas, abegeritis, habebitis, qui dorso atque cervicibus vestris, tanquam jumentis inside-15 bunt; qui vos etiam victores bello suam veluti prædam sub hastâ non bellicâ nundinabuntur; & ex ignorantiâ & superstitione vestrâ, uberem quæstum facient. Nisi avaritiam, ambitionem, luxuriam mentibus, immò familiis quoque vestris luxum expuleritis, quem tyrannum foris & in acie quærendum 20 credidistis eum domi, eum intus vel duriorem sentietis, immò multi indies tyranni ex ipsis præcordiis vestris intolerandi pullulabunt. Hos vincite in primis, hæc pacis militia est, hæ sunt victoriæ, difficiles quidem, at incruentæ, illis bellicis &

is such, which, springing from piety, justice, temperance, in
fine, from real virtue, shall take deep and intimate root in
your minds; you may be assured, there will not be wanting
one, who, even without arms, will speedily deprive you of
5 what it is your boast to have gained by force of arms. Many
were made greater by the war, whom the peace has again
made less. If, after putting an end to the war, you neglect the
arts of peace; if war be your peace and liberty, war alone your
virtue, your highest glory, you will find, believe me, that
10 your greatest enemy is peace itself; peace itself will be by far
your hardest warfare, and what you think liberty will prove to
be your slavery. Unless by real and sincere devotion to God and
man, not an idle and wordy, but an efficacious, an operative
devotion, you drive from your minds superstition, which
15 originates in an ignorance of true and substantial religion,
you will not want those who will sit upon your backs and upon
your necks, as if you were beasts of burden; who, though you
are the victors in the war, will sell you, though by no military
auction, as their plunder to the highest bidder; and will make
20 an excellent market of your ignorance and superstition. Unless you banish avarice, ambition, luxury from your thoughts,
and all excess even from your families, the tyrant, whom you
imagined was to be sought abroad, and in the field, you will
find at home, you will find within, and that a more inexorable
25 one; yea, tyrants without number will be daily engendered in
your own breasts, that are not to be borne. Conquer these
first; this is the warfare of peace; these are victories, hard, it
is true, but bloodless; more glorious far than the warlike and

cruentis longè pulchriores; nisi hìc quoque victores eritis,
illum modo in acie hostem atque tyrannum, aut non omnino
aut frustra vicistis: nam pecuniæ vim maximam in ærarium
inferendi rationes posse calidissimas excogitare, pedestres
5 atque navales copias impigrè posse instruere, posse cum legatis exterorum cautè agere, societates & fœdera peritè contra-
here, si qui majus atque utilius ac sapientius in republica exi-
stimavistis esse, quàm incorrupta populo judicia præstare,
afflictis per injuriam atque oppressis opem ferre, suum cuíque
10 jus expeditum reddere, quanto sitis in errore versati, tum serò
nimis perspicietis, cum illa magna repentè vos fefellerint, hæc
parva vestro nunc judicio & neglecta adversa tum vobis &
exitio fuerint. Quin & exercituum & sociorum, quibus con-
fiditis, fluxa fides, nisi justitiæ solâ authoritate retineatur: &
15 opes atque honores, quos plerique sectantur, facilè dominos
mutant: ubi virtus, ubi industria, & laborum tolerantia plus
viget, eò transfugiunt, & ignavos deserunt. Sic gens gentem
urget, aut sanior pars gentis corruptiorem proturbat: sic vos
regios dejecistis. Si vos in eadem vitia prolabi, si illos imitari,
20 eadem sequi, easdem inanitates aucupari ceperitis, vos profectò regii estis, vel eisdem adhuc hostibus, vel aliis vicissim

the bloody. If ye are not the victors here also, that enemy and tyrant, whom you so late have conquered in the field, you have either not conquered at all, or have conquered to no purpose: for, if, to be able to devise the subtlest expedients for
5 filling the treasury; if, to furnish out sea and land forces, with the utmost expedition; if, to treat warily with the ambassadors of foreign states; to enter, with dexterity, into coalitions and treaties, be accounted by you more grand, more useful, more wise in a state, than to administer uncorrupted justice
10 to the people; than to succour the oppressed, and those who are injuriously afflicted; than to give to every man his free, unshackled right—when you have suddenly found those grand things to be delusive, and the things which are now thought little and are neglected by you shall prove adverse and de-
15 structive; it will then be too late for you to discover how great has been your error. Again, the fidelity of the armies and adherents, in whom ye confide, is uncertain, unless it be maintained by the authority of justice alone: and wealth and honours, the objects of pursuit to most men, easily change masters.
20 Where virtue, where industry, and patience of labour are in greatest vigour, thither do they take their flight; the indolent they forsake. Thus nation presses on nation; or the sounder part of a nation thrusts out the more corrupt. Thus have you thrust out the royalists. If you suffer yourselves to turn aside
25 to the same vices; to imitate them; to follow the same courses; to hunt after the same vanities, you will, in effect, be royalists yourselves, and in your turn will lay yourselves open to these, either to the same as have been hitherto your enemies, or to

opportuni; qui iisdem ad Deum precibus, eâdem patientiâ, integritate, solertiâ freti, quâ vos primò valuistis, depravatos nunc, & in regium luxum atque socordiam prolapsos, meritò subjugabunt. Tum verò, quod miserum est, videbimini, planè

5 quasi Deum vestri pœnituisset, pervasisse ignem ut fumo pereatis: quantæ nunc admirationi, tantæ tunc omnibus contemptioni eritis; hoc solum quod aliis fortasse, non vobis, prodesse in posterum queat, salutare documentum relicturi, quantas res vera virtus & pietas efficere potuisset, cum ficta & adum-

10 brata, duntaxat bellè simulando, & aggredi tantas, & progressus in iis tantos per vos facere valuerit. Non enim, si propter vestram sive imperitiam, sive inconstantiam, sive improbitatem tam præclarè facta malè cesserunt, idcirco viris melioribus minus post hæc vel licebit vel sperandum erit. Sed

15 liberare vos denuò tam facilè corruptos nemo, ne Cromuellus quidem, nec tota, si revivisceret, Brutorum natio liberatorum, aut si velit, possit, aut si possit, velit. Quid enim quisquam vobis libera suffragia & eligendi quos vultis in senatum potestatem tum assereret, an ut suæ quisque factionis homines per

20 urbes, aut qui conviviis unctiùs vos, & majoribus poculis per municipia colonos ac rusticos exceperit, eum quantumvis in-

others; who, trusting to the same prayers to God, the same patience, integrity, and skill, by which you first prevailed, will deservedly bring you under the yoke, corrupted as you then will be, and sunk into royalist excess and folly. Then, as

5 if God had utterly repented him of you, which is a miserable thing, you will appear to have passed through the fire only to perish in the smoke; and then you will become as much the contempt of mankind, as you are now their admiration; and will leave behind you this only salutary lesson, which here-

10 after may haply be useful to others, though not to yourselves, —how great achievements true virtue and piety could perform, when the false counterfeit of these qualities, merely well dissembled, could, in your case, attempt so much and succeed so far in their attempt. But if, either through your

15 inexperience, or inconstancy, or want of principle, achieve-ments so splendid have turned out unfortunately, they will not be the less feasible, on that account, or the less likely to succeed, for the time to come, in the hands of better men. But no man, not Cromwell himself, not the whole nation

20 of those deliverers the Brutuses, if it should revisit us, either could, if it would, or would, if it could, deliver you again, if you are thus easily corrupted. For, to what purpose, in such a case, would any one stand up in your behalf, for freedom of suffrage, and for the privilege of returning whom

25 you please to parliament?—that every candidate may en-tertain the men of his own party in the cities? or, that you may elect the man, however unfit, who should treat you with the most lavish feastings, or the farmers and countrymen, in

dignum eligere possitis? ita non prudentia, non authoritas,
sed factio & sagina, aut ex tabernis urbicis caupones & insti-
tores reipublicæ, aut ex pagis bubulcos, & verè pecuarios senatores, nobis creaverit. Illis nempe rempublicam commenda-
5 ret, quibus vel rem privatem nemo committeret? illis ærarium
& vectigalia qui rem suam turpiter prodegere? illis publicos
reditus, quos depeculentur, quos ex publicis privatos reddant?
an legislatores ut illi extemplò gentis universæ fiant, qui ipsi
quid lex, quid ratio, quid fas aut jus, rectum aut curvum, lici-
10 tum aut illicitum sit, nunquam intellexerint? qui potestatem
omnem in violentia, dignitatem in superbia atque fastidio po-
sitam existiment? Qui in Senatu nihil prius agant, quàm ut
amicis pravè gratificentur, inimicis memores adversentur?
qui propinquos sibi ac necessarios, tributis imperandis, bonis
15 proscribendis, per provincias substituant, homines plerosque
viles ac perditos, qui suarum ipsi auctionum sectores, gran-
dem exinde pecuniam cogant, coactam intervertant, rempublicam fraudent, provincias expilent, se locupletent, ad opu-
lentiam atque fastum ex mendicitate hesterna ac sordibus
20 repentini emergant? quis tales ferat servos furaces, domino-
rum vicarios? quis ipsos furum dominos ac patronos, libertatis
idoneos fore custodes crediderit, aut illiusmodi curatoribus

the borough-towns, with the greatest quantity of drink? Thus
would faction and cramming, not prudence and authority,
create for us the men who are to watch over the state; and we
should have victuallers and hucksters from the city-shops, and
5 herdsmen and graziers from the villages, for our senators.
That is, the concerns of the public would be entrusted to those,
to whom nobody would entrust his private concerns—the
treasury and taxes to such as had shamefully squandered their
own substance, the public revenue to those who would be
10 guilty of peculation, who would convert public into private
property. Can men become all at once the legislators of a nation, who have never learnt what law means, what reason,
what is right or wrong, lawful or unlawful? Who think that
all power consists in violence; dignity, in pride and haughti-
15 ness? Whose first acts in the parliament, are to confer corrupt
favours on their friends, and to take care to thwart their
enemies? Who appoint in the provinces their relations and
dependents to superintend the assessments, and to sequester
property—most of them men of worthless character and des-
20 perate fortunes, who from being the purchasers at their own
auctions, amass immense sums of money, which they convert
to their own use, and thus defraud the public, plunder the
provinces, enrich themselves, and from the beggary and
meanness of yesterday, suddenly emerge to opulence and
25 pride? Who can bear such thievish servants, their masters
deputies? Who would believe that the very masters and
patrons of thieves could be proper guardians of liberty, or
think himself made one jot the more free by such adminis-

reipublicæ (quingenti licet consueto numero sint ex muni-
cipiis omnibus hunc in modum electi) pilo se factum liberio-
rem putet, cùm & libertatis ipsi custodes & quibus custoditur
tam pauci tum sint futuri, qui libertate uti atque frui vel sciant
5 vel digni sint? Libertate autem indigni, quod omittendum
postremò non est, erga ipsos primum liberatores ingratissimi
ferè existunt. Quis nunc talium pro libertate pugnare, aut vel
minimum adire periculum velit? non convenit, non cadit in
tales esse liberos; ut ut libertatem strepant atque jactent, servi
10 sunt & domi & foris, nec sentiunt; & cùm senserint tandem,
& velut ferocientes equi frænum indignantes, non veræ libertatis amore (quam solus vir bonus rectè potest appetere) sed
superbiâ & cupiditatibus pravis impulsi, jugum excutere cona-
buntur, etiamsi armis rem sæpiùs tentaverint, nihil tamen pro-
15 ficient; mutare servitutem fortasse poterunt, exuere non poterunt. Id quod Romanis etiam antiquis luxu jam fractis ac
diffluentibus persæpè accidit; recentioribus multò magis;
cùm longo post tempore Crescentii Nomentani auspiciis, &
postea duce Nicolao Rentio, qui se tribunum plebis nomina-
20 verat, antiquam renovare gloriam Romanam, & rempublicam restituere affectarent. Scitote enim, ne fortè stomache-
mini, aut quemquam præter vosmetipsos inculpare possitis,
scitote, quemadmodum esse liberum idem planè est atque esse

trators of the state (though the customary number of five hundred should be returned, after this manner, from the counties and towns) when there would be so few among the very guardians of liberty, and by whom it is guarded, who
5 could either know how to use, or could be worthy to enjoy it? But last of all, it is not to be forgotten, that those who are unworthy of liberty are commonly the first to show their ingratitude towards our deliverers. Who would now fight, or incur the least danger, for the liberty of such men? It does
10 not suit, it does not fall to the lot of such men to be free. However they may bawl and boast about liberty, they are slaves both at home and abroad, and yet perceive it not; and when they shall at length perceive it, they will disdain the curb like headstrong horses, and from the impulse of pride and little
15 desires, not from a love of genuine liberty (which a good man alone can properly attain) they will try to shake off the yoke. They may make the same attempt by arms again and again; but they will make no progress: they may change their slavery perhaps; but they will never be able to shake it off. This is
20 what very frequently happened even to the ancient Romans, after they had become effeminate and unnerved through luxury: and much more did it happen to the modern Romans, when, after a long interval they affected—under the auspices of Crescentius Nomentanus, and afterwards of Nicolaus Ren-
25 tius, who got himself nominated tribune of the people—to renew their ancient glory, and to restore the republic. For know, that you may not feel resentment, or be able to blame any body but yourselves, know, that as to be free is precisely

pium, esse sapientem, esse justum ac temperantem, sui pro-
vidum, alieni abstinentem, atque exinde demum magnani-
mum ac fortem, ita his contrarium esse, idem esse atque esse
servum; solitóque Dei judicio & quasi talione justissimâ fit,
5 ut quæ gens se regere séque moderari nequit, suísque ipsa se
libidinibus in servitutem tradidit, ea aliis, quibus nollet, do-
minis tradatur; nec libens modò, sed invita quoque serviat.
Quod etiam & jure & naturâ ipsâ sancitum est; ut qui impos
sui, qui per inopiam mentis aut furorem suas res rectè admini-
10 strare nequit, in suâ potestate ne sit; sed tanquam pupillus,
alieno dedatur imperio; nedum ut alienis negotiis, aut reipublicæ præficiendus sit. Qui liberi igitur vultis permanere, aut
sapite imprimis, aut quamprimùm resipiscite: si servire du-
rum est, atque nolitis, rectæ rationi obtemperare discite,
15 vestrûm esse compotes; postremò factionibus, odiis, supersti-
tionibus, injuriis, libidinibus ac rapinis invicem abstinete. Id
nisi pro virili vestrâ parte feceritis, neque Deo neque hominibus, ne vestris quidem jam nunc liberatoribus, idonei poteritis videri, penes quos libertas & reipublicæ gubernatio, &
20 imperandi aliis, quod tam cupidè vobis arrogatis, potestas
relinquenda sit: cum tutore potius aliquo rerúmque vestrarum
fideli ac forti curatore tanquam pupilla gens, tum quidem

the same thing as to be pious, wise, just and temperate, careful
of one's own, abstinent from what is another's, and thence, in
fine, magnanimous and brave—so, to be the opposite of these,
is the same thing as to be a slave; and by the wonted judg-
5 ment, and as it were by the just retribution of God, it comes to
pass, that the nation, which has been incapable of governing
and ordering itself, and has delivered itself up to the slavery of
its own lusts, is itself delivered over, against its will, to other
masters—and whether it will or no, is compelled to serve. For
10 this we have the sanction of law, and of nature herself; since
he who has no command of himself, who, either through im-
becility or derangement of mind, is unable to manage properly his own affairs, is not left at his own disposal; but, like a
ward, is given up to the direction of another; and much less
15 is he set to manage other people's affairs, or the affairs of a
state. Do you, therefore, who have the wish to continue free,
either begin with being wise, or repent without delay. If it be
hard, if it be against the grain, to be slaves, learn to obey right
reason, to be masters of yourselves; in fine, keep aloof from
20 factions, hatreds, superstitions, injuries, lusts, and plunders.
Unless you do this to the utmost of your power, you will be
thought neither by God nor man, not even by those who are
now your deliverers, to be fit persons in whose hands to leave
liberty, the government of the commonwealth, and what you
25 arrogate to yourselves with so much eagerness, the government of others, when like a nation in pupillage, you would
then want rather a tutor, and a faithful and courageous super-
intendent of your own concerns.

indigeatis. Ad me quod attinet, quocunque res redierit, quam
ego operam meam maximè ex usu reipublicæ futuram judi-
cavi, haud gravatim certè, &, ut spero, haud frustra impendi;
meáque arma pro libertate, non solùm ante fores extuli, sed
5 etiam iis ita latè sum usus, ut factorum minimè vulgarium jus
atque ratio, & apud nostros & apud exteros explicata atque
defensa, bonis certè omnibus probata, & ad meorum civium
summam laudem, & posterorum ad exemplum præclarè constet. Si postrema primis non satis responderint, ipsi viderint;
10 ego quæ eximia, quæ excelsa, quæ omni laude propè majora
fuere, iis testimonium, prope dixerim monumentum, perhi-
bui, haud citò interiturum; & si aliud nihil, certè fidem meam
liberavi. Quemadmodum autem poeta is qui Epicus vocatur,
si quis paulò accuratior, miniméque abnormis est, quem He-
15 roem versibus canendum sibi proponit, ejus non vitam omnem, sed unam ferè vitæ actionem, Achillis putà ad Troiam,
vel Ulissis reditum, vel Æneæ in Italiam adventum ornandum
sibi sumit, reliquas prætermittit; ita mihi quoque vel ad officium, vel ad excusationem satis fuerit, unam saltem popu-
20 larium meorum heroicè rem gestam exornasse; reliqua præ-
tereo; omnia universi populi præstare quis possit? si post tam
fortia facinora fœdiùs delicqueritis, si quid vobis indignum
commiseritis, loquetur profectò posteritas, & judicium feret;

As for myself, to whatever state things may return, I have performed, and certainly with a good will, I hope not in vain, the service which I thought would be of most use to the commonwealth. It is not before our own doors alone that I have
5 borne my arms in defence of liberty; I have wielded them on a field so wide, that the justice and reason of these which are no vulgar deeds, shall be explained and vindicated alike to foreign nations and to our own countrymen; and by all good men shall no doubt be approved; and shall remain to the matchless
10 renown of my fellow-citizens, and as the brightest example for after-ages. If our last actions should not be sufficiently answerable to the first, it is for themselves to see to it. I have celebrated, as a testimony to them, I had almost said, a monument, which will not speedily perish, actions which were
15 glorious, lofty, which were almost above all praise; and if I have done nothing else, I have assuredly discharged my trust. But as the poet, who is styled epic, if he adhere strictly to established rules, undertakes to embellish not the whole life of the hero whom he proposes to celebrate in song, but, usually,
20 one particular action of his life, as for example, that of Achilles at Troy, or the return of Ulysses, or the arrival of Æneas in Italy, and leaves alone the rest; so likewise will it suffice for my duty and excuse, that I have at least embellished one of the heroic actions of my countrymen. The rest I pass by: for who
25 could do justice to all the great actions of an entire people? If, after achievements so magnanimous, ye basely fall off from your duty, if ye are guilty of any thing unworthy of you, be assured, posterity will speak, and thus pronounce its judg-

jacta strenuè fundamenta fuisse, præclara initia immò plus quam initia; sed qui opus exædificarent, qui fastigium imponerent, non sine commotione quadam animi desiderabit; tantis incœptis, tantis virtutibus, non adfuisse perseverantiam
5 dolebit; ingentem gloriæ segetem, & maximarum rerum gerendarum materiam præbitam videbit, sed materiæ defuisse viros: non defuisse qui monere recta, hortari, incitare, qui egregiè tum facta, tum qui fecissent, condecorare, & victuris in omne ævum celebrare laudibus potuerit.

FINIS.

ment: The foundation was strongly laid, the beginning, nay more than the beginning, was excellent; but it will be inquired, not without a disturbed emotion, who raised the superstructure, who completed the fabric! To undertakings so grand, to virtues so noble, it will be a subject of grief that perseverance was wanting. It will be seen that the harvest of glory was abundant; that there were materials for the greatest operations, but that men were not to be found for the work; yet, that there was not wanting one, who could give good counsel; who could exhort, encourage; who could adorn, and celebrate, in praises destined to endure forever, the transcendent deeds, and those who performed them.

The End.

NOTES

DEFENSIO SECUNDA

THE title-page of the *Defensio Secunda* bears the date 1654. A reprint of this edition appeared at The Hague in the course of the same year—*Ex Typographia Adriani Vlacq*. The present text has been prepared from photostats of the Columbia University Library copy of the original London edition. All corrections made in the *Errata* have been incorporated into the text, but are not listed in the following notes.

PAGE 14
—22 verâ] vera
PAGE 16
—9 cum primis] cumprimis
PAGE 18
—10 contra humanæ] contrahumanæ
PAGE 28
—19 extrahêre,] extrahêre
PAGE 30
—2 vacat,] vacat
PAGE 34
—9 licuit,] licuit
PAGE 40
—16 causâ publicâ] causa publica
PAGE 42
—9 epistolam cum] epistolam, cùm   —10 rogabat] rogabat, gratiâ] gratia,   —12 voluerint] volue- (end of line) erint (beginning of next line)
PAGE 54
—9 teneat,] teneat   —11 alterâ] altera   —19 carnibus] carnibus,
PAGE 66
—4 propugnatorem?] propugnatorem.
PAGE 70
—2 ipsâ gloriâ] ipsa gloria   —4 quantâ] quanta
PAGE 72
—4 discrucior] discrutior

Page 76
　—3 oculos] oculos,　　　—12 linguâ] lingua
Page 82
　—12 optimè] optime
Page 86
　—14 injuriâ] injuria
Page 88
　—5 impudentiâ tuâ] impudentia tua　　　5–6 tuâ famâ] tua fama
—6 malâ] mala　　nociturum] nosciturum
Page 90
　—9 horrescant] horescant　　　—11 Abde,] Abde　　　—13 audeas]
audias
Page 92
　—4 sunt;] sunt,　　　—5 ratio,] ratio　　　—11 ceventem, More]
ceventem more
Page 94
　—1 audeas] audias　　　—7 causâ] causa
Page 96
　—14 Eâ] Ea　　　—14 legibus,] legibus　　　—17 Audite,] Audite
Page 98
　—18 totâ illâ] tota illa
Page 100
　—16 arriperetur] arriperetur,　　　—17 præceps] præceps
Page 102
　—6 famâ] fama
Page 106
　—7 ullâ] ulla
Page 108
　—23 reppererim] repererim
Page 112
　—14 *Academiâ*] *Academia*
Page 114
　—15 solemne] solẽne　　　—21 sceleratè] scelerate　　　—23 vide,
inquam,] vide inquam　　　—23–24 subversâ] subversa　　　—24
Salmasianâ] Salmasiana
Page 116
　—15 unâ] una
Page 118
　—4 dicta] dicta,　　　15–16 probatissimâ] probatissima　　　—21
cùm] cum
Page 120
　—2 perceptâ] percepta　　　—13 gratiâ] gratia

PAGE 122
—19 Florentiâ] Florentia —23 Româ] Roma
PAGE 124
—4 gratiâ] gratia
PAGE 130
—6 Apologiâ] Apologia
PAGE 132
—3 totâ] tota Mosaïcâ] Mosaïca
PAGE 136
—4 meâ] mea
PAGE 138
—23 *maximè*] *maxime*
PAGE 142
—17 capitis] capitis,
PAGE 144
—4 *parricidis*] *paricidis* —5 te] te, —12 ἐλεγχίστῳ]
ἐλεγχίστω —21 concubitus] concubitus,
PAGE 146
—1 locupletes] locupletes, —10 *invectâ*] *invecta*
PAGE 148
—1 More] Morè
PAGE 150
—13 acceptâ] accepta summâ] summa —16 suæ] suæ,
PAGE 152
—9 suâ] sua —11 agmine] agmine, —17 *virtute*] *virtuti*
PAGE 156
—5 perfugarum] per fugarum —6 quas] quas, causâ] causa
—8 sempiternæ] semptiternæ —9 familiâ] familia —22
providentiâ] providentia
PAGE 158
—2 tantum] tantùm —13 benevolentiâ] benevolentia
PAGE 160
—5 meritò] merito
PAGE 162
—6 meritoria] meritoriæ
PAGE 166
—10 sanctiùs] sanctius
PAGE 172
—7 effutiret] effutiret, —12 eâdem] eadem —21 deditâ
operâ] dedita opera
PAGE 176
—9 venereâ] venerea

Page 178
—17 monitis,] monitis
Page 182
—12 cœlitùs] cœlitùs,
Page 184
—8 nostras] nostras,
Page 186
—9 illâ] illa   —10 victoriâ] victoria   —17 locum] loco
Page 188
—19 sententiâ] sententia
Page 190
—7 amplectuntur;] amplectuntur?
Page 192
—4 cogito?] cogito.
Page 194
—11 Genevensi] Genevense   —19 *maximè*] *maxime*
Page 198
—3 eâdem datâ] eadem data   —10 unde] undè   —17 sanè]
sane
Page 200
—6 discipulus] discicipulus   —16 *relinquetur.*] *relinquetur*
Page 202
—1 fusiùs] fusius   —7 *illâ*] *illa*   —11 Mariâ] Maria
Elizabethâ] Elizabetha
Page 204
—6 naturâ] natura   —11 suâ] sua   —14 fugâ] fuga
Page 206
—7 prudentiâ] prudentia   —11 Presbyteriani] presbyteriani
Page 210
—1 longâ] longa
Page 212
—2 suâ] sua   —9 eâdem infamiâ] eadem infamia   —12
republicâ] republica   —13 administratâ] administrata   —14
orthodoxâ] orthodoxa   restitutâ] restituta   stabilitâ] stabilita
—15 maturâ] matura   firmatâ] firmata   —16 nullâ] nulla
Page 214
—1 delatâ suâ] delata sua   —2 operâ] opera
Page 216
—4 licentiâ] licentia   —15 mutatâ] mutata   —21 jure]
jure,
Page 218
—20 eâdem] eadem

PAGE 220
—10 totâ] tota   —19 concessâ] concessa
PAGE 222
—3 neque] néque   —10 æquius,] æquius
PAGE 226
—9 naturâ] natura   —23 fides,] fides
PAGE 228
—1 summam] summam.   —3 antehac] ante hac   —14 aliâ] aliâ   —22 causâ] causa,
PAGE 230
—3 ipsâ] ipsa   —6 rempublicam] rempubl.   —14 totiésque] totiesque
PAGE 234
—3 amicitiâ] amicitia   —4 famâ] fama   —17 firmare,] firmare
PAGE 238
—8 violentiùs] violentius
PAGE 240
—7–8 invenietis,] invenietis
PAGE 242
—14 solâ] sola
PAGE 244
—1 eâdem patientiâ] eadem patientia   —2 solertiâ] solertia quâ] qua
PAGE 246
—18 locupletent,] locupletent
PAGE 248
—13 superbiâ] superbia
PAGE 250
—4 justissimâ] justissima   —17 vestrâ] vestra

NOTES ON THE TRANSLATION

CHANGES in the English translation have been made only in cases where the meaning of the original translator's English is different from the meaning of Milton's Latin. No attempt has been made to add elegance or to supply omissions of phrases which do not alter the meaning of the text. Notes are here supplied only in the cases of puns or of literary allusions so tangible as to carry a certain connotation for the Latin reader.

PAGE 31
—16 Morus (μωρός) signifies 'fool and profligate.'
PAGE 33
—12–13 An indecent but effective pun. ". . . to engraft a *Morus* ('mulberry' or 'More') in a *ficus* ('fig' or 'feminine genital'), thence to raise *sycomori* ('fig-mulberries' or 'fig-Mores').
PAGE 55
—22–28 Latin authors speak of bad literature as useful only for wrapping fish. Martial, for example, hopes his book will not be put to such use (4.86.8: *nec scombris tunicas dabis molestas*).
PAGE 57
—13–14 The *impression* of the book makes a pun with *compression* of Pontia.
PAGE 63
—27 The passage in Apollonius is 2.181–184.
PAGE 68
—15–20 The passage in the *Iliad* is 9.411–416.
PAGE 74
—3–9 The passages from Euripides are *Orestes* 795 and *Hercules Furens* 1398, 1402.
PAGE 81
—12–13 The allusion is to Horace, *Satires* 2.6.38–39:

> *Tune, Syri, Damæ, aut Dionysi filius, audes*
> *deicere e saxo civis aut tradere Cadmo.*

The sense of these lines is: "Will you, a mere freedman, (the names are typical slave names) dare execute or deliver to the executioner (Cadmus) citizens free-born?"

—17 Oscan is a primitive Italic dialect. 'Croaking' (*coaxare*) is an allusion to the chorus of Aristophanes' *Frogs*.

—27 Orbilius was Horace's martinet school-master (Horace, *Epistles* 2.1.70–71).

PAGE 83

—21–85, 5 The reference is to Quintus of Smyrna (or Calabria) 5.139–164. The quotation is 5.157, 162–164.

PAGE 89

—13 Literally, 'from Pontia though she be with hair'. The form of the name is reminiscent of Pontius Pilate, a contrast is formed with 'shaven' (line 11), and allusion is made to the custom of the ancients that courtesans were depilated.

PAGE 113

—15–18 In Psalms 22.6 David says: "But I am a worm and no man." In Isaiah 66.24 occurs the phrase, "their worm shall not die."

PAGE 115

—27 *Rem publicam* means 'commonwealth' as well as 'public thing'.

PAGE 117

—8 Curius is a Roman name which became an appellative for a bold and moderate man.

PAGE 139

—20 The use of the Greek word for 'hold your peace' is a definite allusion, with an insulting connotation, to Mark 1.25.

PAGE 143

—6 The Greek word employed is reminiscence of Acts 17.18.

—7 *morigeranti* means 'accommodating' or 'More-bearing'.

—14–17 The allusion is to the ancient modes of punishing adulterers.

PAGE 147

—11 The unusual word for 'alien' (*exoticus* = ἐξωτικός) means 'heathen' in ecclesiastical writers.

PAGE 157

—8 'Mores' carries the added meaning of 'fools'.

PAGE 161

—16 Salmoneus was punished by Jupiter for presuming to make artificial thunder.

PAGE 167

—21–169, 6 The citation (partly verbatim, partly otherwise, as indicated) is from *Pro Plancio* 93, 94.

PAGE 177

—25 The proverbially bad Annals of Volusius are called by Catullus (36.1) *cacata charta*.

—28 Lerna was the bog which sheltered the monster which Hercules slew.

PAGE 183
  —21–22 Romans 14.4.
  —24–25 Psalms 69.10.
PAGE 197
  —26–199, 1 Cicero, *Pro Rabirio* 19.
PAGE 206
  —15 *omnis in eum faba cuditur* is a reminiscence of Terence, *Eunuch* 381.
PAGE 209
  —21 Priscian (flourished at the beginning of the sixth century) was the most used Latin grammarian. A sculpture on Chartres cathedral represents Grammar and Priscian.

COLUMBIA UNIVERSITY PRESS
COLUMBIA UNIVERSITY
NEW YORK

FOREIGN AGENT
OXFORD UNIVERSITY PRESS
HUMPHREY MILFORD
AMEN HOUSE, LONDON, E.C.

Date Due
